Islamic Charity

Islamic Charity

How Charitable Giving Became Seen as a Threat to National Security

Samantha May

ZED

Zed Books
Bloomsbury Publishing Plc
50 Bedford Square, London, WC1B 3DP, UK
1385 Broadway, New York, NY 10018, USA
29 Earlsfort Terrace, Dublin 2, Ireland

First published in Great Britain 2021

Copyright © Samantha May, 2021

Samantha May has asserted her right under the Copyright, Designs and Patents Act, 1988, to be identified as Author of this work.

For legal purposes the Acknowledgements on p. ix constitute an extension of this copyright page.

Cover design by www.ianrossdesigner.com
Cover image © World Religions Photo Library / Alamy Stock Photo

All rights reserved. No part of this publication may be reproduced or transmitted in any form or by any means, electronic or mechanical, including photocopying, recording, or any information storage or retrieval system, without prior permission in writing from the publishers.

Bloomsbury Publishing Plc does not have any control over, or responsibility for, any third-party websites referred to or in this book. All internet addresses given in this book were correct at the time of going to press. The author and publisher regret any inconvenience caused if addresses have changed or sites have ceased to exist, but can accept no responsibility for any such changes.

A catalogue record for this book is available from the British Library.

A catalog record for this book is available from the Library of Congress.

ISBN: HB: 978-1-7869-9944-3
PB: 978-1-7869-9945-0
ePDF: 978-1-7869-9943-6
eBook: 978-1-7869-9941-2

Typeset by Deanta Global Publishing Services, Chennai, India

To find out more about our authors and books visit www.bloomsbury.com and sign up for our newsletters.

Contents

Preface	vi
Acknowledgements	ix
Abbreviations	x
Introduction	1
1 The importance of the 'everyday': Theories and methods	7
2 The (il)logic of financial counter-terrorism strategies: From the United States to the global	29
3 'You cannot split Islam from charitable work': *Zakat* and *sadaqah*	59
4 'They keep asking for evidence. We have none... Absolutely none'	79
5 'No one starves in Britain'	99
6 'Actively awaiting the return'	119
7 'Diamonds are made from that pressure'	147
Conclusion: Counter-terror or counterproductive?	169
References	179
Index	193

Preface

At the time of writing, the world is grappling with the new Covid-19 virus. Although the evaluation stage is early, the UK appears to have one of the highest death rates in Europe and one of the highest death rates per capita in the world. Although it is oft repeated that 'we are all in this together', it appears that we are not equally together: we are all weathering the same storm but with different access to shelter (and none).

The emergence of Covid-19 has dramatically affected the charitable sector as demand for services rise, while financial, volunteer and material resources dwindle. In the UK, Muslim volunteers, individuals and charities have been some of the most proactive and among the first responders to the evolving crisis. Lucas Faure has found a similar trend in France where French Muslim charities have been among the first organizations to respond to the crisis and are at the heart of mitigation efforts. Faure has argued that the national implications for the renewed vigour and visibility of the Muslim charitable sector 'challenge negative stereotypes on Islam in France and potentially reshapes their relations with public authorities in the provision of welfare services' (Faure, 2020). In agreement with Faure, Muslim actors and actions in the current crisis could assist in strengthening 'religious and civic identity, and help Muslims become more engaged, politically interested, and active citizens' (Uddin, 2020: 5). From assisting the homeless to providing essential food packages, from outreach projects to combating loneliness, to small grant giving, Muslim charities are at the centre of the fight against the societal and economic consequences of the new virus both domestically and internationally. The efforts to combat some of the various knock-on effects of Covid-19 have resulted in a resurgent effort to focus on Muslim charitable giving 'at home' in addition to overseas humanitarian needs regardless of faith or none (Uddin, 2020: 3). While facing a barrage of unprecedented challenges, Muslim charities have an opportunity to showcase the true value of their services, previously under-recognized, and the shared values of charity and humanitarian work with wider society.

In a report released in August 2020, the umbrella organization the Muslim Charities Forum identified 194 Muslim charities responding to the Covid crisis in the UK (Uddin, 2020: 3). Small, medium and large charities have used the resources they have to mitigate the most dire of consequences whether that be re-appropriating mosque space for the use of food banks, providing care packages to the most vulnerable or assisting care workers with basic personal protection equipment (PPE). Overall, the Muslim Charities Forum identified key services provided by British Muslim charities which include essentials and food for the vulnerable, mental health support, distributing hardship funds, supporting NHS and key workers, burial and bereavement services, PPE distribution and advice services (Uddin, 2020: 8).

It is too early to make any firm conclusions, but it is likely that the Muslim charitable sector will have additional challenges to endure. First, it is becoming increasingly clear that Black, Asian and minority ethnic (BAME) groups are unequally affected by both the disease and the indirect fallout of the pandemic. Given the demographics of the UK and immigration patterns, a large percentage of BAME communities affected by Covid-19 are Muslim. In conjunction with being statistically more vulnerable to the spread of Covid-19 due to a complex intersection of societal and economic factors, BAME communities are already among the poorest groups within UK society. Prior to the recent outbreak, Muslim communities suffered greater levels of poverty than other groups within the UK (Uddin, 2020: 10), which is likely to increase further as the repercussions of our current crisis unfold and economic recession deepens. Thus, usage and need for Muslim charities are likely to increase, while simultaneously decreasing the fundraising base and increasing the health risks for individuals working or volunteering in the sector. However, as Faure has noted, the Muslim charitable sector is dominated by youth and thus their volunteer base faces less severe mobility restrictions than the elderly and vulnerable, potentially providing an important source of volunteers (Faure, 2020). Second, as this monograph will argue, the Muslim charitable sector is particularly susceptible to allegations of charitable misuse, extremism and terrorist financing which is not becoming lessened in the face of the pandemic. Continued counter-terror finance (CTF) measures are likely to decrease the efficiency and ability of Muslim charities to respond to our global crisis. In the era of Covid-19, hampering the efficiency and ability of Muslim charitable distributions will likely affect donations being sent not only overseas but within the UK itself as economic recession and unemployment manifest.

In evidence of Faure's suggestion that Muslim charities and humanitarian organizations during the crisis have 'increased their public visibility and their active partnerships with other associations' (Faure, 2020), British Muslim charities have seen a surge in partnerships and collaborations with other charities, particularly those working domestically within the UK. Examples include the partnership between Islamic Relief (the largest British humanitarian charity which previously worked predominantly overseas) and the National Zakat Foundation (founded in 2011 and distributes charity exclusively within the UK). Muslim Hands has also partnered with FareShare (the longest running food distribution organization in the UK), while Penny Appeal has established a number of partnerships with various local and regional charities including the Salvation Army in Birmingham (Uddin, 2020).

Despite the various ongoing challenges, Muslim charitable givers have also responded to humanitarian need abroad and within the UK. The holy month of Ramadan occurred during the full lockdown in the UK. Typically, mosques and Islamic centres across the UK would utilize the month of Ramadan to collect *zakat* (obligatory alms) from donors via mosques and face-to-face fundraising. The year 2020 witnessed a very different Ramadan where door-to-door charitable collections became impossible and online donations to charities or online money transfers were the only practical option. While undoubtedly small–to-medium charities that lacked an online presence will have seen a shortfall in fundraising in comparison to previous years, other charities with a strong online presence and online donations have been far more resilient. For instance, Islamic Relief is reported to have collected a 30 per cent increase in donations during Ramadan than in 2019 while the National Zakat Foundation witnessed a 43 per cent increase in its online donations (Yusoof, 2020) with applications for its grants being received every fifteen minutes (Uddin, 2020: 10).

Covid-19 has forced many to contemplate our global political and economic norms with new discussions regarding the role of the state in welfare and service provision. The emergence of Covid-19 means that we cannot return to the norms of old. Now is perhaps exactly the time we should be reflecting and seriously considering alternative political, economic and ethical paradigms rather than demonizing them offhand as contrary to 'fundamental British values'.

Attempting to monitor and control the spread of Covid-19, many states, including the UK, are struggling to devise 'track and trace' systems with much of the technology being re-appropriated from counter-terror surveillance mechanisms. States have utilized the opportunity to expand further into our everyday lives extending their grip on the securitization of the mundane. 'Track and trace' systems are (at the time of writing) thought to be crucial in controlling and isolating Covid-19 cases, but scepticism over the government's use of data collected has already raised debates. Suspicion of how the government will utilize the data, who the data will be shared with and for what purpose, threatens to undermine voluntary uptake on 'track and trace' techniques. Nearly two decades of intrusive surveillance, particularly on Muslim and Asian communities in the UK, has potentially increased mistrust between the British government and segments within British society, resulting in apprehension of new 'track and trace' systems. As populations across the globe face grief, shock and uncertainty, the securitization of the mundane is increasing substantially as attentions are diverted to the immediate crisis. It is not just Muslim charities and Muslim individuals who are monitored and surveyed – we are all under the state's gaze. Our ongoing crisis has the potential to recast Muslim charitable giving in the UK beyond suspicion and mistrust towards a common agenda for the common good for Muslims and non-Muslims alike.

Acknowledgements

Enormous gratitude to all those who participated in this research giving time and trust. This work could not have been possible without you. Indebtedness is extended to all who have offered comments and critique, especially the staff and students at the University of Aberdeen, blind reviewers and my 'amigo'. All remaining errors are entirely my own.

Appreciation to the Leverhulme Trust – project entitled '*Zakat* in the UK: Islamic Giving, Citizenship and Government Policy' (Grant F-2015-331) – and the British Academy for funding this research – 'Identifying Political and Transnational Dimensions of Pious Alms Giving (*Zakat*) in the United Kingdom' (BA Grant number SG122527).

I dedicate this book to my family – by blood and by choice – I love you all beyond measure.

Abbreviations

Charity Commission	Charity Commission for England and Wales
CTF	Counter-terror financing
FATF	Financial Action Task Force
FBOs	Faith-based organizations
FWoT	Financial War on Terror
NGOs	Non-governmental organizations
OSCR	Office of the Scottish Charity Regulator
SWIFT	The Society for Worldwide Interbank Financial Telecommunications
USA PATRIOT Act	acronym for 'Uniting and Strengthening America by Providing Appropriate Tools Required to Intercept and Obstruct Terrorism'
WoT	War on Terror

Introduction

Islam has become the new 'folk devil' (Salgado-Pottier, 2008). Since 9/11 and the global War on Terror (WoT), practitioners of Islam have been scrutinized and surveyed in suspicion of disloyalty and as potential disrupters of national social cohesion. In this climate, even seemingly benign, altruistic practices such as charity are viewed as potential threats to national security and have increasingly become subject to counter-terrorism policies. This is evidenced in the words of President Bush, instigator of the Financial War on Terror (FWoT), when he iterated that

> Just to show you how insidious these terrorists are, they often times use nice-sounding, non-governmental organisations as fronts for their activities . . . . We intend to deal with them, just like we intend to deal with others who aid and abet terrorist organisations. (George W. Bush, cited ACLU, 2009: 7)

This work seeks to critically assess the assumptions behind the lesser known 'Financial War on Terror', taking empirical, evidence-based approaches at its core.

Engaging with the 'everyday' sociopolitical activities of Muslims within the UK, the work gives voice to the motivations, apprehensions, hopes and fears of Muslim charitable practitioners and seeks to unearth the consequences of counter-terrorism policies in relation to Islamic charitable giving in the UK. The current perceived consequences of counter-terror policies in the charitable sphere include greater suspicion on Muslim charities from non-Muslim populations, increased politicization of aid/charity to specific causes (e.g. Palestine), disruption to charitable and aid work due to bank accounts being frozen or denied and the loss of standard of life and/or life itself when distribution of aid is restricted, delayed or denied ultimately exposing the violence otherwise invisible in financial counter-terror strategies. A Muslim charity, interviewed on the conditions of strict anonymity, stated that 'yes, people have died . . . but they [policy makers] don't see the human value of their actions or the human cost of their actions'.

The FWoT emerged in the aftermath of 9/11 as a pre-emptive strike against future terrorist action. The idea, following the logic of anti-money laundering, is that if you follow the money, you will find the criminal. In the decades following 9/11 there has been a link made in the media and political rhetoric connecting anything 'Muslim' with terrorism and violence. Following the money trail therefore has, in practical terms, resulted in disproportionate scrutiny and surveillance of Muslim and Islamic associations, institutions and NGOs. This is despite the US government report on 9/11 outlining that 11 September 2001 involved relatively small amounts of finance with no evidence that monies were illicit or channelled through anything other than mainstream banking institutions. 'No charities, Islamic banks, front companies . . . were involved' (Warde, 2007: 64). However, this same report bears some responsibility for the suspicion cast upon Muslim charities. *The 9/11 Commission Report* states that the 'origin of the funds remain unknown' (p. 169) but does not shy from hazarding unevidenced guesses by declaring that 'Al Qaeda also collected money from employees of corrupt charities . . . . Charities were a source of money and also provided significant cover, which enabled operatives to travel undetected under the guise of working for a humanitarian organisation' (The 9/11 Commission Report: 170–1).

The consequences of current policies are multifaceted from stigmatization and suspicion of Muslim charities and Muslim communities generally, to individual losses in status and financial standing, to loss of living standards and lives as end recipients are delayed or denied funds. The non-violent argument made in justification of the FWoT will be demonstrated as a veneer which disguises and hides the real violences occurring.

It will be argued that the reported aim of preventing terrorism is highly unlikely to occur via counter-terror financing (CTF) initiatives largely because the form of violent political activity witnessed in the UK over the last decade need not be high cost nor be traceable. For instance, the murder of the British soldier Drummer Lee Rigby in Woolwich, England, in May, 2013 would not have been detected by following financial flows nor would the freezing or closing of bank accounts prevented the attack. In contrast, the 'side effects' of increased scrutiny of institutions and charities and individual financial patterns are effectively being utilized to securitize everyday activities and attempts to establish normal/abnormal financial behaviour patterns.

This is not to imply that *all* terrorism is low cost. Large political and violent organizations and entities require substantial funds to remain operative, entice recruits and prepare for large-scale operations particularly over extended time periods. Within the context of the UK, substantial literature exists concerning the financing of the IRA during the 'Troubles' (Jonsson, 2007). However, this is not the type of terrorism that has occurred in Britain over more recent decades. The UK government's own statistics clearly indicate a substantial decrease in political violence since the end of the Northern Ireland conflict (House of Commons Library, 2020). The highest number of deaths resulting from political violence occurred from the 1970s to the 1990s with 84 per cent of deaths related to the Troubles. The highest death count was in 1986 which saw a total of 350 deaths because of terrorist acts. In contrast, from April 2003 to the end of March 2019, the UK experienced a total of ninety-two deaths resulting from terrorism (House of Commons Library, 2020: 5). From this period, deaths as the result of terrorism remained low though small spikes occurred, notably in July 2005 with the London bombings and 2017 which saw the Westminster Bridge and Palace attacks, the bombing of Manchester Arena and the London Bridge attack. None of these attacks caused as many deaths by political violence as had occurred prior to the Good Friday Agreement. Contemporary violent political acts that have occurred in the UK have mostly not been perpetrated by large existing organizations but by individuals (so-called 'lone wolves') not directly associated with other entities. The types of terrorist attacks that have occurred in the UK most recently, and those applicable to the current financial counter-terror policies, have consisted of vehicles being used to run people over (the Westminster Bridge and Palace attacks), knife attacks and homemade (yet powerful) explosives (Manchester Arena bombing), none of which could have been detected by monitoring the individual's bank accounts. There is therefore a need to understand the finance and funding of terrorism and political violence within context and in relation to specific actions, groups and individuals (Tierney, 2017: 159). Quite simply not all terrorism is the same and not all violent actors use similar funding strategies or even require the same financial resources.

Chapter outline

Chapter 1 begins with the necessary overview of the concepts, theoretical approaches and methodologies of the research. The chapter will then go on to outline how the work understands 'securitization' and how charitable giving has been 'successfully' securitized within the UK context via counter-terror initiatives. Important concepts such as Butler's (2006) 'petty-sovereigns' are introduced which argue that the purported aim of CTF procedures may not succeed, but the 'side effects' of increased government control prospers, largely through the role of unelected, inexpert and unaccountable 'petty-sovereigns'.

Expanding on how the charitable sector became 'securitized', Chapter 2 explores the development of the FWoT in which charity is embroiled. Tracing the beginnings of the FWoT to just two weeks after 9/11, the chapter demonstrates how the United States forged current CTF policy and spread current counter-terror norms globally. As the chapter title suggests, the assumptions behind the current CTF logic will be critiqued arguing that current CTF measures are disproportionate, inappropriate to the challenges faced and potentially counterproductive. The case of *al-Barakaat*, wrongfully accused of terror financing, demonstrates the hidden violence behind CTF practices.

Chapter 3 explores how Islamic charity is understood by those who practise it particularly focusing on the obligatory article of faith, *zakat* (obligatory alms giving). As the CTF system assumes that informal, non-Western financial flows are inherently 'vulnerable' to abuse, this chapter focuses on the ways individual donors scrutinize where, and to whom, their charitable donations are given, thus mitigating against misuse from the outset. The final sections of this chapter discuss the ways in which Muslim charitable giving can be considered as 'performative' in that it helps construct not only a Muslim person but also a British Muslim person.

Utilizing the example of the UK-based charity Interpal, Chapter 4 will investigate the pressures and limits of the US-led CTF system on UK charity investigations. It shall be argued, following the analysis of De Goede (2017a), that the UK can be considered a 'norm adopter' by modifying global CTF norms to the UK context. Furthering the idea of 'norm adopters', it will be posited that the devolved powers within the UK also develop their own interpretations of CTF duties due to the differences in context, nature and size of their charitable sectors. At least part of the perception of disproportionate investigations into Muslim charities is a result not of the charity regulators themselves but of the various actors and individuals playing their role as unaccountable and opaque 'petty-sovereigns'.

The argument presented in Chapter 5 is that policy makers have made an error in their reading that overseas charity necessitates lingering loyalties to other political entities. Equally, it is too reductionist to argue that charity donated to the UK necessarily indicates an uncritical stance on the British state. This chapter highlights that transnational giving is not peculiar to British Muslim communities and should be read alongside literature concerning migrant and diaspora philanthropy more generally considering the conditions of advanced globalization. Examination of interviewee explanations of charitable giving highlights concerns surrounding obligations to family and kin, religious obligations to the global *ummah* and humanitarian purposes to alleviate suffering and hardship associated with poverty and economic insecurity. Prior to the experience of migration to a Muslim minority state, it would have been likely that individual Muslims donated (specifically their *zakat*) to their local communities and areas. However, with the experience of migration, minority status and the provision of welfare within Britain, many first-generation British Muslims donate their religious alms to their places of origin.

The penultimate chapter will demonstrate that alterations in charitable giving are occurring between Muslim generations, which simultaneously present younger Muslim generations as both an expression and constitutive element of contemporary British society. Muslim charitable giving within the UK is therefore specifically British. The research has found that particularly regarding *zakat* donations, older generations tend to donate to their place (not necessarily state) of origin while younger generations are more likely to distribute their *zakat* either within the UK itself or/and to a wider geographic terrain than their parents and grandparents. Rather than being an either/or choice to donate within the UK or elsewhere, younger Muslims are increasingly likely to do both. Like all charitable initiatives, whether secular or faith-based, what is emphasized in the mainstream media goes a long way in explaining the motivations for transnational giving. Events (whether natural or manmade) which find focus in mainstream media tend to receive higher quantities of charitable donations as Muslims can now identify for themselves who are the most in need. In attempting to mitigate the fickle nature of media attention, charities are using new techniques to encourage charitable giving and in so doing are taking upon themselves the authority to direct the collection and dispersal of charitable obligations. For some individual practitioners, Muslim charities that collect and distribute the religious obligation of *zakat* are taking responsibility in the absence of an Islamic system of governance.

The final chapter investigates the negative repercussions for Muslim charities in the UK resulting from CTF practices. Areas identified by interviewees suggest the three most damaging effects of CTF measures are driving donations 'underground', the reputational risk to individual charitable institutions and the sector as a whole and sustained de-risking initiatives by banks and mainstream financial institutions. Perhaps surprisingly, Muslim charities have responded positively to changes in regulation and increased bureaucratization. As the title of this chapter asserts, it takes pressure to create a diamond. Muslim charities are, however, not only responding to the external pressures for increased accountability and documentation but are proactively seeking further improvements by 'anticipatory accountability' (Iofalla, 2018) as they increasingly emphasize the humanitarian nature of their work that crosses both faith and non-faith communities, in addition to advocating shared 'fundamental British values' (Contest, 2018). The positivity of the sector, despite current CTF measures, is largely a tactical response to ensure their humanitarian and relief efforts remain operable and sustainable in the evolving global CTF system. The resilience of the Muslim charitable sector should not, however, distract from the various violences the CTF system evokes whether that be financial exclusions for charitable practitioners and organizations, reputational damage or restrictions and delays for end receivers.

1

The importance of the 'everyday'

Theories and methods

It's quite amazing... it's like an instinct – people give money without expecting anything in return (Muslim charity worker in interview).

According to the UK government, current de-radicalization measures aim to ensure there are 'no ungoverned spaces' in which 'extremism' and 'radicalization' can stand unchallenged (Home Office, 2018). Security measures have therefore penetrated the mundane aspects of our everyday lives barely noticed by some but conspicuously experienced by others (often based on religious grouping or/and racializations). Particularly important is Kundnani's observation that 'when government widened the perceived threat of terrorism from individuals actively inciting, financing, or preparing terrorist attacks to those having an ideology, they brought constitutionally protected activities of large numbers of people under surveillance' (2014: 12–13). Legitimate and legal everyday activities are now targeted for suspicion and monitored for deviance from 'fundamental British values' following from the UK counter-terror policies contained in CONTEST II (Contest, 2018). Qurashi has argued that 'embedded surveillance is an increasingly mundane feature of late modern life as it is embedded into the routines of everyday life, across private and public spaces' (2018). As the world was drawn to the spectacle of 'shock and awe', Guantanamo Bay, the hunt for Osama bin Laden and more, the small incremental moves into securing the everyday have largely gone unnoticed.

The securitization of the mundane is apparent across the social arena of the UK not least in the Prevent Duty (2015) that guarantees that all public spaces and institutions such as hospitals, schools and universities are scrutinized and surveyed to ensure they stay within the parameters of 'fundamental British values' (Contest, 2018). Not only do surveillance measures penetrate deeply into our daily activities, but they are also championed to monitor and cover a range of both public and private actors incorporating the likes of teachers, doctors and banking employees alongside police, journalists, bloggers and security agencies. Kundnani argues that 'when informants are recruited from communities, surveillance becomes intertwined with the fabric of human relationships and the threads of trust upon which they are built' (2014: 13). Kundnani further warns that 'the power and danger of these forms of surveillance derive from their entanglement in everyday human interactions at the community level rather than from external monitoring capabilities of hidden technologies' (2014: 13).

While the global War on Terror (WoT) generally has garnished much media and academic attention, what has achieved less public scrutiny is the securitization of everyday economic practices which ensure the state monitors and collect data on our everyday economic activities. The rationale being that by monitoring everyone, first, there are no 'ungoverned spaces' and, second, the data collected is thought to establish 'normal' from 'deviant' practices. 'The minutiae of everyday life including ATM transactions, wire transfers and charitable donations are to be securitised, sorted and regulated in this logic' (De Goede, 2012b: 29–30). One problem of such a logic is that our everyday economic practices are so diverse that 'normal' behaviour cannot be established let alone deviancy. Each and every one of us in our lifetimes will deviate from our everyday 'normal' financial activities on rare and special (yet completely 'normal' and legitimate) occasions such as marriages, deaths, buying a house or attending our children's graduations. Essentially, what this means is that counter-terror measures are now in place to monitor our everyday lives and activities in an effort to establish 'deviant' from 'normal' behaviour but with scant evidence that it can succeed in its stated goal. As De Goede has argued, 'legitimate, everyday money flows are no longer considered beyond suspicion but are inscribed with the ability to indicate terrorist intent if approached with the right data mining tools' (2012b: 58). Important to De Goede's assertion is that 'legitimate' financial activities are no longer 'beyond suspicion'. This is further supported by a Financial Action Task Force (FATF) report on terrorism financing, which stated that 'in many situations, the raising, moving and using of funds for terrorism can be . . . almost indistinguishable from the financial activity associated with everyday life' (FATF, 2008). There are indeed no 'ungoverned spaces' and every one of us is being monitored and mapped according to scales of 'normalcy' or 'deviancy' which in reality cannot be empirically established.

Background assumptions and key concepts

This work largely assumes that the secular and the religious, rather than being oppositional dichotomies, are mutually incorporating terms that make little sense without the other (May et al., 2014). It understands the boundaries of the religious and the mundane to be porous so that 'the mundane becomes sacred and *vice-versa*' (Barylo, 2018: 13). Barylo posits that as religious and non-religious practices are so intertwined, separate analysis of these phenomena is difficult. Barylo argues that 'trying to differentiate religion from non-religious actions in the social sciences' would be like 'trying to know if Schrödinger's cat is dead or alive' (2018: 14). Similarly, Barnett and Stein have argued that 'trying to make sense of the relationship between the religious and the secular in the humanitarian world is no easier than doing so in the wider world . . . because the two concepts define one another, constitute one another, bleeds into one another through porous boundaries' (2012: 28–9). Osella has posited that charitable practices are constituted through both Islamic traditions 'and encounters with non-Muslim Others, whether religious, ethnic, secular or political' (2019). According to this position, Muslim charitable practices emerge from the 'routinized practices of the everyday', which allows for the 'emergence of (novel) subjectivities which remain always incomplete and in the process of becoming' (Osella, 2019). Hence, Islamic charitable practices alter and transform during encounters with other traditions and the environment in which it is embedded.

Religion has re-entered the public domain as an alternative or reformed option to challenge existing dominant economic and political paradigms: 'this can be seen particularly in the role of faith-based organizations, who are increasingly filling the gaps left by the neoliberalization of the state, and campaigning for broader change' (Wilson and Steger, 2013: 485). Thus, it is imperative to place the rise and resilience of Islamic charitable giving and the role of Islamic NGOs into the wider global perspective of the general upsurge of the third sector, whether that be faith-based or secular. The policy and media gaze upon Islamic charities and NGOs is, in all probability, far more correlated to the general perception of Islam in Western Europe than any specific peculiarity in Islamic NGOs.

Contemporary Western governance tends to view religion as a coin of two sides: one side dangerous and the other peaceful (Hurd, 2012: 947). Dangerous religion is transformed into an object of securitization and a target of state control and/or violence (Hurd, 2012: 947). Peaceful religion, on the other hand, is deemed to need recognition, reorganization and 'rescued to serve as global problem solvers' (Hurd, 2012: 949). Consequently, some religious views are banished, while others are brought into the system but strongly monitored and controlled by a variety of governmental and societal constraints.

Media portrayals and 'common-sense' popular belief tend to equate religion (of any sect) with dogma, rigidity and group isolationism. Samuel Huntington's controversial, but highly influential, 'Clash of Civilizations' (1993) has intensified the perception that religious differences necessarily lead to conflict and are thus a threat to liberal societies. Such understandings of religion tend to be based on privileging elite textual theology rather than looking to the various ways religious beliefs are interpreted and acted upon by any community of believers. By contrast, privileging practices rather than textual commentary grants the opportunity of exploring how religious actions become contextualized in various environments (specifically in a Muslim-minority British context) and how practices alter and develop over time rather than simply rigidly following dogmatic acts from previous generations. This work therefore takes on board Gunning and Jackson's observation that religion is best 'contextualised as a living community of believers, rather than a set of text-based beliefs' (2011: 383). This is not to suggest that texts and the substance of doctrines are not important but 'not without methodological considerations looking at how the doctrines are played out and the performance of agency' (Sheikh, 2012: 377). Osella (2019) has forcefully argued:

> At the current historical juncture in which transformations of Islamic religious practice continue to be represented and misread . . . as determined primarily by theological debates or textual traditions, it is increasingly important, and indeed

urgent to trace the articulation of Islamic discursive traditions within the broader social, cultural, political and economic environments in which they are debated.

Importantly, privileging religious practice over textual rigidness 'can point towards the possibility of change and provide scholars a better understanding of why adherents within the same belief community can advocate different courses of action' (Sheikh, 2012: 278).

Faith-based charities of all sects and denominations pose challenges to contemporary secular Britain. On the one hand, faith-based charities and NGOs have gained importance and visibility in the era of neoliberal economics which favours decreasing the role of the welfare state in preference for privatization and competition. This is the side of faith-based charities that has been viewed positively and 'in general has been represented as a flowering of global citizenship in healthy counter balance to the power of the nation-state' (Benthall, 2007: 5).

On the other hand, faith-based charities problematize the secular understanding of the British state as religion escapes from its confinement in the private sphere into civil/social society. Essentially, there is an 'underlying assumption in security studies that implicitly associates security with secularisation' (Mavelli, 2011: 179). Any perceived challenge to liberal secularism (real or imagined) is deemed a security issue in and of itself. One such challenge to secularism is the generally accepted understanding that 'most religions perform social as well as psychological functions and meet collective as well as individual needs' (Casanova, 1994: 46). The social and collective function of Islamic charitable giving necessitates that Islam cannot be neatly secured in the private domain as duties and obligations of the faith transcend from the individual to wider society. At least in the case of charity, Islam extends and negotiates between the boundaries of the public and private sphere and local British communities and global Muslim solidarities (*ummah*).

Consequently, governments and policy makers have begun to include and target religious actors and institutions in policy initiatives in an attempt to tame and domesticize religious groups and organizations, resulting in sweeping alterations in religious procedures.

> The move to restore religion has laid the groundwork for an array of legal and administrative initiatives to intervene in religious affairs around the world – creating new religious and political realities. They designate acceptable spaces for religion and acceptable forms of religion that are regulated legally and politically, domestically, and transnationally. (Hurd, 2012: 946)

In the era of widespread Islamophobia and intense scrutiny of anything Muslim or Islamic, the Muslim charitable sector is one domain which the UK government wants to ensure is not an 'ungoverned space' for fears of charitable funds being misused or redistributed for terrorist purposes. The ability to move with ease from the private to civic space grants Muslim charities the opportunity to expel persistent myths associated with Islam and Muslims. It also provides a platform for alternative interpretations of Islam to counter violent narratives from Islamist ideologies. Moving outside of the purely private, yet not fully within the realms of 'high politics', Muslim charitable practice in the UK offers potentials to benefit British society generally beyond isolated Muslim communities.

Many religions, including Islam, are not contained within the arbitrary borders of nation states and thus have important transnational dimensions that criss-cross geographical and political borders. Aspects of identity such as religion, culture and language have inherent transnational dimensions 'that affects the way nations gain influence in foreign countries. Organisational, cultural, or emotional ties among religious groups create trans-border bonds with political impact on foreign and domestic policies' (Jodicke, 2018: 1). It is the acknowledgement of potential cross-border loyalties that initiates the suspicion and fear in some policy makers' minds. However, there is potential to embrace the transnational links that are created and sustained by Muslim charitable giving. Drawing from Nye, religion can be conceptualized as 'soft power' (2004). Nye conceptualized soft power as

> the ability to get what you want through attraction rather than coercion or payments. It arises from the attractiveness of a country's culture, political ideals, and policies. When our policies are seen as legitimate in the eyes of others, our soft power is enhanced. (2004: 12)

In terms of diplomatic soft power, charities and faith-based NGOs can be successful in a range of ways but not least in promoting democracy and human rights (Sheikh, 2012: 379). Charitable donations and the ease in which they can be distributed can create positive perceptions of both a state and its people that in turn can assist in the efficiency of soft power being deemed 'legitimate'. Conversely, if actions are deemed illegitimate (such as the withdrawal, restriction or curtailment of aid and charity) a nation's soft power may be drastically reduced internationally. The positive aspects of Muslim charitable giving are currently in danger of being thwarted by negative press, societal suspicion and the harmful consequences for end-users and recipients. The detrimental consequences of current counter-terror initiatives that have penetrated the charitable sector therefore risks more than just the lives of those actively involved in charity, but also the effectiveness and success of British diplomatic initiatives, especially in countries with sizeable Muslim populations.

Securitization

As one argument of this work is that there is an increased securitization of the mundane activities of everyday life that affects all British community (albeit some more than others), it is necessary to outline what is meant by 'securitization'. The concept of securitization has grown from the 1980s and is associated with the likes of Ole Wæver and Barry Buzan of the Copenhagen School who drew insights from social theory and linguistics to challenge the assumed 'realities' of dominant views of security (Stritzel, 2007: 357). 'Securitization' is understood to hold a relationship between saying and doing. The argument is that security is primarily about naming: 'the utterance itself is the act. By saying it, something is done' (Sheikh, 2012: 383). The point being that an object/subject becomes securitized because they are *said* to be a threat. The real degree of danger is largely irrelevant once an audience *believes* the threat exists. Once the 'threat' has been accepted by an audience, successful securitization has occurred regardless of the actual realities of the threat in question. Saliently, 'successful securitisation cements the ground for extra-ordinary action having provided a legitimising security narrative' (Sheikh, 2012: 384).

A successful securitization narrative ensures that the policies enacted to prevent, or decrease, the said threat becomes legitimated and deemed unavoidable in the name of securing the interests of the nation. This, in turn, renders the critique of securitization problematic, difficult and potentially perceived as 'deviant' against the national interests. Critique therefore becomes a security issue in and of itself. As an issue/object/subject becomes securitized the perception is that danger exists which must be thwarted to prevent worse atrocities occurring. In this logic, then, 'extraordinary' measures which circumvent, or break, 'normal' political and legal procedures become rationalized. Securitization operates outside the domain of 'normal' politics which justifies extraordinary control and containment. In the name of security, hard-fought-for civil rights are in danger of being overlooked, neglected and disregarded. As Amal and Husband have observed, 'once security is invoked, principles of individual rights and liberties become negotiable, rather than absolute' (2013: 245).

Since 9/11, and particularly the 7 July London bombings of 2005, Islam has been constructed as an 'existential threat that requires extraordinary and emergency procedures outside the bounds of regular political procedure' (Cesari, 2012: 430) in British political discourse. In media and political rhetoric, it appears as though the threat of terrorism is on the rise in the UK despite the significant decrease in political violence in Britain since the end of the Troubles in Northern Ireland (House of Commons Library, 2020). For instance, according to a YouGov survey, 74 per cent of British residents believed that the threat of terrorism had increased from 2010 to 2016 in contrast to the evidence (Smith, 2016). Cesari has argued that the main consequences to this securitization are 'increased surveillance and police activity around Islamic actors and organizations; banning groups and deportation of radicals; and greater limitations on the religious practice of Muslims' (2012: 432). Muslims, especially those who assert their religious identity through participation in 'Islamic activities (such as charitable giving), are under increased political scrutiny and control' (Cesari, 2012: 434). Despite the British government denying that counter-terror initiatives stigmatize specifically Muslims, a plethora of academic writing and evidence suggests that whatever the intention, Muslims as a community are targeted in practice with far-reaching consequences for communities, individuals and their ability to conduct their faith (Kundnani, 2009).

This is not to downplay the threat of political violence but simply to suggest that terrorism is perhaps not the main security threat to the UK. According to Baroness Warsi, a British resident is more likely to die, or suffer injury, from poorly erected flat-pack furniture than from a terrorist attack (Warsi, 2017). However, the threat of political violence is very real for many living outside of Western Europe. According to the Global Terrorism Index (2019: 2), South Asia followed by sub-Saharan Africa and the Middle East and North Africa suffer the largest deaths from terrorism mainly from violent Islamist movements such as the Taliban, ISIS and Boko Haram. In comparison, in 2019, Western Europe saw the lowest number of recorded deaths as a result of political violence since 2012 but with a worrying 320 per cent increase in far-right terrorism since 2014 (Global Terrorism Index, 2019: 4). Rather than religion, or specifically Islam, being the motivator for political violence, the Global Terrorism Index suggests the main determinator for terrorism is an environment of conflict. Charities potentially offer a bulwark against violent ideology by providing basic life essentials and acting as a peaceful voice for Islamic action. In doing so, Muslim charities present an alternative to the narratives espoused by violent Islamist groups. Benthall has argued that if aid and humanitarian services were banned from conflict and terrorist zones 'there is a danger of creating a "humanitarian vacuum" that can be penetrated by violent extremist groups' (2012: 83). It can therefore be suggested that encouraging, rather than hampering, Islamic charities could be the most effective way to reduce the recruitment to violent Islamist movements overseas.

By presenting financial and everyday securitization as both necessary and unavoidable, securitization of the mundane is portrayed as apolitical: simply a technical tool to map and scrutinize those with criminal intent but with no effect on those who have nothing to fear. To portray financial counter-terror measures this way is to deny the political and dislocate political agency leaving the effects (both intended and unintended) opaque. Particularly important to this line of argument is the difficulty in challenging the stated position. Who would argue that terrorism should not be prevented nor state with certainty that it is out with the realms of possibility that charitable funds could be used to support or aid terrorist actions? Presented as both necessary and unavoidable, critique of the current securitization of the mundane becomes equated with appeasing terrorism or political naivety.

In the name of counter-terror measures and national protection, our use of ATMs, which banks we service, what charities we give to and what direct debits are made are all collected and mapped by government initiatives. Little evidence currently exists that would point to the effectiveness of such policies in thwarting violent political action or terrorist activities, but where such initiatives do succeed is in their extension and deepening of state power and control. Securitization of the charitable sphere makes possible the greater regulation, reporting and surveillance of charities and charitable actors by the state (Jackson, 2007: 422).

As will be argued, the likelihood of current financial counter-terror initiatives in being successful in decreasing or preventing terrorist action within the UK is slight. In addition to largely being ineffective on the pronounced goals of counterterrorism, there is increased possibility of negative counter effects. Current financial counter-terror initiatives have been coined as 'speculative' by De Goede (2012b) as they aim to intercede *prior* to any criminality and thus specifically and consciously target legitimate practices. In regard to charities, De Goede has stated that 'the outcome of this targeting is speculative in the sense that it does not produce the security it professes to strive for but instead intensifies conditions of insecurity both for the charitable organisations and the constituencies they aid and serve' (2012b: 153). Insecurity is increased as speculation and suspicion intensify, and measures are put in place that deepen the challenges of charitable donations with consequences at national and international levels. Moreover, 'the overall effect of this chain of securitization is to produce opportunities for investigation, policing and prosecution' (De Goede, 2017a: 2014). The intended goal of reducing or preventing violent political action may not succeed, but the 'side effects' (Ferguson, 1994[1]) of increased state control are emerging.

Violence

Behind the assertion that the financial counter-terror initiatives aimed at charities and charitable giving are simply a necessary precaution against terrorist financing is arguably a form of violence which categorizes some financial actions as 'normal' and others as 'deviant' and in requirement of scrutiny and surveillance. While current policy claims to do no harm to those who have nothing to fear, the consequences of the financial counter-terror initiatives are insufficiently explored and mapped. While perhaps not the stated intention of financial counter-terror policies, in practice these initiatives have had enormous negative consequences that stretch from individual donors, charitable institutions to end recipients both within, and without, the UK. This research essentially argues that, despite the rhetoric claiming that the Financial War on Terror (FWoT) is a 'soft' mechanism in the fight against terrorism, there are consequential violences which are currently largely hidden and unaccounted for. This work understands 'violence' as more than just physical harm.

Violence can be understood in several senses – physical, psychological, emotional and conceptual (Bishop and Philips, 2006: 377). The disruption of financial flows and the inability to act within the national and global economy can be considered a form of violence. De Goede has argued that

> money and language perform parallel functions in modern society: both entail a system of signs and symbols that render possible social exchange and interaction . . . . In effect, then, the currency interrupted is not the hard-financial flows to terrorists but the currency of social interaction and political participation from which the sanctioned person becomes excluded. (2012b: 163)

While this work recognizes the criticisms of extending the use of 'violence' beyond the physical, it nonetheless believes the broadening is legitimated by the intersections between physical and non-physical violences with the latter often resulting in the former and vice versa. Jackman has posited that 'a physically harrowing experience . . . or bodily injury is often consequential for the victim in large part because of the long-term impact on his or her psychological, material or social welfare. Indeed, the boundaries between different types of injury are fundamentally clouded' (2002: 393).

Institutional and systemic violence is far more opaque than immediate physical violence perpetrated by one individual on another (Aisenberg, 2011: 17). The

---

[1] The author has drawn from James Ferguson's conception of 'anti-politics' which was devised as a critique of dominant economic development projects in the global South. The author has loosely adapted Ferguson's main argument of development practices to the realm of financial counter-terror initiatives.

invisibleness of institutional violence results in the acceptance of certain policies and initiatives from the public at large as their negative consequences are not seen. This coincides with Jackman's argument that 'forms of corporate violence have been harder to recognise – specifically, actions that result from the fragmented or cumulative activities of multiple actors, in which the agent or victims are faceless and/or amorphous, or in which there is either a temporal lag or a probabilistic relationship between the actions taken by agents and the outcomes experienced by the victims' (2002: 399). This is particularly relevant given the practice of counter-terror financing (CTF) is carried out by a range of actors and institutions both public and private. Moreover, in line with Jackman, much of the violent consequences of British financial counter-terror initiatives are felt outside of the British state itself as transnational donations are delayed, disrupted or ceased. It has so far proved impossible for charities and NGOs to quantify the consequences of disruptions of aid distributions as charities lack the resources, time and skill sets to conduct this type of research. The effects of disruptions to aid, as Jackman asserts, may involve a 'temporal lag' between the harm experienced and the passing of legislation further obscuring the correlation between counter-terror measures and harm. Many of the directly harmed victims are the intended recipients of aid that are 'faceless' and largely geographically separated from Western governments that initiate such policies and their domestic audiences. Not only this, the true consequences of CTF will not be felt or seen immediately but may escalate and bubble away unnoticed in the medium to long term.

Performativity

Drawing from work on performativity and belonging, this monograph will, to an extent, combine the terms of politics, practice and ritual arguing that these physical movements and gestures (picking up the phone to make a donation; dropping coins into a collection box; etc.) can be considered 'performative' (Butler, 1988; Lambek, 2013).

Performativity implies that we are not born a particular way but *become*. While Butler focuses primarily on the construction of genders we can apply her theory to religion in that none are truly born into a religion but become a member of the religion through various acts of worship and ritual: the performance of Muslim norms is what leads a person to being a Muslim. As Mahmood has articulated, 'for many pious Muslims, these embodied practices and virtues provide the substrate through which one comes to acquire a devoted and pious disposition' (2013: 72).

Outward behavioural forms 'were not only the expression of their interiorized religiosity but also a necessary means of acquiring it' (Mahmood, 2005: 147). Mahmood continues by stating that 'in other words, action does not issue forth from natural feelings but *creates* them . . . it is through repeated *bodily* acts that one trains one's memory, desire, and intellect to behave according to established standards of conduct' (2005: 157). In the case of Muslim communities of the UK several sets of norms and objective realities are conditioning the Muslim individual simultaneously. The first is obviously the norms and practices of Islam while the second are the norms and constraints of British society generally. Both act to various degrees to constrain and shape the individual. In many instances, the influence of Islam was not 'unconscious' but actively cultivated in the individual with self-awareness and critique. The effects of living in a British secular society were often the less consciously apparent. Not that Muslims were unaware of the challenges of being Muslim in contemporary secular Britain but that the effects this had on their practice were less explicitly articulated. Specifically, in the case of Muslim charity, the influence of both Islamic and British charitable norms can be evidenced from the below conversation with a practising Muslim in Glasgow who explicitly links Islamic obligations and responsibilities to wider British charitable norms and non-Muslim charitable causes (such as the Big Issue).

> *Zakat* is one of the Five Pillars and as a Muslim, I hold the Five Pillars.... Ever since we were little in my household charity was a really big thing. My Mum encouraged us to go out in the community to give back, whether it was time, or whether it was money. I think in terms of Islam anyway, charity isn't just money. It is *sadaqah*: giving of yourself, your time, your wealth, and I think I have always seen my Mum as an example of that. It seems so silly, but she was very cautious to ensure we understood as children. I remember, you know, those charity appeals that came on TV. Now there are loads of them and most of them aren't even Muslim charities, just you know, generic UK charities but I think that I could guarantee anytime an appeal would come on my Mum would pick up the phone or she would get us to pick up the phone and dial so that we would be involved in it and she would speak about the importance of charity.... Anytime we used to go out as kids, she'd make me give the money to Big Issue and things like that.

The interaction between both Muslim and non-Muslim charitable practices was an oft-repeated pattern from those interviewed for this research. For instance, a young male charity shop employee based in Bradford retold how his mother would send him to their elderly poor neighbours with regular meals. The individual stated that looking out for and feeding neighbours (Muslim or non-Muslim) was simply a 'daily routine'. The interviewee believed that notions of charity were embedded in Muslims from an early age with the form and type of charity being donated depending upon the immediate context of both the giver and the receiver.

Part of the challenge in the post-9/11 and 7/7 British context is the perception that British norms and values are at odds with certain Islamic values and practices which in turn relates to how British Muslim citizens and residents are viewed by the wider British society. At stake is whether Muslims can simultaneously be 'Muslim' and 'British' by coinciding with vague notions of 'fundamental British values' (Contest, 2018). As Butler observes,

> To be a subject at all requires first complying with certain norms that govern recognition – that make a person recognisable ... non-compliance calls into question the viability of one's life, the ontological conditions of one's persistence ... condition in advance who will count as a subject, and who will not. (2009: iv)

Importantly, 'shared performance of patterns of behaviour not only produces a communal appreciation of belonging, but it simultaneously produces particular kinds of subjects which cannot be disassociated from the collective project' (Bell, 1999: 48). The performance of Muslim norms, of which charitable giving is an important aspect, therefore both produces the British Muslim community and helps shape British Muslims as 'British' as practices are both contained and constrained within the UK context. Particularly since 9/11 and 7/7, British Muslims are conscious of themselves as being perceived as Muslims and increasingly constrained by the suspicion and stigmatization of contemporary counter-terror initiatives that frames Muslims as a threat to wider society.

Petty-sovereigns

De Goede (2012b) utilizes Butler's concept of 'petty-sovereigns' in her analysis of the operation of financial counter-terror policies. 'Petty-sovereigns' describes a plethora of actors who hold some autonomy in specific areas and exercise certain powers yet are not accountable nor absolute sovereign in all spheres. The 'petty-sovereigns' of the FWoT range from government agencies and officials to bank assistants and university librarians as they are legally coerced to survey, monitor and report 'deviant' action. Warde has noted that 'the financial war gave rise to a new class of "financial warriors", in the United States and overseas – political officials and bureaucrats in charge of waging and promoting the financial war' (2007: 14). What Warde refers to as 'financial warriors' can easily be conceived of as petty-sovereigns. The unaccountability of these petty-sovereigns is augmented by the fact that the burden of implementing and practising many counter-terror financial initiatives 'fall on the private sector' (Rumaniuk, 2008: 248). The range of actors and institutions recruited as petty-sovereigns is increasing as the financial counter-terror initiatives expand further and deeper into our everyday lives with 'new financial sectors and new industries (such as travel agencies, car dealerships, and jewellery businesses) – without much evidence to support such expansion' (Warde, 2007: 49). Unaccountability and the lack of transparency grow as does the range of actors, institutions and sectors embroiled in counter-terror measures. Not only are these petty-sovereigns unaccountable, they are also largely untrained and being asked to identify and monitor potential 'terrorists' for which no profile currently exists. Engagement with counter-terror measures is now a statutory requirement in the UK under the Prevent Duty established in 2015 but the remit is vague and definitions incomplete leaving much scrutiny and reporting left to individual, inexpert interpretations. In an era of widespread Islamophobia, many Muslims and Islamic institutions are being reported to counter-terror boards (such as Prevent) for simply being Muslim and part of a 'suspect' community. Racializations, stereotypes, Islamophobia and more combine to ensure that the perceptions of inexpert petty-sovereigns detrimentally affect Muslim communities far more than any other religious or ethnic community in the UK despite government rhetoric denying the targeting of Muslims.

Islam

While much literature exists regarding the beliefs and practices of Islam, many misunderstandings still linger in the minds of mainstream British (and other) societies. Islam is the third of the Abrahamic religions which like its cousins, Judaism and Christianity, centre around the belief in a single creator God. Islam is the second-largest religion in the world exceeded only by Christianity but growing faster in terms of adherents and new converts (Lipka, 2017). According to data from the Pew Research Centre, the growth in Islam globally is largely a result of Muslims having on average more children than other religious groups and the general youth of practitioners who relatedly are at the age where having children is more likely (Lipka, 2017). Islam has central beliefs and obligations shared across the global community of Muslims (*ummah*). This is demonstrated most saliently in the 'five pillars' of Islam which constitute the declaration of faith (*shahada*), prayer (*salat*), obligatory alms (*zakat*), fasting (*sawat*) and pilgrimage (*hajj*). Despite these central tenets it would be erroneous to understand Islam as a single homogenous faith. Like all world religions an enormous variety exists regarding interpretations and practices not least in the Sunni/Shia divide but also within these sects are different legal schools (*madhabs*). The differing sects and legal interpretations vie against each other for the 'correct' interpretation of the Islamic faith. As a global religion that emanated from the Arabian Peninsula, Islam is now firmly grounded across the globe and as such differences in interpretation and practices have emerged in different geographic locales. As Mahmood has noted, 'Islam . . . is not a single "cultural formation" but . . . a discursive tradition whose practitioners struggle over what it means to live in this world, a struggle furthermore, that unfolds in a field of power in which the historical development of "secular liberalism" commands considerable force and weight' (2013: 141). Thus, this work does not understand British Muslim communities as a homogenous unified group but an array of practitioners with differing interpretations and practices though all sharing an abstract faith in the Five Pillars.

Barylo understands Islam as being capable of 'extracting information from different contexts, which reshapes its organisation and makes it integrate into its environment differently' (2018: 17), thereby resulting in various practices and understandings. Recognition of the heterogeneous nature of Islamic interpretation and practice does not invalidate the core characteristics of charitable giving which transcends internal divisions between Muslim practitioners. Despite the plurality of practice there is a 'common underlying humanitarian ethos grounded in Islamic discourse, structural dynamics rooted in religious practices, and a set of shared historical experiences shaped by the current geopolitical climate' (Barzegar and El Karhili, 2017: 14). Shared concern regarding charity is also emphasized by Benthall who posited that 'all Islamic charities share a family resemblance: for example, the way they draw on the potent religious idioms of zakat . . . in their references to the religious calendar and quotations from the Koran and hadiths' (2007: 1–14). Thus, when this monograph uses terms such as 'Islamic ethos' it is not attempting to describe an essentialist, homogenous Islamic faith but a broad and overlapping focus on charity and humanitarianism across the differing *Islams*.

Islamic charity in UK

There are currently over 1,600 Muslim charities registered with the Charity Commission for England and Wales with an estimated combined annual income of

£275 million (Yasmin and Ghafran, 2019: 5). Religious organizations and communities have played an important role in the development of charity and delivery of services for hundreds of years within Britain (NCP, 2014). However, much of the contemporary growth of faith-based charitable organization has been witnessed since the 1990s (Barnett and Stein, 2012: 5). Muslim charitable giving in the UK dates from the first Muslim migrants to Britain, although specifically Muslim charitable institutions and organizations became more visible from the early 1980s onwards, in part because of the integration of Muslims into the wider British society. While all charities need to register with the independent regulator the Charity Commission (or the Scottish equivalent Office of the Scottish Charity Regulator [OSCR]), a large minority of Muslim charitable giving remains individually and informally donated, especially in the case of *zakat*. It is particularly the informal and (assumed to be) unrecorded financial flows that immediately raise suspicion in contemporary neoliberal economic frames. De Goede has asserted that 'money and transactions that are relatively invisible within the regular channels of Western record keeping and reporting are quickly considered to be suspicious in themselves' (De Goede, 2012b: 95) regardless of the intended use of such funds.

According to a joint survey between JustGiving and ICM, Muslims donate to charitable causes more than any other religious group within the UK, averaging annual donations of £371 per head in contrast to the national average of £165 (Ainsworth, 2013; Khimji, 2014: 2). While some *zakat* donations are informally and personally distributed, Muslim charities in the UK have in recent decades seen an upsurge in both donations, and the number and types of charitable organizations in existence, with some focusing on small highly localized projects, others aiming to alleviate suffering at the national level, and still others focused on international humanitarian efforts. Benthall notes that Islamic charitable organizations and NGOs emerged as 'the result of a confluence of two historical movements' dating back to the 1970s – the two historical moments being the rise of NGOs in general and 'the Islamic resurgence' (2007: 6). Further instigations for the growth of Muslim charitable and welfare organizations were provided by the conflict in Afghanistan in the 1980s and the Bosnian crisis in the early 1990s, resulting in many Muslim charities arising as a consequence 'that mixed humanitarianism with religious and political aims' (Benthall, 2007: 6).

Benthall does not err in the explanation for the rise of specifically Muslim charitable and social institutions in the UK. However, from the noted events it would read that Muslim charities were concerned largely with events and tragedies concerning Muslim issues only. The reality is that large and internationally renowned charities such as Islamic Relief and Muslim Aid began, in part, as an attempt for Muslims to assist in wider humanitarian efforts. The spark for Islamic Relief and Muslim Aid, for instance, was not the events that can be considered simply 'Muslim' but the crisis that hit the continent of Africa in the 1980s. As broader British society responded to the African crisis with events such as 'Band Aid', British Muslims felt they could also contribute by creating organized and professional charities that would assist in Muslims fulfilling their religious obligations while additionally providing an Islamic response to humanitarian catastrophes. From the beginning then, there is a symbiotic relationship between the rise of Muslim charitable institutions and the charitable practices and motivations of wider British society as the civil sphere allows for 'interdependencies' between social and religious groupings as Casanova (1994: 42) recognizes.

There are several types of Muslim charities working within Britain from large international organizations (such as Islamic Relief, Muslim Aid, and Muslim Hands UK) to small grassroots initiatives like mosques and local Islamic organizations. Approximately 50 per cent of UK Muslim charities report an annual income of less than £10,000 (Kroessin, 2009: 7).

In many ways, the services provided by Muslim charities are identical to those provided by secular and other faith-based organizations (FBOs) with the obvious exceptions of specific Islamic alms such as *zakat* and providing food for religious festivities (Benthall, 2018: 19). There is an emphasis, particularly in overseas aid, on providing provisions for orphans, widows and clean water facilities. While coinciding with secular aid projects, the emphasis on orphans, widows and water can be derived from the Qu'ran. The Qu'ran, for instance, promises rewards for kindnesses directed towards orphans while also warning of severe punishment for neglect or mistreatment (Khan, 2012: 105). Significantly, the Prophet Muhammad was an orphan.

It is impossible to outline all the services and provisions that the various Muslim charities in Britain provide; however, the following discussion gives a 'flavour' of the vibrant and diverse subsector but is by no means exhaustive.

Visibility of the Muslim charitable sector was also augmented in the 1980s by the emergence of energetic and charismatic philanthropists such as Dr Hany El-Banna and Yusuf Islam (perhaps better known as the musician and songwriter, Cat Stevens). El-Banna founded Islamic Relief, the Humanitarian Forum and the umbrella organization the Muslim Charities Forum, among others. Yusuf Islam established the charity Small Kindnesses and acted as chairman for Muslim Aid from 1985 to 1993.

Both El-Banna and Islam have received awards in merit of their philanthropy, and both have also been at the receiving end of allegations of terrorist financing. Yusuf Islam, for instance, was denied entry into the United States in 2004 for being on a 'watchlist' for allegedly providing funds for Hamas after previously being denied entry into Israel in 2000 (Frith, 2004). Islam subsequently won substantial libel damages against *The Sun* and *The Sunday Times* both of which suggested that Islam's denied entry to the United States was justified. Despite being awarded an OBE in 1994, El-Banna has been subject to allegations of 'extremism'. These allegations largely hang on claims of affiliation with the Muslim Brotherhood. The Muslim Brotherhood, however, is *not* a designated terrorist entity. Claims of El-Banna's 'extremism' have been made while explicitly stating that no illegality or criminality took place (Webb, 2018). For instance, a report published by The Henry Jackson Society infers links between El-Banna and the Muslim Brotherhood on the basis that El-Banna once read the controversial book *Milestones* by Islamist ideologue Sayyid Qutb (Webb, 2018: 65). Numerous allegations of links to the Muslim Brotherhood and Hamas are made within this report between several charities included under the Muslim Charities Forum umbrella. The report, however, explicitly states that it 'focuses on abuse by those charities that support the spread of harmful non-violent extremist views that are not illegal' (Webb, 2018: 4). The views are considered 'harmful' not because they promote violence or because of illegal association with terrorist entities but simply because they differ from the 'normal' mainstream liberal standards of contemporary British society.

Islamic Relief and Muslim Aid represent two of the largest international Muslim charities in the UK and are therefore worthy of some explanation. Islamic Relief was founded in 1984 by Dr Hany El-Banna (OBE) in Birmingham, England. Dr El-Banna was born in Egypt and relocated to Britain to serve as a medic in the NHS, establishing Islamic Relief with other medics and activists to provide disaster and emergency responses to the most vulnerable in Africa. Likewise, Muslim Aid was founded in 1985, has won the 'International Charity of the Year' at the Charity Times Awards and works in twenty-seven different countries (Muslim Aid, 2020). Both charities have concentrated their humanitarian work overseas with focus on children, safe water, education, sustainability and women's empowerment.

According to research conducted by Khan, Islamic Relief has attracted Muslim donors 'because of its reputation as a reliable, trusted and well-organised charity and because they believed it promoted a positive image of Muslims and their contributions to British society' (2012: 91). Importantly, and coinciding with the arguments made in subsequent chapters, Khan argues that 'the fact that Islamic Relief is a Muslim FBO with its headquarters and almost all fundraising offices in Western Europe . . . no doubt contributes to shaping the organisation's identity, and Islamic Relief presents itself simultaneously as both Muslim and Western' (2012: 91). Islamic Relief conforms to humanitarian 'best practice' by emphasizing its commitment to non-partiality and non-discrimination in line with secular aid agencies. Equally, while Muslim Aid draws from an Islamic ethos, it provides services based on need. Islamic Relief was the first Muslim charity in the UK to be represented in the Disasters Emergency Committee and British Overseas NGOs for Development (BOND) (Khan, 2012: 102). Other partners for Islamic Relief include the World Food Programme, UN Women, CAFOD, Tear Fund and Age International. More recently, in the Covid-19 era, Islamic Relief support organizations have been further augmented with the likes of Shelter, FareShare, Oxfam, Crisis and the British Red Cross (Islamic Relief, 2020). Consequently, Islamic Relief has succeeded in gaining trust from individual Muslim donors in addition to secular governmental and non-governmental agencies such as Britain's Department for International Development (DfID). Similarly, Muslim Aid has succeeded in attracting external funders and partnerships which include the European Union and the United Nations Development Programme. Within the UK, Muslim Aid has partnered with local entities such as the Salvation Army and Tower Hamlets Council.

Financially, Islamic Relief consistently raises millions annually reporting a record £128 million in 2018 (Islamic Relief, 2019) overshadowing Muslim Aid's 2018 income of £24.5 million (Muslim Aid Trustee Report, 2019: 20). Overwhelmingly, Islamic Relief has concentrated on humanitarian efforts outside of the UK but has gradually encroached upon British charitable provisions through UK partnerships which in 2018 contributed to food banks, a vegetable garden scheme and distribution of clothing and blankets to the UK's homeless among other projects (Islamic Relief, 2019). Muslim Aid also has embarked upon the UK sector, being among the first responders to the 2017 Grenfell Tower tragedy (Muslim Aid, 2020). Despite being internationally renowned, Islamic Relief has not escaped the attention of financial counter-terror initiatives stating in their Annual Report of 2019 that 'the obstacles and delays we face when moving funds to provide timely assistance to those in need are having a direct impact on people's lives' (Islamic Relief, 2019: 39).

In contrast, the charities National Zakat Foundation, Penny Appeal and al-Mizan Charitable Trust were all founded approximately a decade following the tragedy of 9/11 and thus represent the 'next generation' of British Muslim charities. All three charities appealed particularly to the younger and second-generation Muslim practitioners interviewed for this research. Unlike Islamic Relief, the National Zakat Foundation and al-Mizan provide assistance to the poor and needy in Britain exclusively, while Penny Appeal provides both nationally and internationally. Since its launch in 2011, the National Zakat Foundation has distributed approximately £16 million in charity across the UK focusing on hardship relief, housing, education and providing shelters for women of domestic abuse. In 2018 alone, the charity raised £4,629,679 in voluntary income (National Zakat Foundation, 2019). The focus on the UK, as will be demonstrated in the following chapters, is an emerging shift in Muslim *zakat* charitable practices. For the National Zakat Foundation, focus on the UK is an explicit understanding of the poverty and economic failures of the British political system. In its 2019 Annual Report, the National Zakat Foundation justifies its focus on Britain by stating that 'almost half of all Muslims living in the UK are in poverty' (National Zakat Foundation, 2019).

Penny Appeal celebrated its ten-year anniversary in 2019 and was co-founded by the young and dynamic Yorkshire-born Adeem Younis on the back of his hugely successful digital dating site SingleMuslim.com. Penny Appeal appears to allure young and modern British Muslims. Like most Muslim charities, Penny Appeal focuses on orphans, women, education and safe water provisions but includes some innovative campaigns such as 'Adopt a Gran'. In addition to aid distribution in the UK, which has seen the provision of winter kits to the homeless, Penny Appeal also tackles emergency and disaster appeals overseas. Overseas projects include the familiar states of Syria, Yemen and Palestine (among others) in conjunction with perhaps more surprising geographies such as Australia, South Africa and New Zealand (Penny Appeal, 2019).

Essentially, al-Mizan is a grant provider for vulnerable and disadvantaged individuals and families in need within the UK. Grants are provided based on need and regardless of faith, cultural background or ethnicity. Those eligible for grants can seek assistance with funding towards education, training, employment, medical costs and subsistence. Similar to Penny Appeal, the al-Mizan Trust provides some innovative projects which blend British secular life with Islamic ethos of charitable giving such as 'back to school' backpacks for school children, 'winter warmer packs' for the homeless and uniquely 'mother's day baby kits' for new mothers (al-Mizan Charitable Trust, 2019). With a reported income of £55,504 in 2019, al-Mizan represents one of the newer and medium-sized Muslim charities that have emerged in the UK over the past decade.

The brief and select biographies of British Muslim charities indicate that Muslim charities do not serve Muslims alone nor work in isolation from other organizations of whatever faith or none. That being said, an argument has arisen which posits that Muslim charities could possess advantages in some areas that non-Muslim charities do not have. One potential positive for Muslim charities working overseas (and with Muslim communities in the UK) is the argument for 'cultural proximity'. Cultural proximity assumes that a commonality (in this case, a common religion) between the aid giver and aid receiver provides an 'operational advantage' (Benthall, 2012: 68). The claim that cultural proximity can be advantageous and increase efficiency and trust levels is made by both Islamic charities and non-Muslim charities that have faced difficulties in aid distribution in Muslim-majority areas (Benthall, 2012: 68). This is particularly significant as currently the largest portion of overseas aid from Western states is directed to Muslim-majority states such as Afghanistan, Iraq, Syria and Yemen (Barnett and Stein, 2012: 7). Some explicitly Christian aid agencies have found mistrust from the Muslim communities they seek to assist, caused in part by historical Christian missionary work and past and present Western political interventions (Barnett and Stein, 2012: 7). Claims regarding the advantages of cultural proximity, while important, should not be overdetermined as the various interpretations of Islamic practice can themselves be a point of conflict. Additionally, some of the largest international charities, such as Islamic Relief, are signatories of the Code of Conduct for the International Red Cross and Red Crescent Movement, which stipulates that charitable provisions be based on need alone and cannot discriminate on aspects such as faith or none (Benthall, 2012: 68). Arguments for cultural proximity should not, therefore, be read that Muslim charities only (or should only) assist Muslims or that other FBOs only serve fellow religious practitioners. The claim for cultural proximity simultaneously defends the need for specific FBOs while also legitimating partnerships and understandings between different faith-based and secular bodies. For instance, Benthall has argued that cultural proximity does not detract from the 'practical potential of non-Muslim agencies, both religious and secular, to work effectively in Muslim field areas . . . and to collaborate effectively with Islamic aid agencies – as do, for instance, Oxfam, CAFOD, the United Methodist Committee on Relief' (Benthall, 2012: 83).

None of this is to argue that misuse of charitable funds cannot occur. Charitable abuses occur across the sector (faith-based or secular) (Benthall, 2016: 3) and none are immune to the possibility of abuse. Nonetheless, it should be recognized that misuse of charitable funds is rare and is not confined to Muslim charities alone. When misuses do occur, they are even less likely to involve connections to 'terrorism' or political violence, at least since the end of the Afghan *jihad* in the early 1990s. Compelling evidence certainly exists for the re-appropriation of charitable funds towards violent political goals prior to the 1990s, specifically concerning charities based in the Gulf states and Saudi Arabia particularly. For instance, both the International Islamic Relief Organization (IIRO) (based in Saudi Arabia and not to be confused with Islamic Relief UK) and the World Assembly of Muslim Youth provided financial resources to the Afghan *jihad* in the 1980s. According to Benthall, 'the charge sheet against IIROSA's branches during the 1980s and the 1990s is extensive' (2018: 2–3). In the 1980s, IIROSA was one of many charities based at the Afghan/Pakistan border which contributed to military as well as humanitarian assistance (Benthall, 2018: 19). However, at the time support for the Afghan *jihad* was considered to coincide with Western anti-communist interests. Support, militarily and financially, towards the *mujahideen* in Afghanistan was encouraged by Western states rather than deemed as providing support for terrorism. There is no 'record of the US government expressing the slightest disquiet' that charitable resources were used to support the anti-Soviet war in Afghanistan (Bokhari, Chowdhury and Lacey, 2014: 202). As Benthall has argued, 'during the Soviet-Afghan war, the Western powers, and especially the United States, set a lead for others to follow, only to turn later against Islamic charities with draconian counterterrorist measures' (2018: 19). IIRO is now dramatically reduced and confined to working within Saudi Arabia. Robust evidence for charitable funds being directed towards support to contemporary political violence is far more difficult to ascertain from the 1990s onwards.

It must, however, be noted that the charitable sector in the UK has witnessed a worrying increase in cases of fraud (secular and faith-based) seeing a rise from £1.9 billion in 2016 to £2.3 billion in 2017 (Crowe, 2017). The Charity Commission recently published evidence that half of all British charities have been victims of fraud stating that 'while there is no evidence that charities are at greater risk of fraud or financial crime than any other type of organisation, the risk of fraud in charities appears to be growing' (Charity Commission for England and Wales, 2019a). It must also be noted that fraud does not equate with terrorism or political violence with 59 per cent of fraud cases within the charitable sector being less than £1,000 and eight out of ten cases were identified by the concerned charity itself (Charity Commission for England and Wales, 2019b). According to the Charity Commission for England and Wales, the greatest risk concerning fraud in the charitable sector is the reputational damage to individual charities and the charitable sphere generally (Charity Commission for England and Wales, 2019a).

Methodology

To take the *practice* of religion as seriously as theological dogma requires allowing active Muslims a voice of their own, Ammermon states, 'looking for lived religion does mean that we look for the material, embodied aspects of religion as they occur in everyday life, in addition to listening for how people explain themselves' (2014, 190). The theoretical framework thus relates to the methodology of semi-structured in-depth interviews with individual Muslims, charitable organizations, mosques and Islamic institutions. Complementing interview material will be data received from regulatory bodies such as the Charity Commission for England and Wales and the OSCR, academic literature and published reports by charities, governments, NGOs and think tanks. It should be noted that charities in the UK are legally required to publicly submit annual reports which are an extremely useful resource for obtaining quantitative data on how much financial resources are available to the Muslim charitable sector and how the monies are distributed. Equally it should be noted that these reports range dramatically in depth and scope with the larger and more financially secure charities issuing glossy, visual reports while the smaller charities often provide little more than the minimum legal requirement. Another limitation of charitable annual reports is that under current charity regulation in the UK, they are not obliged to detail which donations are given as general charity (*sadaqah*) and which are received specifically as religious alms (*zakat*).

A range of charities, Islamic institutions, religious scholars and practising individuals were consulted constituting a wide range of Muslim practitioners from a diverse socio-economic background, ethnicity and sects. The intention was to gain insights not solely into institutions and individuals directly donating or distributing charity but also to individuals and institutions that disseminate theological understandings of charitable purposes and acts (hence the inclusion of the Muslim World League that in addition to disseminating theological understandings of charity has *sadaqah* and *zakat* collection boxes in its main London office). Research began in 2013 with assistance from the British Academy small grants. Further in-depth research has been conducted from 2016 to 2019 as part of the Leverhulme Trust Early Careers research project. Many institutions, charities and individuals permitted interviews on condition of anonymity which itself is indicative of the apprehension, suspicion and fear currently felt within certain spheres of contemporary British communities. Charities and institutions which were consulted and agreed to being named include Islamic Relief, the Muslim Charities Forum, the National Foundation of Zakat, Interpal, the Islamic Centre of England, Zakat House, Penny Appeal, the Muslim Association of Britain, the Muslim World League and the London Central Mosque. Additionally, the Charity Commission for England and Wales agreed to answer written questions via email while the OSCR agreed to an extensive face-to-face interview. A number of other charities, both large and small, also contributed with face-to-face interviews but did so only on the condition of anonymity. The author is thus ethically bound to not explicitly name institutions and individuals that have been paramount in this research. In some cases, the fear of repercussion was not merely perceived but a direct result of previous UK government interventions, scrutiny and media allegations. Consequently, most quotations used in this work derived from interview transcripts remain anonymous to coincide with ethical procedure and protect participants and organizations from harm.

Over thirty in-depth semi-structured interviews were conducted across England and Scotland with over one hundred more informal participants ranging from mosque attendees to charity employees/volunteers to individual practising Muslims. Consultation with *Sunni*, *Shia* and *Ahmadiyya* communities were sought but in line with contemporary British demographics, practitioners of *Sunni* Islam were the majority of those interviewed. As the research focus was on Islamic institutions, mosques and Muslim charities an obvious limitation to the work is that it potentially has missed the practices of Muslims not associated with any mosque or institution. Another limitation to this work is that the number of participants does not allow for quantitative evaluation. This work therefore undertakes qualitative analysis, understanding the subjectivity that risks.

What is, or is not, considered a 'faith-based' charity is notoriously hard to define. Faith manifests in many different forms, intensities and rhetoric. The New Philanthropy Capitol (NCP) distinguishes between three different levels of faith-based charities: (1) Central faith charity – where faith is integral to charities work in both mission statements and projects; (2) mission-based charity – where faith is a central component of the intent and understanding of charitable actions but does not affect the projects and end-users of the charity; (3) historical faith charity – where faith is important to the initial charity project but has become of historical rather than contemporary relevance (Wharton and Las Casas, 2016: 10).

As methodologically difficult as it is to distinguish what is, or is not, faith-based it is even more tricky to break the faith-based categories down further to specific faiths. Neither the Charity Commission nor OSCR require details of which religion or faith a charity seeks to base its values on. To establish specific faith-based charities requires searching the Charity Commission and OSCR's website for key words and terms. However, even this does not roll out the methodological lumps. Certain charities I spoke to, while they considered themselves humanitarian rather than faith-based, were acutely aware of how they were *perceived* by their majority donor base.

An example of this is the Yorkshire-based charity Penny Appeal which does not have the words 'Muslim' or 'Islamic' in the title, does not profess any particular faith in its guiding statements, assists in over thirty countries globally on the criteria of need, not religion, ethnicity or sect, and as such is easily conceived of as simply a charity aimed at poverty alleviation. Yet, many of its donors perceive it as a 'Muslim' charity or certainly that is how many of my respondents understood it. Penny Appeal collects charitable donations under many project titles considered largely 'secular' such as 'adopt a Gran', but also has a '100% *zakat*' collection fund. By including *zakat* within its donations, it is directly meeting a need required by its majority donor base and to deny any association with 'Islam' would de-legitimize its ability to take responsibility for its donor's religious obligations. Of note is that Penny Appeal's headquarters is established consciously in the founder's hometown of Wakefield, Yorkshire, providing over 200 jobs to the local community and involving over 3,000 volunteers. Office staff were notably of a diverse selection of British peoples many of whom were non-Muslim or of no faith whatsoever demonstrating the potential of social integration and cohesion despite my 'loose' inclusion of this particular charity (and others) as 'Muslim'.

The methodological quagmire of categorizing what is, or is not, to be considered a faith-based charity or 'Muslim' charity only feeds further into the theoretical assumptions. Teasing apart what is secular and what is religious is not always possible or indeed desirable. The strict opposing categories of 'secular' and 'religious' are unhelpful when investigating the various ways in which religion manifests itself in action at different junctures and levels. Many of the charities I interviewed considered themselves primarily humanitarian rather than religious per se, yet this does not detract from the founders of the charities who, driven by values and ethics of faith, put that faith into action by beginning the charity in the first place. For example, a founding member of a medium-sized charity based in London and founded in 2010 stated,

> I don't think we really see ourselves as a 'Muslim' charity, but more that it just happens to have been set up by a bunch of Muslims. It follows some Islamic principles like helping people in need, compassion and generosity and things like that, but I don't think we use our Muslim identity as much as other charities.

The same participant acknowledged that most of the charity's donor base were Muslims despite the lack of emphasis on the charity's 'Islamic' credentials. This would, by and large, fit into the NPC's category of 'historical faith-based charity' yet the term 'historical' implies faith had meaning and motivational value in the past but not the present which is not necessarily the case for either Trustees or donors despite the lack of religious rhetoric elsewhere. The wishes of the majority donor base are extremely important to any charitable organization. As Petersen addresses,

> Organisations do not formulate and present their ideologies to an undefined or abstract other, but address particular *audiences* with the purpose of motivating and encouraging them to support their organization . . . . Here issues of legitimacy are central: if audiences do not consider organisations to be legitimate, they will not support them. (2015: 40)

Taking a broad definition, 'Muslim' charities are understood as (1) a charity that specifically categorizes itself in name or goals as 'Islamic', (2) humanitarian but understands faith as the prime motivator behind charitable actions, (3) humanitarian in nature and does not state faith as its goal or prime motivator and yet is understood as 'Muslim' by the majority of its donors and the general public. While the definition is intentionally broad, it must be noted that this wide categorization does not come without its own perils. A charity that self-ascribes as 'Muslim' commented,

> While we call ourselves Muslim charities and the Muslim sector . . . we are a humanitarian organisation. When it comes to beneficiaries, we don't look at their faith . . . we just treat people equally . . . really in a way the Islamic charity label works against us because of the way things are. People see the word 'Islamic' or 'Muslim' and it becomes a negative – 'they must have links to terrorism'.

The terrain of Muslim charities and charitable practices within Britain cannot be considered as a homogenous whole and the pluralities of beliefs and practices must be accounted for in addition to the differing size, financial resources and scopes of charitable causes. Emphasis should also be granted to the fact that many within the charitable sector dislike the sub-categorization of 'Muslim' charity, arguing this creates a false distinction. Yet, like a recent report on the Muslim Humanitarian Sector argues, 'the political reality that governments, media and development practitioners in fact already categorise practitioners and subject them, whether intentionally or not, to a particular set of practices and presumptions' (Barzegar and El Karhili, 2017, 11) thereby justifies the use of the term 'Muslim charity' while acknowledging that distinction can at times be harmful.

The following chapter will explain in more detail how the charitable sector became embroiled in the FWoT through global CTF systems. It will also explore how CTF policies, derived from the United States, have expanded into the United Kingdom examining some of the consequences for charities that operated in the United States and the limits of US coercive powers.

2

The (il)logic of financial counter-terrorism strategies

From the United States to the global

Three events sparked current British counter-terror measures: the attacks of 9/11 in the United States, riots in Northern England in 2001 and the London July bombings of 2005 (MacDonald, O'Regan and Hunter, 2013: 445). Globally, the spectacle of 9/11 fostered an international will to challenge global terrorism resulting in the still evolving global counter-terror system. However, the domestic challenges to the UK ensured that, in practice, global counter-terror norms have been adapted to the UK context. While 9/11 was perpetrated by actors largely of non-US citizenship, the riots in Northern England in 2001 and the bombings of 7/7 were largely instigated by British citizens who grew up, were educated and worked within the UK. As a result, British counter-terror measures are concerned about the sense of attachment and belonging that particularly minority ethnicities and religious groups have towards the British state.

In the weeks following 9/11, while controversy grew internationally regarding military retaliation, less controversy manifested in relation to the non-military response in the form of the Financial War on Terror (FWoT). States that were quick to criticize further military expansion had far less qualms concerning financial measures to disrupt and prevent terrorist activities. Projected as a non-violent, 'soft' approach to counter political violence, the FWoT preceded the physical war on terror and continues to grow and expand globally. The impact on Muslim charitable giving from current counter-terror financing (CTF) measures is derived from the focus on both formal financial institutions and informal financial procedures.

As the following discussion explains, formal banking and financial institutions are instructed to take a risk-based approach and submit Suspicious Transfer Reports (STRs) while simultaneously the non-governmental, charitable and voluntary sector has been identified by international counter-terror norms as 'particularly vulnerable' (FATF, 2010) to the misuse of funds for terrorist activities. These measures, in both the formal and informal sectors, are having negative but asymmetric consequences on numerous charities and informal transfer systems which the following chapters will explore in more detail.

The main premise to the FWoT follows that of anti-money laundering (AML) and highly publicized prosecutions of criminals and drug traffickers in the United States. The assumption is that if we follow the money trail, we can find the terrorists and prevent further political violence. As detailed in Chapter 1, the current CTF policies aim to be anticipatory and preventative in what De Goede asserts as 'speculative security' (2012b). Financial counter-terror policies are designed 'to arrest, detain and prosecute suspects at the earliest possible stage and ideally prior to criminal activity' in what De Goede refers to as 'banal pre-emption' (2012b: xxviii). The pre-emption is labelled 'banal' as it relies upon the surveillance and data collection of everyday financial activities permeating all aspects of daily life and mundane financial transactions.

While many international states were decidedly uncomfortable with the violent spectacle of what became 'shock and awe', the logic of cutting off financial funds to would-be terrorists appeared on face value 'like a neat and peaceable way to help prevent future attacks' (El-Fatah, 2009: 7). The premise that 'stopping the money would stop terrorism' was taken on board globally as an accepted counter-terror strategy (De Goede, 2012b: xvi).

This chapter will outline the emergence of the counter-terror finance system which arose from the United States and spread globally before examining how the UK had adapted and accommodated global CTF norms within the context of British challenges. It can be posited that while Britain undoubtedly receives (rather than instigates) much of the CTF norms, this does not prevent these norms being re-inscribed within the British context.

The FWoT was introduced by President Bush just two weeks after the events of 9/11 in the 'Terrorist Financing Executive Order' of 24 September 2001, preceding the military War on Terror (WoT). Under this order it became 'juridically possible to pursue terrorist financiers *as terrorists*. The order does not require proof that suspects *knowingly* assisted terrorist activity' (De Goede, 2012b: xxiv). Like the military WoT, the FWoT can be considered pre-emptive in that it seeks to intervene prior to terrorist activity. While on face value this may seem like a responsible policy which seeks to prevent damage to life and property, it disguises the collateral damage resulting from such policies which affect individuals and organizations that have nothing to do with terrorism or criminal activity. The anticipatory nature of CTF initiatives results in government action prior to criminality which blurs the boundaries between what is legal and illegal and, in some cases, reverses the legal burden of proof from the prosecutor to the prosecuted. As De Goede notes, 'the objective is to enable pre-emptive intervention in the spaces of everyday life, including charitable donations ... and everyday banking' (2012b: 187). The pre-emptive character of the FWoT leaves no space uncovered resulting in the surveillance and monitoring of everyday financial actions across all demographics within society.

The now-established global norms regarding financial anti-terror policies have largely been derived from the United States which, following 9/11, expanded its AML policies to include terrorist activity (Stanley and Buckley, 2016: 85). Combined with the expanded powers of the Financial Action Task Force (FATF) and the enactment of the Material Support Act, in conjunction with additional pressures on banking systems to 'know your customer' (Keatinge, 2014), the United States has acted as the initiator and coercive power in financial counter-terror policy norms. It is beyond the scope of this work to detail all US counter-terror policy and thus what shall be explored will detail that which is most pertinent internationally and specifically to the charitable sector. Particular attention will be given to the expanded remit of the FATF which has become the global policeman for financial counter-terror regulation.

Financial Action Task Force (FATF)

The FATF is a Paris-based organization originally set up in 1989 to coordinate a global response to the money laundering of drug profits (Tom Keatinge, 2014). After the events of 9/11, FATF's remit was expanded to include CTF drawing from the same logic of AML. FATF acts as a global regulator evaluating countries to determine the extent and efficiency in which they are implementing FATF's recommendations (Keatinge, 2014: 29). As a global institution FATF has enormous influence on domestic CTF initiatives exemplified by the UK Terrorist Asset Freezing Act 2010, which is entirely consistent with FATF recommendations.

In October 2001, only a month after 9/11, the FATF mandate was expanded from AML to include new provisions on CTF. FATF used the technique of 'naming and shaming' (Warde, 2007: 40) to force countries to adopt CTF regulations and procedures. An additional nine special amendments were added to FATF's existing forty recommendations formally expanding the remit far beyond money laundering. The new FATF regulations now instructed all countries to criminalize the financing of terrorism, freeze and confiscate terrorist assets and impose strict controls and surveillance on banks and non-traditional finance systems (Warde, 2007: 48). The Special Recommendations of FATF 2001 identified non-profit organizations (NPOs) as 'particularly vulnerable' to financial misuse for terrorism (FATF, 2010: 3) and thus the intervention into the charitable sector in the name of counterterrorism began. Despite FATF removing the advice in Recommendation VIII in 2016 that NPOs were 'particularly vulnerable' to terrorists, the perception of charities as susceptible to terrorist or criminal misuse has continued as evidenced in the UK's adoption of the Charities (Protection and Social Investment) Act 2016 which explicitly connects terrorism with charity surveillance (Bolleyer and Gaiya, 2017: 658). The revised FATF recommendations temper the issue of 'vulnerability' without removing it completely but simply suggest that countries identify for themselves which NPOs are 'vulnerable to terrorist financing abuse' in order to 'protect' NPOs and charities from 'terrorist financing abuse' (FATF, 2019: 11). Despite softening the association of charities as 'particularly' vulnerable, the conception has been ingrained into the global CTF assemblage (Walker, 2018: 1086).

Like the Prevent strategy in the UK, FATF focuses on the 'vulnerability' of spaces, particularly those associated with the third sector. According to FATF,

> NGOs possess characteristics that make them particularly attractive to terrorists or vulnerable to misuse for terrorist financing. They enjoy the public trust, have access to considerable sources of funds, and their activities are often cash-intensive.

Furthermore, some charities have a global presence that provides a framework for national and international operations and financial transactions, often, in or near areas most exposed to terrorist activity. Finally, charities are subject to significantly lighter regulatory requirements than financial institutions or publicly-held corporate entities. (2010: 20)

Importantly, the financial provisions inherent in FATF recommendations allow for 'the freezing of assets even before conviction' (Warde, 2007: 25). FATF special recommendations assert that 'terrorist financing offences should not require that the funds were ... actually used to carry out or attempt a terrorist act(s)' (FATF, 2010: 5). The legal burden of proof is thus reversed as it becomes incumbent on the accused to prove their innocence before financial assets can be unfrozen. As Judith Turbyne, Head of Engagement at Office of the Scottish Charity Regulator (OSCR), stated, it is 'difficult to prove a negative' (in interview with author, 2017). It is undeniable that a possibility exists that charities can be financially abused, but possibility does not translate effectively into probability. The evidence that 'terrorist and terrorist organisations exploit the NPO sector to raise and move funds' (FATF, 2014: 20) is not as compelling as political rhetoric suggests, as this work will demonstrate. The evidence that does exist is scant and demonstrates that terrorist abuse of charities is the exception rather than the norm. For instance, data from the Charity Commission demonstrates that 'the number of cases in which there is evidence to prove charities have been involved in supporting terrorist activity whether directly, indirectly, deliberately or unwittingly, is very small in comparison to the size of the sector' (Charity Commission, 2008: 5). The Charity Commission states that incidences of charitable abuse in connection to terrorist activity are 'rare' with the most damning effects being a deterioration of 'public confidence in charities' (Charity Commission, 2017). While the literature concerning counter-terror initiatives in the UK stresses 'proportionality' in prevention and response to terrorist activities, the undocumented and unanalysed consequences of current initiatives may counter such claims. Scant attention to the consequences of counter-terror legislation on charities renders invisible the societal and economic violence which may outweigh the attributes of prevention policies where the risk to the general public is more marginal than policy rhetoric would suggest.

In effect, by freezing or confiscating assets a societal violence is done to the charity or institution accused while simultaneously the intended beneficiaries of aid and welfare are denied the funds intended to ease their suffering resulting in further violence largely unseen and unreported by Western media. As the legal burden of proof is reversed the securitization of charity is complete as it breaks and circumvents 'normal' legal and political procedures.

US CTF measures

In addition to the expansion of FATF's remit, the enactment of the US Material Support Act has had enormous repercussions for the charity sector as a whole and specifically on Muslim charities based within the United States. The Material Support Law, section 2339A, prohibits 'providing material support to terrorists' while section 2339B prohibits 'providing material support or resources to designated foreign terrorist organisations' (Doyle, 2016: 2). In practice, the US PATRIOT Act combined with the Material Support Act provided additional tools aimed at terror financiers and granted permission to the FBI and other law enforcement agencies to expand wiretapping, detention and surveillance (El-Fath, 2009: 2). The 'secret' Terrorist Finance Tracking Programme was managed by the CIA under the supervision of the Treasury Department (El-Fath, 2009: 2–3) and became public in June 2006 after a leak to the *New York Times*.

One problem concerning the Material Support Act is that 'material support' is defined differently in different contexts making understanding and applying the concept by charities difficult (Charity and Security Network, 2019). The primary definition of 'material support' is contained in the Anti-Terrorism and Effective Death Penalty Act (ADEPA) which differs from the definition contained in the Immigration and Nationality Act (INA) (Charity and Security Network). According to Aziz, the rationale of the Material Support Act is that

> humanitarian aid delivered to non-combatant civilians living under the control of a terrorist organisation can be illegal based upon the unproven theory that it frees up resources to redirect towards violence. This punitively denies many innocent beneficiaries abroad of food, water, and shelter. (2011)

Holder v. Humanitarian Law Project has proven to be an important case that upholds the 'material support' statute and sets a legal precedent for future cases. The plaintiff, the Humanitarian Law Project, had provided advice and training to foreign groups and organizations that sought an entry or return to non-violent political action and negotiation. With the tightening and extension of laws concerning support to terrorist entities, the Humanitarian Law Project was forced to cease its work for fear of persecution (Ulmschneider and Lutz, 2019: 801). The Humanitarian Law Project was seeking to assist Turkey's Kurdistan Worker's Party and Sri Lanka's Liberation Tigers of Tamil Eelam (LTTE) in peaceful conflict resolution, specifically seeking to train groups to use humanitarian and international law for peaceful dispute resolution, to engage in advocacy work and to teach organizations how to petition bodies such as the UN (Global Freedom of Expression, 2020). In June 2010, the Supreme Court upheld the 'material support' statute by 6-3 resulting in attorney David Cole commenting that 'this statute is so sweeping that it treats human rights advocates as criminal terrorists, and threatens them with 15 years in prison for advocating nonviolent means to resolve disputes' (cited in Charity and Security Network, 2010). The upholding of the material support statute has had enormous repercussions for charitable, human rights and freedom of speech organizations that extends well beyond the Muslim sector. In a joint statement on the tenth anniversary of *Holder v. Humanitarian Law Project*, twenty-two civil society organizations in the United States astutely warn that 'historic moments like the signing of the Good Friday Agreement in Northern Ireland and the end of apartheid in South Africa would not have been possible without engaging the Irish Republican Party or the African National Congress, both listed terrorist organisations at the time' (cited in Charity and Security Network, 2020).

Of concern is that 'material support laws', as enacted in the United States, do not statutorily require proof that the defendant had a specific intent to support terrorism and therefore targets and scrutinizes a broad range of everyday, legitimate activities (Aziz, 2011). This issue became particularly important after the so-called Society for Worldwide Interbank Financial Telecommunications (SWIFT) controversy that reached its peak in 2010. After several subpoenas from the United States, the massive database of Brussels-based SWIFT – which links 7,800 banks and financial institutions globally – was tapped for information on suspected terrorists. The CIA gained access to SWIFT data which handles approximately 80 per cent of global wire transfer traffic (De Goede, 2012a: 215). Over concerns of privacy and security for European citizens the terms of transatlantic data transfers were renegotiated after the Dutch MEP Hennis-Plasschaert rejected the initial EU–US agreement.

The USA PATRIOT Act (acronym for 'Uniting and Strengthening America by Providing Appropriate Tools Required to Intercept and Obstruct Terrorism'), 26 October 2001, amended the Material Support Act to include the 'prohibition against providing "expert advice or assistance" to designated foreign terrorist organisations' (Freedman, 2011). The USA PATRIOT Act significantly expanded the definition of money laundering, decreased the evidence bar, raised penalties and vastly expanded the global reach of US AML and CTF policies (Warde, 2007: 43). The USA PATRIOT Act no longer required a direct link between assets and violent acts and reversed the burden of proof allowing Treasuries to freeze accounts before trial (De Goede, 2012b: 36). In line with the effects of securitization that break or circumvent established political and legal procedures, De Goede has suggested:

> If the practices of speculative security enable asset freezing without trial, destruction of livelihoods before the presentation of evidence, and prosecution of terrorist facilitators before actual plots are hatched, it is useful to understand these developments as a sovereign suspension of law that erases any legal status of the individual. (2012b: xxviii)

The logic of the 'financial war on terror', and extending this to charities, is often presented in the following way. Typically sweeping assertions are made with no supporting empirical evidence such as the below.

> The most important source of financial support . . . came from continuous fundraising efforts that date back to the 1980s: charities, NGOs, mosques, special fundraisers, intermediaries, facilitators, and direct solicitations of wealthy individuals. *Zakat* . . . contributions are largely unregulated, seldom audited . . . . And can be skimmed off for other purposes, including the commitment of acts of terrorism . . . funds can be diverted without knowledge of the donors. (Biersteker and Eckert, 2008: 9)

There are salient aspects of the above that should be noted. First, during the 1980s there was indeed evidence that charitable and fundraising monies were utilized for a number of causes, including political, such as the Afghan *jihad* against the Soviets

(Benthall and Bellion-Jourdan, 2009: 71). At the same time, however, Western governments found this unproblematic and encouraged financial flows in the Cold War struggle against Soviet Communism. Indeed, some monies found its way to, what was at the time, the embryonic leadership of al-Qaeda. This is certainly the case of the Saudi charity al-Haramain Islamic Foundation which emerged during the Soviet-Afghan conflict and closed in 2004 in the aftermath of 9/11 (Bokhari, Chowdhury and Lacey, 2014: 199). It is without doubt that *zakat* funds were used to provide both humanitarian and military support to the Afghan cause. *Zakat* can be dispersed for 'causes for Allah' which can include both violent and non-violent causes so long as the violent recourse was authorized by official and appropriate authorities (Bokhari, Chowdhury and Lacey, 2014: 202), which was certainly the case for the Afghan *jihad* which received numerous supporting *fatwas* from leading Islamic scholars and jurists. With hindsight this would, on face value, appear to be a problem and potential threat of Muslim charitable giving. However, with hindsight should also come a long memory, as far more funds were given to the Islamic fighters of Afghanistan via the CIA (Kepel, 2003: 137) and states such as Kuwait and Saudi Arabia (Alterman, 2009: 64) than from any charitable institution.

During the Afghan *jihad* the *mujahideen* were viewed as freedom fighters against the Godless Soviets as opposed to carrying the label of 'terrorists'. Yet, historic association with individuals who were not designated as terrorists at the time but have since been categorized as such has been the basis of allegations of 'extremism' and 'terrorist' affiliation. A pertinent example of this is the case of the Benevolence International Foundation, a US-based Muslim charity closed in the immediate aftermath of September 2001. In this case, the Benevolence International Foundation was accused of historical association with terrorist *individuals*: evidence regarding any links to terrorist or criminal *activity* was tenuous. The sentencing judge was not impressed with the evidence supplied by the US Treasury and the individual was not found guilty of charges relating to terrorism. The judge is recorded as saying 'nor does the record reflect that he attempted, participated in, or conspired to commit any act of terrorism . . . . The government failed to connect the dots' (cited in Warde, 2007: 141). Not that the lack of evidence of terrorist funding prevented the closure of the charity. Current financial counter-terror legislation therefore assumes that charities and institutions are garnished with clairvoyance and can predict who will be considered 'terrorists' in the future and thus can avoid working with them in the present to safeguard against future prosecution.

Another feature of the quotation from Biersteker and Eckert worthy of additional attention is the assumption that *zakat* is 'unregulated' and 'seldom audited'. This assumption is again contained within the FATF special regulations which state that 'money or value transfer systems have shown themselves vulnerable to misuse for money laundering and terrorist financing purposes' (FATF, 2010: 13). The assumption that non-Western forms of giving and informal financial transactions are undocumented and unregulated was proven entirely incorrect in the case of al-Barakaat: a remittance service based in Somalia. The misguided attack on al-Barakaat began at the behest of the United States when on 7 November 2001, US enforcement agents descended on al-Barakaat offices initiating charges of terrorist offences linked to al-Qaeda (El-Fath,

2009: 3). Accusations were later established as baseless and al-Barakaat was declared innocent of terrorist charges. After a long legal battle, the company was discreetly exonerated (El-Fath, 2009: 3).

The case of al-Barakaat

The case of al-Barakaat is of interest for many reasons. Not only were the assumptions behind the FWoT proved entirely false in this case, but it also revealed cracks in the global counter-terror financial system in addition to providing a warning regarding the counterproductive consequences of financial strikes which potentially decrease rather than increase US and global security.

The initial closure of al-Barakaat and the seizure of its assets were publicly deemed a triumph by President Bush who stated that 'today's actions disrupts al-Qaida's communications, blocks an important source of funds . . . and sends a clear message to the global financial institutions. You are either with us, or with the terrorists' (Bush, 2001). In total, sixty-two institutions and individuals had their assets frozen in connection with this case (Warde, 2007: 95). In contradistinction to the high profile the initial closures had in US media, the exoneration of the company that occurred after a lengthy and costly legal battle was discreet to the point that al-Barakaat is often still raised as a 'successful' case. As El-Fath astutely notes, 'the high-profile closure of the company was presented as a triumph, yet it brought devastation to one of the world's poorest countries' (2009: 11). The case of al-Barakaat may not be well known in the Northern Hemisphere but is renowned in Somalia which resulted in 'a strong sense of injustice done to the company and the country' (Warde, 2007: 97).

To understand the detrimental and disproportionate consequences of closing al-Barakaat, one must appreciate the context in which it operates in Somalia. Somalia is often perceived as a weak, fragile or 'failed' state particularly following the government collapse in 1991. The downfall of the government precipitated the collapse of much of the Somali state including the banking and financial sector. In this context, al-Barakaat assumed a major importance and presence in Somalia's economy by providing money transfers, communications and employment. Al-Barakaat held 60 offices in Somalia itself, with a further 127 offices abroad across 40 different countries with even the UN utilizing al-Barakaat's services for the delivery of finances to Somalia (El-Fath, 2009: 13). In the context of no government and no functioning state, the financial services of al-Barakaat proved essential to the lives of hundreds and thousands of Somali people relying on the firm for employment, communications and cash transfers. The company had been Somalia's largest employer and operated Somalia's only water purification plant. Closure of the company resulted in around 700 individuals losing their jobs. Particularly important was the movement of remittances from the Somalia diaspora which al-Barakaat facilitated. The UN estimated that remittances alone were approximately $500 million in 2001, over ten times that received in foreign aid (El-Fath, 2009: 16) with much of the financial movement facilitated by al-Barakaat. Following the closure of al-Barakaat, remittances received in Somalia fell by half (Warde, 2007: 101).

In contrast to the assumptions, it was discovered that records of all transactions had been kept and no links to terrorism could be found, resulting in a discreet overturning of the initial court verdict. Despite al-Barakaat's importance to Somalia, all countries accepting of the US hegemonic stance on CTF initiatives complied with the US decision to freeze the company's assets. However, it soon became apparent that scrupulous records were indeed kept, resulting in states such as Canada and Sweden concluding that there were no grounds to sustain claims of links to terrorism and thus the first chink in the armour of the counter-terror financial system emerged (El-Fath, 2009: 14).

It was assumed that as an informal financial transfer network al-Barakaat would not have written records and thus open to abuse. However, contrary to assumptions it emerged that scrupulous record keeping of all transactions were kept with the FBI concluding that al-Barakaat's cooperation with the investigation was 'exceptional' (cited in Warde, 2007: 99). Following from al-Barakaat's 'exceptional' cooperation, scrupulous record keeping and no evidence of criminal or terrorist activity, many states including Canada, the Netherlands and the UK could not justify the continued closure of al-Barakaat. With no compelling evidence and pressure from other states, the United States and the UN discreetly removed al-Barakaat's listing as a terrorist entity in 2006 resulting in an official relaunch of the company in 2014.

The case of al-Barakaat is a reminder of the violences being carried out under the justification of CTF initiatives. It could be argued that as al-Barakaat have been removed from terrorist listings and have since relaunched, little real damage has been done. However, this is to neglect and underestimate the harm and suffering that the Somali population endured during the years of al-Barakaat's closure. In the name of Western national security, the Somali population lost a vital life source resulting in portions of the population becoming collateral damage on the ongoing war on terrorism initiated by the Global North. The irony of course is that the perceived injustice, worsening economic conditions and deteriorating security could potentially provide the spark for further political and terrorist violence. The potential for security threats remains an increased possibility as El-Fath notes that beyond the economic impact of closing al-Barakaat 'the symbolic impact – the perception that Somalia was unfairly treated – may have been the most significant and may have played a role in the rise, four years later, of Islamism in Somalia' (2009: 16). Demonstrating the violent consequences of CTF initiatives, the case of al-Barakaat also suggests tensions between evidence provided by the United States and the burden of proof necessary for European courts of law. It can therefore be considered that European states are 'norm adopters' as opposed to simply appropriating US CTF measures en masse and unchanged.

The case of al-Barakaat links to Muslim charitable giving generally as both are deemed to be 'particularly vulnerable' to terrorist abuse and both assumed to lack rigorous record keeping and financial regulation. It shall be argued that the assumption of Muslim charitable giving, and *zakat* specifically, as 'particularly vulnerable' to terrorist abuse is a misreading of *zakat* and charitable practices in the UK. While individually donated *zakat* is difficult to trace, the amounts given per individual are incredibly small since *zakat* is 2.5 per cent of one's annual savings (note: *savings* not earnings). Moreover, when *zakat* is donated to charities and institutions regulation and audits do occur. Every charitable entity in the UK must register with one of the UK's independent charity regulators and thus scrutiny of *zakat* is ongoing and regular.

Charitable closures: The example of the Holy Land Foundation in the United States

The US approach towards CTF in charities has relied on prosecutions. Contrastingly, the UK has taken a more regulatory approach indicating that while the United States may be the hegemon in counter-terror, the norms and practices are not taken by other states without adaptation and accommodation. The United States' emphasis on prosecutions has resulted in almost all the major Muslim charities in the United States being forcefully closed since 2001. As well as closures, charities' assets have been frozen and individual employees charged with support for terrorism. Charities forcefully closed include the Benevolence International Foundation, the Global Relief Foundation and the Holy Land Foundation for Relief and Development (Sidel, 2011: 121). By 2010, 176 Muslim charities and individuals were arrested or indicted for terrorist-related activity in the United States and 'a significant number were prosecuted not for violence but for "expressive" and charitable activities that the government considers "material support" for terrorism – but which would likely have been considered lawful before 9/11' (Kundnani, 2014: 24).

The Material Support Act was crucial in the prosecution of the Holy Land Foundation (HLF) based in the United States. Charges held against the HLF and its leaders resulted in 42 criminal offences for material support for terrorism and a combined sentence of 180 years imprisonment. The HLF had been established in 1988 by American citizens of Palestinian heritage for the primary purpose of providing food, clothing and education for children within Palestine (Fitzgibbon, 2015). The core charge against the HLF was that they funnelled monies through Hamas-controlled *zakat* committees to support families of suicide bombers. Originally the jurors failed to see the evidence that *zakat* committees were run by Hamas or that the HLF knowingly financially assisted Hamas. Nonetheless, a retrial in 2008 sentenced and convicted the defendants to a combined 180 years in prison (Sidel, 2006: 1131; Freedman, 2011: 1132). Pertinently it has been noted that a variety of NGOs and government bodies have also utilized Palestinian *zakat* committees to efficiently distribute charitable funds across the Occupied Territories including the Red Cross and the United Nations Agency for Development (Kundnani, 2014: 268). None of the *zakat* committees used by HLF had been proscribed as terrorist entities nor had individual members been deemed 'terrorists' (Fitzgibbon, 2015). Like the case of the Benevolence International Foundation, the HLF was guilty by association. 'Evidence' crucial in the conviction of individual employees of HLF consisted of links extended family of ex-employees had to Hamas members, demonstrated in the statement issued from the US Justice Department that condemned the HLF because 'Hamas's political chief . . . who is married to a cousin of . . . HLF's former chairman of the board' (cited in Glass, 2018). Here there is no attempt to link particular employees of HLF themselves to violent or criminal acts but simply that tenuous links via extended family through *former* chairman are enough to implicate guilt. Nancy Hollander, the attorney for defendant Shukri Abu Bakr, stated that the US government 'traced every penny from the Holy Land Foundation directly to charity . . . . Yet, because this charity went to families in Palestine, it was a crime' (cited in Fitzgibbon, 2015). Worryingly, the retrial relied on 'anonymous' so-called expert testimony. Neither the jury nor the defence were permitted to know who the 'experts' were or the basis of their expertise. This led Linda Moreno, lawyer for defendant Ghassan Elashi, to publicly state that

> the unprecedented use of anonymous experts by the government . . . along with the admission of unauthenticated hearsay evidence, secured a conviction wholly lacking in integrity. The constitutional right to confront the evidence was ignored and demeaned. (cited in Fitzgibbon, 2015)

None of the five HLF employees who were charged under the Material Support Act were accused of violence or encouraging violence (Downs and Manley, 2013). The US Material Support Act is being utilized to coerce other states to initiate charges and prosecutions of Muslim charities at the behest of the United States (as in the case of UK-based charity Interpal discussed in Chapter 4).

Despite the undeniable influence and coercive measures by the United States to initiate prosecutions abroad there are limits to the United States' intrusion into external states' sovereignty (as the case of Interpal demonstrates in Chapter 4). As De Goede has argued, 'asserting that the finance security-assemblage is transnational does not mean that it exists above and beyond the nation-state' (2012b: 33).

Financial counter-terror initiatives go global

Following the immediate events of 9/11 and the US extension on existing AML legislation to include terrorist financing, the United States quickly sought an international CTF initiative. The financial war was from the beginning intended as a global one. In accordance with US desires, the G-7 members pledged to pursue a 'comprehensive strategy to disrupt terrorist financing around the globe' (cited in El-Fath, 2009: 2).

One of the first and most important global actors cajoled into the counter-financial system was the UN. In September 2001, the UN Security Council passed Resolution 1373 requiring all member nations to scrutinize their financial systems for terrorist financing. The FATF was officially appointed the global organization for CTF regulation, coercion and enforcement (Warde, 2007: viii). Coupled with the tragedy of 9/11 still being fresh in state actors' minds and the seemingly 'soft' approach of financial measures, the UN was quickly brought into the counter-terror system. The UN Security Council Resolution (UNSCR) 1373 requires all 191 member states to suppress the financing of terrorism. Specifically, UNSCR 1373 required states to criminalize 'active or passive support for terrorists' prior to an act of terrorism. States are in addition required to 'freeze funds expeditiously, share operational information, and provide technical assistance to enhance multilateral cooperation in the area' (Ramaniuk, 2008: 236). UNSCR also established the Counter-Terrorism Committee (CTC) to implement its provisions. The CTC emphasized extending measures beyond the formal financial sector to include the operations of charitable organizations and the activities of informal value transfer system such as the case of al-Barakaat (Ramaniuk, 2008: 237). The UN also holds a global list of designated terrorist entities and individuals that have been criticized for their 'lack of due process and transparency' in both the listing and de-listing process (Rumaniuk, 2008: 247). Once on the list (and an individual or organization may not know they have been designated as such) consequences include seizing and freezing of financial assets in addition to 'civil and criminal penalties' (ACLU, 2009: 7).

From the United States to the United Kingdom

Disregarding Britain's current Brexit debacle, the UK can be viewed in line with the EU generally in being understood as a 'norm-taker' essentially accommodating to US counter-terror initiatives to a large degree. However, while a 'norm taker' Britain has not simply adopted these norms wholesale without adaptation and thus can be considered a 'norm adopter'. The US and UK approaches differ in terms of emphasis in that the United States favours criminal prosecutions while the United Kingdom relies more on direct regulation and surveillance largely via the independent charity regulators, specifically the Charity Commission for England and Wales (Sidel, 2011: 121). Chang describes the different approaches by the United States and the United Kingdom as the 'sledgehammer' and the 'scalpel', respectively. One approach appears more explicitly adversarial with a preference for prosecution while the other deemed 'more precise and appears more collaborative and nurturing of the sector' (Chang, 2020:1). Despite this, Chang is critical of the UK's more ambiguous approach offering an interesting and nuanced argument which essentially posits that the impact of how the UK has interpreted and operationalized CTF measures may be deeper than their US counterparts precisely because of the ambiguities. Chang argues that there is a

> disconnect between law and law's on-the-ground impact: impact does not necessarily flow from an accurate understanding of the law. It seems to be an ambiguous process that is influenced by the social and political context and may be led by perceptions and emotions stirred by the law. (Chang, 2020: 3)

While the financial terror system has been largely directed from the United States, the United Kingdom had existing legislation and mechanisms to intercept and freeze material possessions associated with the 'Troubles' in Northern Ireland. Provisions for financial proscriptions have existed in the UK from at least 1936 in the Public Order Act which was revised several times in response to Northern Irish terrorism (Bolleyer and Gaiya, 2017: 664). Other pre-existing measures included the Northern Ireland (Emergency Provisions) Act 1973 and Prevention of Terrorism (Amendment) Act

1989 which criminalized financial contributions to terrorist acts (Ryder, Thomas and Webb, 2018: 784). Importantly, the Terrorism Act 2000 was adopted prior to 9/11 which criminalized fundraising, money laundering and the failure to disclose information pertaining to terror financing among others (Ryder, Thomas and Webb, 2018: 784). However, these mechanisms were infrequently utilized prior to the London bombings as 'it was recognised that terrorist attacks do not cost much and because targeting monies was thought to be an inefficient way to prevent attacks' (De Goede, 2012b: 40). Even after the 7/7 bombings the evidence supported previous findings that terrorist acts were relatively inexpensive. The official report into the London 7/7 bombings concluded that 'the operation did not cost much and was financed by methods that would arise little suspicion' (cited in De Goede, 2012b: 21).

The general measures of counterterrorism provided in the UN resolution 1373 were implemented in the UK by a number of orders and acts such as the Proceeds of Crime Act 2002 which 'requires that law enforcement is alerted where there is a suspicion of money laundering or terrorist financing through the submission of a Suspicious Activity Report' (HM Treasury, 2018: 11) and orders such as the 2006 Terrorism Order (later replaced by amended and revised orders). Both require that assets of those involved in terrorism be frozen indefinitely and no funds be available to them, thereby effectively excluding such persons from economic society prior to criminal charges or prosecutions.

UK counter-terror policies

The underlying logic of the FWoT was accepted by the UK without critique evidenced by the prime minister of the time, Gordon Brown, claiming that 'if fanaticism is the heart of modern terrorism, finance is its lifeblood' (Brown, 2001). The overarching counter-terror initiative within the UK is known as CONTEST. Just as the United States amended the existing AML legislation to include terrorist-related crimes, the UK extended existing counter-terror legislation initially created for northern Irish terrorism specifically to any form of political terrorism. It is therefore assumed that all terrorists are alike despite hugely diverse ideologies, tactics and goals. While there is no space to detail in depth the many criticisms of this in existing literature, it is worthy of note that many have questioned the applicability of extending counter-terror laws designed for a specific type of criminality in a precise temporal frame to a universally applicable framework that covers an array of diverse entities, ideologies and strategies. Pertinently, different organizations that engage with political violence 'fund their operations in different ways' (Neumann, 2017: 95). Neumann strongly suggests that any CTF strategy should be 'tailored to the group and the theatre being targeted' (2017: 97).

As the counter-terror initiatives have developed and grown over the decades since 9/11, CONTEST has focused upon 'vulnerable' individuals, 'especially "vulnerable" youths who have not committed a crime but are still deemed "extremists"' (Elshimi, 2015: 111). So much so that de-radicalization techniques are focused on 'extremism' rather than terrorism or criminality.

Both the terms 'vulnerability' and 'extremism' have been criticized for definitional vagueness. 'Vulnerability' as defined in the Prevent Duty Guidance 'describes the condition of being capable of being injured; difficult to defend; open to moral or ideological attack . . . the word describes factors and characteristics associated with being susceptible to radicalisation' (HM Government, 2015: 22). The imprecision of the term 'vulnerability' ensures the concept is open to interpretation and essentially could include every individual in British society at some point in their lifetime. The definition of 'extremism' has also received enormous criticism (see, for instance, Kundnani, 2009) especially as it moves away from violent action to include 'vocal opposition' and brings in 'fundamental British values' as an additional controversial aspect that also requires careful definition. 'Extremism' is defined legally in the UK as 'vocal or active opposition to fundamental British values, including democracy, the rule of law, individual liberty, and mutual respect and tolerance of different faiths and beliefs' (HM Government, 2011a). This 'effectively moves the object of policy-makers towards other concerns beyond solely reducing the potentiality of violence: particularly ideas, behaviours and practices . . . become problematic' (Elshimi, 2015: 111). It is the emphasis on 'ideas, behaviours and practices' that is most important regarding the Muslim charitable sector specifically and British Muslims more generally. To be able to identify 'radical' or 'extremist' behaviour there must be some kind of conception of non-radical and non-extreme behaviour or to be blunt, what is 'normal'.

What is considered 'normal' tends to be what the majority of the population do, or do not do, or the values they hold or refute. As a minority population, Muslims (especially pious practitioners) act and behave in ways that perhaps their non-Muslim fellow citizens do not (such as the wearing of religious attire, public prayer or mosque attendance). Few allegations of support for terrorism since the 1990s have been evidenced or resulted in prosecution. Most incidents which have seen the use of counter-terror legislation in the charitable sector are associated with 'radicalization' and 'extremism'. These two concepts are poorly defined but as the above notes they fall short of violence and often criminality.

> the most significant problem with current assumptions about de-radicalisation conceptually is the failure to divorce the behavioural and cognitive dimensions . . . it is based on the misleading assumption that radical views predict radical behaviour. (Elshimi, 2015: 113)

It is important to note Elshimi's observation that there is an assumption that radical views necessarily result in radical action. The rationale is that non-violent extremism 'if unchallenged, can lead to a slippery slope towards violent extremism' (Miah, 2015: 106). There is simply no evidence that suggests that holding a view on a particular matter will necessarily lead to an associated action. Equally, it is often assumed that the reading of 'radical' material will increase the chances of an individual being 'radicalized'. However, once again no causal relation has been established between reading and action. In fact, as a social scientist, I (and my colleagues globally) have read and absorbed countless horrific texts and publications yet never have I been motivated to carry out the types of violence I have read about. Statistically, graduates from the social sciences are less likely to embark upon political violence or terrorism than graduates of, say, medicine, engineering or IT (Hoffman 2010; Hudson 1999). What is being governed, controlled and surveyed is not criminality and violence but ideas and behaviours. Elshimi forcefully argues that current UK de-radicalization promotes 'the adoption of liberal values and not merely the abandonment of violence' (Elshimi, 2015: 114). The key therefore is not criminality or violence but coercion of the public at large towards liberal values which necessitates Muslims (and other pious believers) being viewed as a 'problem' due to the secular bias inherent in Liberalism itself.

Prevent

Within the broader counter-terror policies of CONTEST, the sub-policy of the Prevent project is perhaps the most controversial and has received most public and academic scrutiny. As one of the so-called four 'Ps', 'Prevent' stands alongside Pursue, Protect and Prepare as initiatives to shield British society from terrorist threats (HM Government, 2018). Prevent is supposed to do exactly what the title of the project suggests, which is to prevent terrorism from occurring in the first place primarily by identifying individuals 'vulnerable' to being drawn into 'radicalization' and terrorism and intervening prior to the point of criminality and violence. The Prevent programme is yet again speculative as it aims to intervene before any criminality has occurred. The initial Prevent programme received enormous criticism from an array of British society resulting in adaptations and reformulations in Prevent 2011. A major criticism pertinent to this work is that the initial Prevent project focused almost exclusively on Muslim terrorism and violence undermining others threats such as white nationalism and separatist movements. Spencer critiques the original counter-terror narrative:

> These documents tell a simple story. The problem is something called 'radicalisation', which is a process that happens to Muslims and which, in its causes, is more or less completely endogenous to the Muslim Populations. (2010: 293)

In the years following Prevent's re-packaging, the government has been keen to avoid being perceived as targeting Muslims specifically. Yet, the Prevent programme is a governmental attempt to turn the 'hearts and minds' of British Muslims (and now other sectors of British society) away from the violent narrative of al-Qaeda- and ISIS-related groups. A central feature of the initiative is its discourse on integration which is articulated through the prism of shared values, Britishness and tackling segregation (Miah, 2015: 25). Hence, the heart of the debate is really whether, or not, Muslims in Britain can coincide with and share in 'fundamental British values'.

Despite the government rhetoric which emphasizes a focus on all forms of terrorist and extremist ideology, in practice, the emphasis of Prevent remains on Muslim communities broadly. As noted by De Goede, the actual practice of reporting is placed in the hands of non-experts which De Goede refers to as 'petty-sovereigns'. While the British government may emphasize that it takes all forms of terrorism and political violence equally seriously, the public perception is generally one that deems Islamist violence the higher risk and this feeds into reporting behaviours. A brief glance at the referrals to the Prevent programme confirms that records indicate that individuals suspected of Islamist terrorism (specifically men) are statistically more likely to be reported to Prevent than any other grouping. The 2017/2018 statistics reveal that the largest single referral grouping was for suspected Islamist terrorism at 44 per cent followed by 18 per cent for right-wing terrorism in a total of 7,318 referrals. Remarkably out of the 7,318 referrals only 394 were deemed sufficient to receive support for de-radicalization. For those for whom support was deemed necessary, there was an almost equal balance between those concerned with Islamist and right-wing terrorism at 45 per cent and 44 per cent, respectively (Home Office, 2018: 14). Thus, 'in practice, the *Prevent* Strategy and Duty primarily target the Muslim population' (Dudenhoefer, 2018: 170–1).

Radicalization

As the Prevent initiative is concerned with preventing vulnerable individuals from becoming 'radicalized' into 'extremism' it is essential to unpack what is meant by radicalization. Prior to 9/11, the term 'radical' had been used in conjunction with a variety of political inclinations, including 'radical feminism', the 'radical right', 'radical democracy' but rarely associated with Islam or Muslims (Kundnani, 2014: 119). Saliently, the term 'radicalization' has little meaning on its own but is instead a relational concept in that it 'does not necessarily convey any meaning in isolation. In fact, its connotations depend to a great extent on what the majority of society defines as mainstream' (Dudenhoefer, 2018: 159). Thus, we are reliant on understanding radical in terms of its relation to what we actually mean to be 'normal'. As Dudenhoefer elaborates 'the definition of "radical" varies according to the shared norms of the majority of the populations' (2018: 181).

Counter-terror initiatives like Prevent, instead of detecting extremists and radicals, actually create the conditions for a certain type of 'normality' which coerces and forces individuals to appropriate conceptions of 'normality' or risk being designated a 'radical'. It is salient to remember the words of President Bush who stated 'you are either with us, or with the terrorists' (Bush, 2001) which leaves no middle ground. Elshimi has argued that the dichotomy between normality and radicalism

> constitutes the regulatory ideal for subjects. The process of 'normalisation' works directly through invisible and continuous practices of control . . . . It operates essentially by making a totalising grid of 'normality' in which the clinical assessment of all anomalies/deviancy is made. (2015: 120)

Whether the government intends it or not, the popular and media conception is to link Islam and Muslims generally to terrorism, radicalism, extremism and violence. As Elshimi explains,

> The birth of the concept of radicalisation in the UK was precipitated by the existence of a 'problem' emanating from the internal diaspora population, specifically, British citizens of Islamic faith, in the aftermath of the London bombings. The

'crisis' was primarily characterised by ... the looming existential threat of violence ... and the social, cultural, and political incompatibility of the ideas and practices of the Muslim population, particularly certain trends and interpretations of Islam, with mainstream political, cultural, and social spaces. (2015: 118)

As outlined in Chapter 1, the Liberal conception is that for national security, religion should be firmly secured in the private domain lest it disrupt the liberal plural functioning of modern society. As religiously inspired political violence has hit the headlines, governments in Western Europe and the United States have sought to incorporate religion and specifically Islam into 'counterterrorism and deradicalization programmes, training police and security forces in what Islam "really means"' (Bosco, 2014: 6). In practice this has meant incorporating and promoting what is considered 'good Islam' while criminalizing and disrupting anything considered 'bad Islam'. What this has meant in practice is that private 'secularized' versions of Islam which are in line with secular liberal values are claimed by the government to be the 'authentic voice' of Islam (Bosco, 2014: 6). As Manchanda states,

The rhetorical structure of the discourse conflates political violence with *Muslim* terror. Policy makers and the media may issue advisories to avoid conjoining Islam and terror, but they are meaningless in the face of an impressionable rhetorical discourse on 'radicalisation' which the 'Good Muslim' becomes mythic and even praying five times a day makes one suspect of being a 'Bad Muslim'. (2010: 44–5)

Githens-Mazer interprets this discourse as one that 'exceptionalises "Muslim culture" ... which is constructed by political elites and the media as constituting a threat to "traditional British values"' (2012: 560). Constant associations of Islam with terrorism have resulted in Muslim communities in their entirety being perceived as a suspect community which, in this narrative, risks the plural and liberal fabric of British society. By emphasizing vague ideas such as 'vulnerability' to 'radicalization' facilitates the imaging of an inherent relationship 'between challenging ideas and the propensity for violence' (Githens-Mazer, 2012: 556). Pertinently, the fabrication of Muslims as 'suspect' seeps into perceptions of who is likely to be a terrorist and thus feeds into who is likely to be flagged for suspicious transaction and activity reporting.

UK charity regulators: Charity Commission for England and Wales and OSCR

The role of British charity regulators will be covered in more detail in Chapter 4, but a brief explanation of how the Charity Commission is secured within the counter-terror system is required. The Charity Commission for England and Wales functions as the main regulator of charities within the UK and to a lesser extent its Scottish equivalent, the OSCR. The Charity Commission is an independent government department that both registers and regulates charities in England and Wales. The

Charity Commission has three specific objectives: first, to ensure charities know what they are supposed to do; second, that the public knows what the charities do; and finally, that charities are regulated, monitored and held to account (Keatinge, 2014: 38). Since 9/11, and particularly in 2014 when the Charity Commission's overview was broadened, the Charity Commission has acted at the forefront of CTF for the charitable and third sector. The Charity Commission's position of regulator and surveyor of charities and terrorism was augmented in 2016 with the introduction of the Charities (Protection and Social Investment) Act, which strengthens the powers of the Charity Commission further and creates new offences associated with charity trusteeship (Bolleyer and Gaiya, 2017: 661). While numerous charities have faced investigation from the Charity Commission since 2001, few have witnessed prosecutions or closures in comparison to the United States. Even among the charities I spoke to that had been under investigation, they accepted the role of the Charity Commission and perceived it to be evidence-based. The Charity Commission has a range of powers to deal with charities that breach charity legislation from technical assistance, advice, removing trustees, freezing funds to charity closures (Sidel, 2011: 137). Mostly the Charity Commission has aimed at improving, rather than closing, charitable institutions and has focused on removing problematic trustees and providing assistance to charities in meeting their regulatory requirements. Despite all the charities that participated in this research acknowledging and accepting the role of the Charity Commission, trust between the sector as a whole and the Charity Commission has been eroded, though not irrevocably. Blurring the boundaries between regulating and policing in line with counter-terror measures has led to suspicion from some charitable workers that the Charity Commission is no longer truly independent of government policies. A long duration of mutual respect between the charity sector as a whole and the Charity Commission is in danger of expiring. As one charity worker stated in interview,

> The latest programme that the Charity Commission are following is not secret. They are following the Prevent agenda from the Home Office. The government are pushing this. Until a few years ago the Charity Commission has been unique, neutral, supportive, effective to make sure the operations are operating properly but when it starts being influenced by political interfering agendas like the Prevent one, this basically does not really help generally.

As trust between the regulators and charities decreases, it becomes less likely that charities will themselves ask for assistance from the Charity Commission resulting in greater insecurities rather than less. This point was made explicit by one interviewee working for a Muslim charity in London who reported:

> Someone made a comment to me recently when he said that: 'once upon a time the Charity Commission used to be your friend, now it's like the police.' And I found that an interesting comment because what he was trying to say is that: if, as a charity, you weren't sure about something or you wanted to get advice, you wanted to improve, you could come to the Charity Commission with an open,

friendly relationship, knowing that this is of course in the interest of improving the charity. Now charities will not go to the Charity Commission for advice because they see them as someone who polices charities rather than supporting charities. And I don't mean that they shouldn't police charities. What I am trying to say is that the relationship dynamic has changed over the past few years, especially with the political scene.

The neutrality and supportive functions of the Charity Commission are being questioned with consequences for the sector as a whole. It is worth stating that the initial hypothesis of this research was that the changes in charity laws and regulations would have been the greatest challenge to British charities, but admittedly this hypothesis was wrong. Indeed, increased regulation and requirements have challenged British charities but by far the most detrimental alteration since the rise of CTF has been banking changes and 'de-risking' strategies.

Banking and 'de-risking': 'Know your customer'

One of the most cited challenges by the charities and organizations that participated in this research in the current era of CTF is alterations in banking procedures which necessitate banks verifying the identity of account holders and checking names against the designation lists provided by both national and international governments and institutions including the UN, EU, US, Israeli and other national lists (De Goede, 2012b: 178). The designation lists have proved highly contentious given it is not always clear why a person has been designated nor how to contest the designation. In the current CTF global system, banks are required to match their customers with the terrorist designation lists but names are given without accompanying identification information such as date of birth or address. As many names contained within the designation lists are highly common, many innocent people who simply happen to have the same name as a designated terrorist have found themselves turned away from banks who are not only expected but are encouraged to 'err on the side of caution' (Warde, 2007: 103). FATF recognizes the potential for harm if financial institutions are overly cautious proclaiming that CTF could have the 'unintended consequence of excluding legitimate consumers and businesses' (FATF, 2017: 5).

Questions about the reliability and accuracy of designated lists are compounded by the legal processes, or pertinently, the lack of such legal processes, to contest the inclusion of individuals or organizations designated (Belew, 2014: 236). According to the Office of Foreign Assets Control (OFAC) in the United States, 'the OFAC designation process is entirely one-sided. If a designated entity is not reading Treasury Department press releases, it may not even know that it has been put on the list' (cited in Belew, 2014: 236).

Furthering the controversy regarding designation lists is the exponential growth of private companies compiling and selling designation lists to clients, such as banks and other financial institutions. As a variety of designation lists exist internationally, private companies have emerged that consolidate the various global lists into one single searchable (and saleable) product. Thomson Reuters's 'World-Check' is the example par excellence of private designated list compilers.

Established in 2000, World-Check provides the largest database of designated individuals and entities serving over 4,500 institutions including 49 of the world's largest banks (Hayes, 2013). World-Check then sells access to this database for the purpose of protecting businesses and individuals against the threat of money laundering and terrorist financing and allows clients to comply with current CTF pressures (Charity and Security Network, 2016). Lists are compiled from the various governmental and international bodies as well as police and security agencies. However, and most controversially, World-Check does not simply gather pre-existing lists but 'they also "add value" during the list compilation process by providing their own open-source intelligence and risk-analysis' (De Goede, 2016: 69). The criteria and protocols for inclusion on the World-Check designation lists are entirely unclear and opaque. In 2016, for instance, an investigation revealed that many of the individuals listed as 'terrorists' by World-Check were based on open internet sources such as Islamophobic personal blogs and other various unreliable sources (Charity and Security Network, 2016). The fact that World-Check utilizes open-source information on the internet ensures that a variety of unverified and unreliable data is included in their list compilation. World-Check recognizes that their standards for inclusion are lower than most governments (De Goede, 2016: 77). Web-based accusation therefore can form the unsubstantiated basis for inclusion on a terrorist list with enormous repercussions for the individuals and organizations concerned. This is particularly important given that around 80 per cent of World-check's lists are based on informal information and open-source data (De Goede, 2016: 78). Once on the list (and a person may only realize they are listed once their bank account is frozen, denied or closed) it is extremely difficult to be delisted. There is currently no official forum or procedure where a World-Check designation can be contested (De Goede, 2016: 81).

Restrictions on financial access can be experienced by NGOs and charities in three related ways: (1) restrictions on receiving or transferring funds; (2) restrictions or loss of ability to store funds when bank accounts are frozen or closed; (3) requests to open new bank accounts being denied (Keatinge, 2014: 41). As will be explored in Chapter 7, many charities report that overseas donations are often delayed, blocked or returned (Keatinge, 2014: 42).

One of the unintended consequences of increased restrictions on charities associated with counter-terror legislation is the loss of financial access and agency by organizations operating in 'high-risk' areas (Keatinge, 2014: 41). Muslim NGOs and charities often work in areas that increase the perception of being 'at risk' as they work in fragile or conflict zones. Keatinge argues that 'restricting the activities of NGOs on terror-finance grounds may not be proportionate when they are working on notable and life-or-death issues' (2014: 35). Essentially, in an attempt to limit or prevent violent harm in our own state we risk inducing disproportionate harm on others who already suffer physically and economically in high risk areas. At best, violence is thus not prevented but simply geographically relocated beyond Western audiences' visions.

Banking strategies, in what is now commonly referred to as 'know your customer' regulations like much else in the CTF system, derive from the United States. The USA

PATRIOT Act granted the US Treasury expanded powers to exclude any bank, business or country from use of America's financial system that did not exert sufficient control over terrorist financing. 'The tightening of "know your customer" rules resulted in banks making unreasonable demands on broad categories of customers to ensure that they were free of "alleged links to terror"' (Warde, 2007: 110).

Instigated by the United States, new reporting requirements have been propagated, primarily through FATF, that require banks to 'know your customer' and report on suspicious transactions (STs) (Ramaniuk, 2008: 244). Failures in following the 'know your customer' regulations and reluctances to report on STs can result in banks and financial institutions receiving large penalties and/or lawsuits and prosecutions for not doing their due duty in the prevention against terrorism: 'for instance, family members of the victims of 9/11 collectively attempted to sue a total of six charities in the US for their alleged support to the perpetrators of 9/11' (Gunning, 2008: 94). The level of punishment for failing to show due diligence combined with the fragile world economy following the 2008 financial crash have together coerced banks into adopting de-risking strategies. Banks, attempting to avoid such costly and public reprobation, have displayed extra cautions in the practice of 'know your customer' regulations with a disproportionate consequence on Muslim individuals and institutions.

FATF guidance report states:

> Institutions will need to identify higher risk customers, products, and services, including delivery channels, and geographic locations. These are not static assessments. They will change over time, depending on how circumstances develop and how threats evolve. (FATF, 2012)

Clearly the previous discussion infers that certain customers, services and geographies are deemed more vulnerable to terrorist risk than others, but as the criteria for judgement is both opaque and constantly in flux, actors and institutions are constantly having to guess what is, or is not, acceptable in any given time. Again, in such a tumultuous environment banks are erring on the side of caution with destabilizing effects for charities and their ability to distribute funds.

Banks and their frontline employees have, as a result of CTF practices, been positioned to enforce government policy (Keatinge, 2014: 15). As the practitioners of 'know your customer' in addition to requirements to report on suspicious behaviours, bank employees can be understood as 'petty-sovereigns' as outlined in Chapter 1. Important, pre-emptive interventions are thus being taken by individuals ill-prepared to identify terrorist or criminal behaviours. The lack of a terrorist profile assists in increasing the danger that petty-sovereigns make decisions based on personal bias, media representations and the pressure to increase reporting of STRs. Hassan and Liberatore argued that 'access to financial services has become increasingly discriminatory, based on perception rather than factual information' (Hassan and Liberatore, 2016: 35). The petty-sovereigns associated with banks are being tasked to identify terrorists or would-be terrorists prior to criminality. One of the difficulties in leaving terrorist profiling in the hands of the petty-sovereigns of banking employees was raised early by the National Commission on Terrorist Attacks which reported that the inability to develop meaningful indicia of a . . . terrorist fund-raising operation creates a risk that financial institutions could rely primarily on religious, geographic, or ethnic profiling . . . . In addition to doing little good, this type of profiling may subject customers to heightened scrutiny without legitimate basis and could even extend to refusing to service customers meeting a certain profile. (Roth, Greenburg and Wille, 2003: 57)

Many of the concerns raised by the National Commission report have been born into reality with numerous charities and individuals participating in this research outlining increased banking regulations and scrutiny to be the biggest challenge to charitable operations resulting from the CTF system. Existing published literature concurs with my own research that many charities and individuals have had their accounts frozen or terminated with little or no explanation as to why. As Warde confirms, 'although such customers could in theory go to another bank, "Know your Customer" investigations by other institutions would create suspicions, turning them into "high-risk" customers and effectively shutting them out of the banking system' (2007: 111). Being shut out of the national, and international, banking system is to essentially expel individuals and institutions from the economic realm with real social consequences. Economic and social exclusion here is understood as a type of violence with real emotional, professional and personal consequences on individuals. As Warde articulates, 'the impact on customers who faced this predicament was significant: they could not pay their bills or cash their pay checks; their outstanding cheques bounced, ruining their credit. They were essentially excluded from the legal payment system' (2007: 103).

In 2014, a number of UK charities had their bank accounts closed by mainstream banks including HSBC, Co-operative and Barclays (Keatinge, 2014: 43) essentially denying the organization or individual the right to participate in the national and global economy. In July 2014, Finsbury Park mosque's account with HSBC was closed on the stated reason that it was outside the bank's 'risk appetite' (Keatinge, 2014: 89). HSBC's decision to terminate the mosque's account was met with anger by the local community resulting in a 300-strong protest (Keatinge, 2014: 90). This exclusion, given the importance of banking in modern society, can be viewed as violence.

Hypocrisies

Some of the charities that were willing to participate in this research felt that charity aimed at specific territories (most specifically Palestine) was being needlessly 'politicized' increasing the challenges of distributing funds efficiently and in a timely manner. The British-based charity Interpal in writing stated that the needless politicization of aid was being directed by the United States in tandem with Israel and directly and adversely affected the ability to fundraise and distribute charitable alms (Ibrahim Hewitt, in correspondence with author, 2017). Interpal's interpretation is entirely consistent with the findings of Milton-Edwards who has articulated that Israel has strongly identified with counter-terror measures emerging from the United States and 'increasingly framed the work of Muslim charities as part of the existential threat facing the West' (2017: 161). In writing, Interpal did not elaborate further the nature of the politicization of charitable distribution across Palestine, but Milton-Edwards is far more explicit stating that 'the securitization of Palestinian zakat committees was part of a wider policy to inhibit Palestinian autonomy and portray Islamic faith agency as terrorist' (2017: 161). The deepening of perceptions associating Islam broadly with terrorism, and the entirety of Palestine as a 'vulnerable' territory, simultaneously increases the sufferings and violence emerging as a consequence of drawing charity into the securitization lens. Milton-Edwards claims that 'such perception of the *zakat* committees effectively altered the place of faith-based Muslim charity and left the most vulnerable communities in Palestinian society . . . exposed to deepening hardships' (2017: 162).

In a sense, it is not surprising that charity has been politicized and arguably has a long tradition of being so. Particularly from the Marshall Plan onwards, the Western aid system has consistently been deeply connected to domestic and foreign policy and security aims (Benthall, 2007). Deeper historical experiences also connect European colonial adventures with Christian missionaries and associated 'charitable' projects (despite the tensions between colonial administrations and Christian missionaries). Historical experience mixed with recent military interventions in the Muslim world has led to rises in suspicions regarding the motives of aid distributions. Western, particularly non-Muslim, aid to Muslim-majority states is occasionally viewed with suspicion and distrust by the intended recipients of aid. 9/11 increased distrust on all sides: Muslim and non-Muslim. In Muslim-majority countries the motives of Western donors are occasionally distrusted with old suspicions re-emerging that aid is a thinly veiled cover for neo-colonial economic penetration or to spread Christianity. There is now also a widespread perception that aid, and the WoT, is interrelated with the West aiming to subvert Islamic movements and replace them with secular governments and/or institutions (Van Bruinessen, 2007).

Illogic of CTF

CTF is based on five core assumptions. The first is that it assumes that all 'terrorists' are essentially the same so that measures are supposed to be equally effective against groups with varying organizational forms, strategies and aims. Second, there is an assumption that formal and informal financial institutions are sources of terrorist fund transfers without much tangible empirical evidence in support. Third, it is assumed that regulation regarding formal financial institutions can be extended to informal financial networks. Fourth is the oft repeated and taken as 'common sense' inferences that informal transfer systems, particularly those outside of Western states, play an essential role in the financing of terrorism. Lastly, there is an implicit assumption that there are links between organized criminality and terrorism (Biersteker and Eckert, 2008: 7).

Of course, there are established and well-documented evidence of links between some terrorist entities and organized crime, but as Walker has stated, not all acts of political violence seek 'funds from underhand means' (Walker, 2018: 1088). The Irish Republican Army (IRA), for instance, initially relied heavily on criminal activity such as theft, extortion and smuggling, in addition to financial resources from other states (such as Libya under Colonel Ghaddafi) (Tierney, 2017: 163). However, again this is not the type of terrorism that has occurred in Western Europe in recent decades. None of the recent attacks in Western Europe have cost more than $30,000 and most have cost considerably less (Neumann, 2017). Research found that over 90 per cent of violent Islamist actors from 1994 to 2013 in the West were self-funded and used a wide range of fundraising methods, most of which avoided the official financial system entirely (Neumann, 2017). Neumann suggests that the problem with the current CTF system is that it 'implies a set of financial methods that all terrorist groups employ. Nothing could be further from the truth' (2017).

One of the main concerns of current CTF legislation is that funds are being misdirected towards terrorist groups with, or without, donor knowledge. Suspicions of ill-intent are magnified in some geographical areas more than others, for instance Palestine and specifically Gaza are frequently mentioned as terrorist havens. Any charitable or humanitarian funds directed to Palestine (and other so-called failed-states) are met with intense scrutiny and investigations. Gaza is currently run by the political group Hamas after they won the controversial 2006 elections in Palestine. Internal Palestinian tensions, particularly between Fatah and Hamas, have resulted in the stagnation of the democratic process with no further elections since 2006. Hamas have been designated a terrorist entity by the United States and European Union among others. As such, Western states fear that charity directed to Gaza will be misdirected to Hamas' military wing. Even when charitable aid is used legally and as the donors intended, it may still raise concerns. One strand of thought argues that any monies towards social and welfare causes in Palestine simply frees Hamas' remaining funds to be utilized for military, violent and terrorist actions (Levitt, 2006). As Aziz states,

> Humanitarian aid delivered to non-combatant civilians living under the control of a terrorist organisation can be illegal based upon the unproven theory that it frees up resources to redirect towards violence. This punitively denies many innocent beneficiaries abroad of food, water, and shelter. (Aziz, 2011)

Undeniably, this results in real violence towards the intended recipients of aid as food, water and shelter are withheld.

The FWoT relies on the unsubstantiated and unproven assumption that terrorism is for profit and that to stop terrorism first governments must stop the finance. The root assumptions are that 'terrorists are motivated by money, acts of terror require substantial financing and financiers are a necessary part of any terrorist attack' (Warde, 2007: xv). As Warde (2007: xviii) points out, a very troublesome aspect for the above assumption is that many recent terrorists have simultaneously been suicide bombers which highly problematizes the idea of terrorist acts as 'for profit' or at least that the perpetrator will be the main benefactor. Those adamant of the 'terrorism for profit' trope argue that even suicide bombers act for financial gain as the claim is that 'terrorist' organizations financially reward the family of suicide bombers (Levitt, 2006: 58). This framing is particularly relevant to Palestine once again as Muslim charities tend to emphasize welfare provisions for children and orphaned children (derived from religious texts and the model of the Prophet Muhammad, himself an orphan). Orphans, generally defined in Islam as a child that has lost her father (the breadwinner), are a global feature of Islamic charitable efforts (Benthall, 2012: 78). The charities that work in Palestine insist that the welfare provisions provided to orphans are not based on the political preferences or actions of their parents. It is almost inevitable that the children of violent political actors have indeed been in receipt of food, shelter and other charitable efforts not because of their parent's actions but in spite of them. In Islam, and other faiths and non-faiths, a child is not deemed responsible for the actions of their parents, and retrospective punishment on innocent children is deemed (unsurprisingly) illegitimate. It simply cannot be sustained that social and welfare provision for orphans – even the children of suicide bombers – is evidence of support to violent political action rather than simply being humanitarian.

While it is a fact that Hamas are currently a designated entity by some states, it is also a fact that they are the de facto government in the Gaza strip. Therefore, under current international political norms, no aid can enter Gaza without Hamas's endorsement as the de facto authority in the area. The context of Palestine is particularly complicated as under international humanitarian law occupied populations have a right to resist occupation and under the Geneva Convention, civilian populations are entitled to humanitarian relief and aid (Belew, 2014: 240).

Another crucial factor of these assumptions is that terrorist actions cost substantial amounts of money. This point has most frequently been simply accepted rather than positioned next to the evidence. It is true that *some* terrorist actions do require substantial funds, but this does not translate that *all* political violence requires large sums. As Belew notes, 'terrorist organisations . . . operate in many different areas of the world, appeal to different causes, and function in different manners' (Belew, 2014: 240). For instance, ISIS emerged as one of the best funded terrorist organizations globally with a reported budget in 2015 of $1.7 billion largely derived from trade in oil and antiquities, kidnappings, human trafficking and extortion (Neumann, 2017). ISIS required substantial funds as it acquired territory and large numbers of recruits. The acquisition of territory also made possible the furthering of its financial resources as it gained access to oil and other reserves in Iraq and Syrian geographies under its control. Due to the large finances and resources gained by territorial acquisition, ISIS had little need to subvert the highly monitored Western charitable sector (Walker, 2018: 1088). However, most terrorist offences within the UK, and other states in Western Europe, have not involved large sums of money (Neumann, 2017; Warde, 2007; De Goede, 2016). For instance, if we consider the 2016 Bastille Day attack in Nice, the Berlin Christmas market tragedy and the 2017 Westminster Bridge attack we must also note that none cost over £300 which was the price of the truck rental in Nice (Neumann, 2017: 96). In short, the current CTF system would not have detected nor prevented this kind of attack from occurring. In regard to the London bombings of 7/7, Warde states that the materials used to create the home-made bomb were widely available and inexpensive 'none of the banking transactions . . . were out of the ordinary, no "dirty money" or cross-border transfers were involved' (2007: xxi). The 2005 London transport bombings are estimated to have cost as little as £8,000 (Keatinge, 2014: 38–9). Saliently, according to El-Fath, 'if there is a pattern, it is probably that the cost of mounting an attack keeps decreasing – that far from being the lifeblood of terror, money is now a minor aspect of terrorism' (2009: 19).

In addition to money being marginal to the forms of terrorist violence witnessed in the UK in recent years, the correlation between terrorist financing and money laundering is tenuous. Terrorist financing should not automatically be assumed to be synonymous with criminal money laundering as the logics are oppositional.

> Money laundering is about hiding and legitimising profits from illegitimate and illegal activities. The money is dirty first and enters the system to be 'cleaned' . . . . In the case of terrorist financing therefore the logic is the complete opposite. The money is clean and becomes dirty with the terrorist act itself. (Warde, 2007: xxii)

Terrorist violence is rarely about profit and much more likely to be driven by political and ideological motivators (Keatinge, 2014: 40). There is little evidence that terrorist attacks that have occurred in the UK recently are financially sourced by criminal activity and thus the monies utilized for the act are 'clean' to begin with and are not substantial amounts. Consequently, it is unlikely that terrorist acts that have occurred within the UK in the current British context would have been detected, let alone prevented, by surveillance and data mining of financial accounts and activities. As Warde acknowledges, 'all the evidence suggests that "clean money" was used to commit these crimes . . . . Clean money, by its very nature, is consistent with a customer's profile and cannot be spotted by financial institutions' (2007: 46–7).

Effectiveness of countering terrorist financing

The illogical assumptions behind CTF questions both the proportionality and effectiveness of current policies. Given most terrorist activities within the UK do not follow money laundering and criminal rationales involve small and insubstantial amounts of money, which is unlikely to be detected by financial institutions and agents, and is politically rather than materially motivated, it is questionable whether the current CTF package is capable of detecting criminal intent prior to the act. The *Monograph on Terrorist Financing* produced by the National Commission in the United States is particularly damning concerning the effectiveness of current CTF strategies. The report uses the perpetrators of 9/11 as an example stating that 'nothing the hijackers did would have altered any bank personnel to their being criminals, let alone terrorists . . . no financial institution filed a suspicious activity report (SAR) and even with the benefit of hindsight, none of them should have' (Roth, Greenburg and Wille, 2003: 53). The report continues arguing that 'the 19 hijackers hid in plain sight: none of their transactions could have revealed their murderous purpose, no matter how hard the banks looked at them' (Ibid.: 56).

Following from the unlikeliness of CTF in preventing violent attacks, are the collateral damages, which have hit a range of individuals and actors not associated with terrorism and violence, justifiable and proportionate?

There is very little evidence that financial crackdowns initiated since 9/11 have had a substantial impact in decreasing terrorist activities. For instance, between 2000 and 2009 only thirty-six people were charged with terrorist financing offences with only eleven convictions (Ryder, Thomas and Webb, 2018: 787). The effectiveness of current CTF policies has been questioned by the British House of Lords when the Select Committee on Economic Affairs stated 'the evidence suggests that the amounts of money frozen are so small, both in absolute terms and relative to the probable resources of the targets, that it is doubtful whether asset freezes are effective' (cited in Ryder, Thomas and Webb, 2018: 784). Determination of the effectiveness of CTF policies is difficult to measure and often relies solely on quantifying the extent that CTF measures are used rather than the effect they have on terrorist entities or activities. For instance, the number of Suspicious Activity Reports (SARs) are meticulously counted and the dramatic rise in reporting of suspicious activities is itself often seen as evidence of success despite only a small percentage (0.27 per cent in 2013) of SARs being connected to terrorist financing (Ryder, Thomas and Webb, 2018: 794). The amount of finances which have been frozen is recorded as decreasing yearly falling from £100,000 in the UK in 2011 to £61,000 in 2014 (Ryder, Thomas and Webb, 2018: 789). According to Neumann, the current CTF strategy 'has probably deterred the terrorists from using the international financial system. But there is no evidence that it has ever thwarted a terrorist campaign' (2017: 94). Similarly, while financial counter-terror policies have 'successfully' closed all the major Muslim charities in the United States there is little evidence this has had any effect at all on thwarting terrorist operations. For instance, while the HLF ceased acting as a charity and five of its employees were charged and convicted for material support to Hamas, fifteen years after their closure 'Hamas are doing fine' (Glass, 2018).

However, unintended consequences such as global perceptions and pushing monies underground may have increased insecurities rather than lessened them. In terms of global perceptions, current policies risk denting 'the image' of the UK in 'the Muslim world' (El-Fath, 2009: 1). El-Fath continues by arguing that a real potential consequence of those harmed by the CTF system who have nothing to do with terrorism or criminality could endanger national interests and 'the security of the world in the long term' (2009: 7). El-Fath argues that not only are current CTF policies inefficient and unlikely to decrease terrorist activity, they are in fact counterproductive, adding to perceptions of harm, grievance and marginalization thought to be correlating variables in violent action 'which is likely to increase recruitment and support, including financial, for terrorism' (2009: 20). In agreement, Walker has argued that hindering the work of charities, especially humanitarian overseas engagement, is 'contrary to the public interest because a failure to intervene might worsen the generation of terrorism' (2018: 1104).

Moreover, a concern frequently raised by the participants of this research is the fear that monies and financial sources are being driven underground due to the restrictions and high surveillances imposed on the formal financial system. According to Keatinge, 'restricting financial access drives money flows out of the formal system into informal networks, decreasing rather than increasing security' (2014: 40).

One major consequence of the CTF system is the financial exclusions occurring, often impacting individuals and organizations innocent of violent, criminal or terrorist activity. FATF is entirely aware of the potential for the unintended consequences and asserts that it is 'committed to financial inclusion' and recognizes that CTF could force individuals to 'conduct their transactions through unregulated channels when they lack access to formal financial services' (FATF, 2017: 5). Financial exclusions are evidenced by those shut out of the official financial sector by either asset freezes or denials of bank accounts. However, higher costs of informal financial transfers in addition to delays and restrictions on charitable distributions further the financial exclusion and extend it beyond the borders of the UK. According to Stanlley and Buckley, 'financial inclusion involves the delivery of financial services at affordable costs to all sections of society' (2016: 84). Financial exclusion thus can be considered as not only the exiling from official financial systems but also the systemic exclusions based on costs and affordability. It is beyond the remit of this research to detail in depth the global repercussions, but it is acknowledged that 'CTF threatens financial inclusion in the developing world' (Stanlley and Buckley, 2016: 85). Neumann has argued that CTF measures and banking de-risking strategies have 'resulted in the de facto exclusion of entire countries, mostly poor ones such as Afghanistan and Somalia, from the global financial system' (2017: 95). Particularly, the increased regulations, surveillance and restrictions on informal financial transfers have increased associated costs which are disproportionately affecting the world's poorer demographics as they are already excluded from the formal financial system as half the world's adult population do not have access to formal bank accounts (Stanlley and Buckley, 2016: 86). De Goede has argued that financial exclusions have a 'symbolic denunciating function' which works through discourses of 'otherness' positioned against rational liberalism (2018: 337). Importantly De Goede strongly asserts that

> this seemingly technical financial measure has substantial impact on individuals' lives: without access to their resources, use of a bank account, opportunity to buy insurance or receive salaries, the measure fully disables a meaningful life in a modern society. A financial blacklisting measure is a mode of political and societal exclusion ... and functions as a form of 'modern exile'. (2018: 337)

Equally, Walker has also questioned the proportionality given the increased obstacles for charities to continue their work and argues that 'the impediments created for the work of charities are alleged to be out of proportion to these risks, giving rise to explanations about official motivations which are less about counter-terrorism and more about the state assertion of control over non-government actors' (2018: 1088).

Summary

This chapter has sought to provide a backcloth to the still evolving global CTF system. Initiated by the United States, within weeks of the destruction of the Twin Towers, the international community were quick to follow the seemingly non-violent 'soft' approach offered by CTF initiatives. Through various global mechanisms and institutions such as the G-7, the United Nations and importantly FATF, US-instigated counter-terror norms now cover the international stage.

However, high-profile closures of US Muslim charities (such as the Benevolence International Foundation and the HLF) and global informal transfer systems (such as al-Barakaat) raised questions for the international community regarding required levels of evidence and proof. As such, the UK can be conceived as a 'norm adopter' in that it has appropriated many of the CTF initiatives derived from the United States and FATF, but adapted them to pre-existing British CT measures and the UK context. Consequently, while there are global norms to CTF measures there are adaptations and differences in practice and implementation. This is evidenced by the United States favouring charitable prosecutions and closures in contrast to the United Kingdom's focus on regulation, guidance and protecting charitable organizations.

Despite the differences in application of CTF policies, important elements of the global CTF system remain within UK policy such as the conception of 'vulnerability' and the presentation of the dichotomy between 'radical'/'extreme' and 'normal' behaviour. 'Radical' and 'extreme' may fall short of terrorism or political violence but are still presented as a threat to contemporary British society. Thus, due to the nature of the threat, discourse is articulated as necessitating regulation and surveillance. But regarding British Muslim charities and charitable giving, what is being surveyed? The remainder of this work accepts El-Fath's basic premise that 'policies based on inappropriate understanding are bound to be counterproductive' (2009: 20). It is the effort to increase appropriate understandings of Muslim charity and how Muslims practise the pillar of *zakat* that the next chapter turns to.

3

'You cannot split Islam from charitable work'

Zakat and *sadaqah*

Islamic charity since 9/11 'has acquired some notoriety' with journalists and politicians alike drawing 'the conclusion that a number of Muslim charities were using humanitarian programmes as a cover for "terrorist" activities' (Benthall and Bellion-Jourdan, 2009: 1). Yet, according to Benthall, 'the blame attached to the sector for the funding of violent extremism since 2001 has almost certainly been exaggerated' (2016: 3). This coincides with the understanding of the Charity Commission for England and Wales, in a written response to the author in 2017, which stated that 'we are clear that incidents of abuse of charities for terrorist purposes are rare, but when these do occur [they] significantly threaten public trust and confidence in the sector'. With such suspicion and fear of Islamic charity ongoing, the positive aspects of Islamic charitable giving, not least its civil function and the possibility for social cohesion, are being lost in the mire of accusations, defences and media headlines. Setting aside specifically Islamic or Muslim charities 'the rise of NGOs in general has been represented as a flowering of global citizenship in healthy counter-balance to the power of nation states' (Benthall, 2016: 30). This monograph concurs with Benthall's assertion that 'a significant opportunity to defuse the purported "clash of civilizations" is thus being lost' (2016: 36). Looking to the positive contributions Islamic charitable giving offers, this chapter focuses on how understandings of Islamic charitable practice can serve an important role in civil society and assist in the process of social cohesion and the creation of British Muslim persons.

The focus of this chapter is largely on *zakat*, the obligatory alms giving contained within the five pillars of Islam. *Zakat* has been identified as particularly 'vulnerable' to terrorist misuse, hence the attention to this practice. However, it must be firmly acknowledged that *zakat* is a relatively small portion of Muslim charitable donations as most charitable offerings are given as *sadaqah* (general charity). Individual *zakat* donations are usually small amounts donated on an annual basis (usually during the holy month of Ramadan) consisting of only 2.5 per cent of an individual's annual *savings*, not income. By first outlining the current context of *zakat* debates, this chapter will then go onto delineate how the charitable concepts of *zakat* and *sadaqah* are understood and practised by Muslims within the UK. Attention will be given to the categories of rightful recipients of *zakat* and the efforts Muslims make in knowing the most deserving of their charitable donations. The final section of this chapter discusses the ways in which Muslim charitable giving can be considered 'performative' in that it helps construct not only a Muslim person but also a British Muslim person, which holds the potential to bridge differences between, and within, British communities.

Contextualizing Islamic charitable giving in the UK

Muslims living in the UK have been forced to defend, contemplate and evaluate their religion to an unprecedented scale in the last decades with the rise of 'Islamophobia' (Tell Mama, 2017). As Strindberg and Warn have argued, 'the "Muslim question" in the public sphere has come to be framed primarily in terms of cultural incompatibility and terrorism' (2011: 170). Githens-Mazer further argues,

> This discourse has meant that the social construction of risk associated with Islamically inspired violence has become intimately bound up with debates over 'community cohesion' . . . . This discourse exceptionalizes 'Muslim' culture (objectifying and essentializing a vast array of identities, theological outlooks, and experiences), which is constructed by political elites and the media as constituting a threat to 'traditional' British values. (2012: 561)

The argument posited is that whatever differences exist between Muslim and non-Muslim communities in Britain (and indeed the differences *within* Muslim demographics), the charitable ethos of Islam serves as an important bridging tie between various communities (religious and secular). Islamic charity is perceived, by those who practice, to be for a 'common good' for the benefit of all God's creations. Through the practical implementation of this ethos, active citizenry and progress towards shared values and beliefs can be utilized as a frame for more positive social cohesion strategies.

Islamic scripture and contemporary charitable practices demonstrate that humanitarian aims of relief and prevention of human suffering align with British historical charitable giving and thus with 'fundamental British values'. Interestingly, Muslim individuals frequently mentioned in interview the influence of mainstream media in their charitable decisions ranging from awareness of issues to where and whom to donate to. Both individual donors and charities were aware that aid and charitable projects which received the most attention were those highlighted in the media. Many interviewees mentioned growing up with British appeals on the television such as 'Comic Relief' and 'Children in Need'.

This then suggests that it is conceivable that a synthesis between an Islamic charitable ethos and British norms of charitable giving has in some communities created a synthesis of Islamic and British values. If, as Mahmood (2005) has argued, Muslim persons can be created through 'performative acts', then can the performative actions of making charitable donations over the phone, responding to 'Children in Need', dropping pennies into a collection box, etc., assist in the creation of a British Muslim person? This chapter suggests that a synthesis of values is already occurring within the domain of charitable giving where an Islamic charitable ethos recognizes an alignment of values in British charitable giving. Through the performative practice of charitable giving Muslims are reaffirming both their faith and their Britishness, and in so doing are in the process of constructing what it means to be both British and Muslim.

The aim is, therefore, to investigate the actual lived practices of charitable giving by British Muslims with a focus on the concerted efforts individuals make in ensuring their charitable sacrifice is received by the rightful recipients. In the struggle to ensure their religious duties and obligations are fulfilled, arguably, British Muslims are themselves providing the first instance of scrutiny to make sure their financial sacrifices are not misused or abused. In doing so, British Muslims, through religious practice, militate against the charges against them that they are facilitating financial flows to violent movements – charges which pre-suppose that the identities of charitable recipients are hidden through the nature of clandestine, charitable giving.

Islamic charity can be divided between two main categories: *zakat* (obligatory alms) and *sadaqah* (voluntary alms). *Zakat* is one of the five pillars of Islam and thus is meant to be practised by all Muslims that can afford it and meet the eligibility criteria. *Zakat* constitutes the objective reality of private Muslim religiosity while simultaneously being an annual, public obligation. Mainstream liberal secular bias results in religious activities (of all faiths) that seemingly transcend the private domain into the public, being generally viewed with suspicion. The ability of the practice of *zakat* to transcend public/private divides situates Muslim practices in the larger discussions regarding the boundaries between the secular and the religious (Philpott, 2000).

In today's contemporary environment, *zakat* is a topic of public policy. President Obama's 2009 Cairo speech announced that 'in the United States, rules on charitable giving have made it harder for Muslims to fulfil their religious obligation. That is why I am committed to working with American Muslims to ensure they fulfil zakat' (Obama, 2009). Designed as an outreach speech aimed to build bridges between Muslim peoples and non-Muslim America, one consequence was scathing criticism against Obama. For instance, the Center for Security Policy wrote,

> We're still shaking our heads in disgust over Obama's pledge to ease the scrutiny on *zakat* payments to Islamic charities . . . . All too often, the destinations of *zakat* payments are to jihadists, simply because Shariah mandates it. That is the reason the federal law enforcement and intelligence authorities in the US have scrutinized Islamic charities to such a degree . . . . This is in fact how our enemies are being funded. (Holton, 2009)

Without offering evidence to support the argument that 'too often, the destination of *zakat* payments are to jihadists', the Center for Security Policy's analysis concludes that the funding of violent movements, via *zakat*, is not only encouraged by *shariah* law but is a mandate. But is this how Muslims within the UK practice the pillar of Islamic charitable giving? To answer this question, I draw from Roy, who has argued,

> It is the believers' practice of their religion that decides, and not the secular exegesis of sacred texts. The question is not: 'What does the Quran really say?' but rather: 'What do Muslims say about what the Quran says?' (2017: 56)

While theological scholarship already exists regarding Islamic charitable giving, it tends not to focus on the UK or be read by policy makers and think tanks because of their theological tone and specialized terminology (Azim, 2005). This is, therefore, not an attempt at theological exegesis. A theological exegesis regarding the obligation of *zakat* tells us much about how *zakat ought* to be understood but tells us little about the *actual* practices and behaviours of Muslim individuals and communities in Britain today. In investigating the actual practices and meanings attached to charitable giving, errors and misperceptions in public and policy debates can be made visible. The positives of informal economic and welfare structures can be highlighted and the assumptions that informal structures and more dangerous and less transparent and accountable can be countered.

The following sections will attempt to explain Islamic charitable giving as understood by British Muslim practitioners themselves. Select quotations are given from research interlocutors which express the typical views of Muslims interviewed for this research.

Islamic charity: *Zakat* and *sadaqah*

As used in the Qur'an, the term *zakat* often refers to charity in general (*sadaqah*), but a combination of subsequent Islamic legal literature has distinguished *zakat* (obligatory alms) from *sadaqah* and other charitable giving. 'In other words, while all zakah is sadaqah, only the sadaqah which is fard [compulsory], is zakah' (Azmi, 2004: 52). As a Glaswegian practising Muslim in her thirties articulated in interview, '*zakat* is obviously an obligation which you have to fulfil at least once a year. . . . that's the fundamental difference: *zakat* is an absolute must and *sadaqah* is something you should do as an extra.'

Zakat is considered obligatory for all Muslims: the Qur'an positions it next to prayer over thirty times firmly establishing its importance to Islamic practice as one of the five pillars of the faith. As one interviewee claimed, 'for Muslims to be Muslims they must fulfil the five pillars. If you don't fulfil this, you are not a Muslim.' To most participants in this research, to really be deemed a Muslim, the obligation and sacrifice of *zakat* must be fulfilled, if a person is able to do so.

Zakat literally means 'to grow' or 'to increase' (Benthall, 1999) with the inference being that giving *zakat* does not ultimately diminish an individual's wealth but will in due course allow it to grow with God's pleasure. The etymological origins of *zakat* connote several meanings such as 'to cleanse' or 'to purify' (Hudiyya Foundation). Thus, the giving of *zakat* is deemed to purify oneself and one's financial resources. The concept of *zakat* as both purification and growth was understood by all those interviewed moving beyond just theological understanding to become a motivational factor in charitable giving. A Sunni interviewee interpreted the motivations for giving *zakat* in terms of purification and growth in the following way:

> *Zakat* is not given as a task, it is an obligation, you are fully hearted, you are happy about it. You wait for the time to give it because you know it is going to purify your earnings, your family life: everything. . . . We believe it [money] will come back to you.

The above quotation from a Muslim practitioner helps link the meaning of *zakat* to that of non-Muslim charity. The English word 'charity' stems from the Latin *caritas* meaning 'love for humanity' (Marusek, 2019: 15). Importantly, charity in Islam, and specifically *zakat*, is not just a temporal societal good but also a form of worship to God as one of the five pillars of Islam. As a prominent mosque director articulated, 'it is not just a charity it is a kind of worship – giving to poor people, fighting poverty – it is worship in Islam'.

The globally renowned and controversial modern theological scholar al-Qaradawi interprets the primary aim of *zakat* as eliminating poverty and destitution from society:

> The objective of zakah distribution is to realize an adequate and suitable standard of living and to help Muslims stay above the poverty level.... Using contemporary terms, the other needs must include education, health care, and other social necessities that can only be determined by time and locale; no absolute can be applied to all cases. (al-Qaradawi, 2000: 5)

Al-Qaradawi is an Egyptian-born theologian whose major study *Fiqh al-zakat* provided the main theological basis for the formation of modern Islamic charitable organizations (Benthall, 2016: 181). Al-Qaradawi's influence on Islamic charity in the UK can be evidenced by the frequent references to his theology by Sunni interviewees. For example, a senior mosque leader insisted I have a copy of al-Qaradawi's seminal work (he later sent an electronic version and telephoned to ensure I had received it). Qaradawi's thoughts are thus pertinent to Muslim charities working in the UK as well as elsewhere. Al-Qaradawi's relative understanding of poverty has provided justification for Muslim charities to disperse *zakat* funds within the UK. However, many of the interlocutors for this research (particularly older participants) tended to prioritize 'absolute' poverty, especially when comparing the economic and life conditions in the UK to other geographies. For instance, a Sunni practitioner originally from Iraq stated,

> There is a relative definition of the term 'poverty'. A poor person in the UK may not be able to warm their house 24/7, probably cannot afford luxury items or to go to the restaurant . . . while people [elsewhere] have no shelter, no bread: they dream of milk for their children . . . so poverty is relative.

The debate between 'relative' and 'absolute' understandings of poverty helps account for why much of *zakat* collection within the UK is distributed overseas and will be explored in more detail in Chapters 5 and 6. However, it is pertinent for the reader to understand that while many interviewees understood the rise of relative poverty within the UK itself, the levels of poverty were often judged less severe than in other geographical regions outside of Britain.

In simplistic terms, *zakat* should be given on all savings held for a year and becomes obligatory when an individual's assets exceed a certain minimum value, or *nisab* (Azmi, 2004: 61). *Zakat* is not dependent on one's earnings (thus not equitable with income tax) but on an individual's savings over and above household expenditures. Therefore, what is deemed 'zakatable' is any money left over after paying for essential provisions such as shelter (rent/mortgage), food, utility bills, employment tools, tuition fees and other essential items. In the contemporary economic system of capitalism, *zakat* in its simplest calculation is held to be 2.5 per cent of an individual's savings held for one year.

Zakat is sometimes referred to as an Islamic system of taxation, yet this interpretation was met with criticism from some of the individuals who participated in this research. The main distinction between *zakat* and a government tax can be expressed as follows: '*Zakah* [zakat] is the divinely granted right of the poor on the wealth of the rich: tax is the non-divine right of the state to collect money to meet state needs' (Azmi, 2004: 61). Thus, the distinction between *obligations* from the state and *obligations* from God is inherent in such understandings. This sentiment was echoed by Fadi Itani in 2013 (then of Zakat House) who stated,

> It is not a tax, it is not a charity, it is a right of the needy and an obligation for the people who have the ability, the wealth to help them. A symbol of the Islamic social justice.

Thus, 'obligation' here needs to be understood in non-state-centric terms and in relation to obligations to God and fellow humans. This has been referred to as a 'triad' as *zakat* is 'orientated toward the Other in need, the self, and God, all at once' (Mittermaier cited Schaeublin, 2019: 126). This is not to say that religious and state obligations are in opposition. The defining feature of 'charity' in UK legislation is the requirement of 'public benefit' (Charities Act, 2011), which complements the practice and understanding of *zakat* as a religious obligation for the benefit of the community.

More than simply a voluntary gift, *zakat* is an obligatory practice which the needy have a right (*haqq*) to receive. While there is no earthly coercion mechanism to ensure that the right (*haqq*) of the poor is given, the believer will ultimately fear God's punishment if their religious obligations are not met. Ultimately, *zakat* is fundamentally linked to both reward and punishment. To give *zakat* is a purifying act with heavenly rewards. In contrast, to neglect the duty of *zakat* is thought to invoke divine punishment. As one participant working within an international Muslim charity lamented, 'a Muslim can go to hell' if the poor are not fed. He claimed that charity 'is embedded into the faith of Islam. You cannot split Islam from charitable work – it is integrated'. Hence, any curtailments on Islamic charitable giving could be perceived as threats to the practice of religious freedom itself as charity and Islam 'cannot be split'. Current financial counter-terror legislation which increases difficulties in the giving of *zakat* could be deemed as a threat to the freedom of religious practice and tolerance within the UK.

Eight categories of rightful *zakat* recipients

Not only is *zakat* obligatory and the amount of *zakat* set in terms of percentage of one's yearly savings, the recipients of *zakat* are also stipulated within the Qur'an. The Qur'an instructs,

> Zakah expenditures are only for the poor and for the needy and for those employed to collect [zakah] and for bringing hearts together [for Islam] and for freeing

captives [or slaves] and for those in debt and for the cause of Allah and for the [stranded] traveller – an obligation [imposed] by Allah. (al-Tawbah 9:60)

Therefore, the Qur'an instructs there are eight rightful recipients of *zakat* which include the poor, the needy, *zakat* administrators, those in need of being brought closer to Islam (often interpreted as new converts to Islam), slaves, debtors, travellers/pilgrims and those in the cause of God. As one respondent from the Muslim Association of Britain stated,

> Allah has told us who can receive *zakat* – no one can change those categories. This is where things are restricted in a way but also flexible. The first two categories of needy and poor are important without doubt and the ones mentioned most frequently.

Despite the stated importance of all categories, among all participants, it was clear that the emphasis of individual giving was largely on the first two categories: poor and needy. In fact, many lay Muslims struggled to remember all eight categories of rightful *zakat* recipients – indeed, one Imam in interview counted seven and could not recall the eighth. For the vast majority of those interviewed, it was perceived that the poor and needy have a right (*haqq*) to receive *zakat*. Moreover, it was deemed easier for the individual donor to evaluate who is considered 'poor' or 'needy' than for other categories such as those in debt (which may be private debt and thus not public knowledge) or those working in the way of Allah (which can be differently interpreted and thus contested).

Perhaps the most controversial category in the post-9/11 environment is the seventh category of '*fi sabil Allah*' (lit: 'in the cause of Allah'). Most religious legal scholars agree that this category can include the use of the lesser *jihad* or armed fighting in the name of Allah, which theologically requires strict conditions to be deemed legitimate. Within Islamic practice, however, this category most frequently encompasses all good deeds acted with the intention of sincerely struggling or striving (the greater *jihad*) for God's cause through non-violence (al-Qaradawi, 2000: 57). Only one participant (a Shia scholar based in Nottingham) emphasized this category and interpreted the meaning of '*fi sabil Allah*' to be 'endeavour work', which for him comprised the funding of religious education and training the next generation of Shia scholars. He stated that 'my own emphasis is on "*fi sabil Allah*": in the way of God and the cause of God and for the sake of God'. In terms of practical significance, as the only participant to have emphasized this category, I asked how donors had responded to the weight given to this category in his mosque in which *zakat* donations were collected. The Imam replied, 'some people did object to this, they don't really give us *zakat*, they don't really accept this . . . . So, yes, this is a real challenge'.

The point being that in *practice* Muslim charitable giving tends to focus primarily on the 'poor and needy' and charitable organizations struggle to find donors for the remaining categories even if these are interpreted as striving for the future of Islamic scholarship and knowledge. Returning to the quote given earlier in the chapter from the Centre for Security Policy in the United States which stated that *shariah* mandated the giving of monies towards *jihad* (Holton, 2009), it can be revealed that this interpretation is contrary to the views expressed by the interlocutors of this research. First, as established there are eight categories of rightful recipients of *zakat* and an individual donor need not give to all eight categories and therefore need not give towards the category of '*fi sabil Allah*' at all. Second, '*fi sabil Allah*' need not be interpreted as the lesser or armed *jihad* as assumed by the Centre for Security Policy and is most frequently interpreted as non-violent striving for the cause of God. Third, in practice Muslims tend to favour the first two categories of the poor and the needy, barely mentioning the other potential categories for donations. And fourthly, Muslims are bound to pay heed to the laws of the state in which they live. Derived from thinkers such as Ibn Khaldun, a Muslim proto-sociologist of the fourteenth century, Muslims living in a non-Muslim state are obliged to follow the laws of the land provided they are free to practice their religion (Ibn Khaldun, 1958). The injunction to follow the laws of the land in which they reside was articulated by many of the participants of this research. For instance, a practising Muslim in Bradford stated, 'as a Muslim, it is my religious duty, that I support the state where I live.' Equally, a mosque attendee in Scotland stated in interview, 'the law of the land prevails wherever you are ... you have to follow what the state has ordered you to do – the law of the land. That's your contract with the state you are living in.' Thus, Muslims living within the UK are obliged to adhere to the legal requirements of the country, not only in state terms but also as a religious requirement to prevent *fitna* (chaos). *Fitna* or chaos needs to be avoided as Ibn Khaldun asserts that it is only through a functioning and secure political system that Muslims can freely and safely practice their religious obligations (1958). Thus, as the British state has deemed it illegal to provide funds for terrorist groups it is religiously obligated that Muslims adhere to this legislation in both state and religious terms.

'Knowing' charitable recipients

The first instance of scrutiny against the misuse of charitable funds emerges from the donor's responsibility of knowing the correct recipients of *zakat*. The importance of knowing who the correct recipients are is tied to the completion of the obligation of *zakat*. It is not enough to simply give *zakat*, but *zakat* must be given to, and *received* by, at least one of the eight stipulated categories. For some legal schools, if *zakat* is given but it does not reach one of the rightful recipients then the obligation, and thus the spiritual rewards, is incomplete. Not only is *zakat* perceived to be the 'right of the poor', it is also a strong obligation of the wealthy to give. All respondents insisted that the obligation of *zakat* is not fulfilled by simply donating monies; the funds must also be received by the correct recipients, and thus a strong mechanism of accountability is in motion in simply making the decision regarding who, or to where, *zakat* donations will be distributed. For instance, the director of London Central Mosque explained,

> The Muslim himself should try to find the right people to give them the money. So, if I pass the money to someone who is going to do my *zaka*t, for instance if I decide to give to Nigeria or Syria and I have to do it through Mr. X, I have to decide if Mr. X is really going to give it to this family. You have to search the right way to

do it: the true way . . . . Even for relief we always stipulate it should be used for a particular purpose, we say for example, this is for the orphans and we need a list of the orphans names.

Another participant echoed much of the above sentiment,

> We need to give and make sure you are giving to the right people. When you give it to a charity you are authorizing them to perform on your behalf an obligation and this is not a joke. I can't give my money to someone I don't know will be doing the duty on my behalf properly. So, I need to make sure – this is how serious it is. I cannot give money and close my eyes. If it goes to the wrong person you have not performed your duty, and this is something quite serious. Your obligation hasn't been fulfilled if you didn't really make sure.

The point here is *zakat* is more than simply an obligation; it is a form of worship and purification and, also, the right of Allah and the poor (Schaeublin, 2019: 127). The concept of the right of Allah and the poor stems from the belief that any wealth a person possesses in this world is granted by Allah, and Allah has the authority to withdraw this wealth at any moment. As one respondent stated,

> We have the notion that the money is not ours. The money comes from God, the will of God. In the end it is not ours. A portion is there for other people and you have to give that portion otherwise you are a thief; you have stolen from other people.

Wealth and material belongings ultimately belong to God and are simply held in trust by human beings. As the wealth held by any individual is Allah's, then to withhold *zakat* is not just sidestepping a religious obligation but also restricting the rights of the poor (Schaeublin, 2019: 127). As one interviewee articulated, 'I have to know and make one hundred per cent sure that my money goes to the poor people.' While every participant stressed the importance of the right of the poor to receive *zakat*, it cannot be forgotten that the obligation to give *zakat* is, for Muslims, integrally linked to the salvation of the soul and rewards in heaven. In this there is a resemblance (though I am cautious of taking comparisons too far) to medieval alms giving in Christianity. As Gronemeyer has stated, often the purpose of charity was not merely to relieve the poor or for societal economic justice but for the soul's deliverance.

> It is easier for a camel to pass through the eye of a needle than for a rich man to enter the kingdom of Heaven . . . . From this bleak point of view, to be in need of help applies not to the recipient of gifts, but to the giver, for it is the salvation of his soul that is at stake. (1995: 55)

The importance of the fulfilment of the obligation of *zakat* and the fulfilment of the rights of the poor essentially act as a strong buffer against misuse of charitable funds. Taking into serious consideration the spiritual character of *zakat* allows the non-

Muslim insight into the vigorous attempts individual Muslims make in their decision-making regarding *zakat*. To ignore or marginalize the religiosity of *zakat* practice is to disregard the efforts Muslim individuals and communities already make in attempting to minimize misuse of economic funds. Ahmed Uddin in 2013, then an employee at the National Zakat Foundation, strongly argued,

> [It is] really important to get it right. Donation money is taken really seriously – it is given to us as a trust and abuse of that trust . . . well, there are various verses in the Qur'an and *Hadiths* that say if you abuse that trust you will be in major sin. . . . if you have exploited that wealth the consequences of that . . . (deep sigh). Idealistically every Muslim charity that is dealing with donations has to be very rigorous right down to the penny. It should be accountable to every penny, so if someone asks how much you are spending on each project, we have to make that information available.

It is not simply a case of wishing to stay within the legal confines of British law and the Charity Commission guidelines (though this is also true), but the actual theological aspects of *zakat* and other Islamic charity obligations fall into the same aims of transparency, accountability and rightful use of alms as existing British legal frameworks.

Distribution mechanisms

Of concern to governments and policy makers are the ways in which *zakat* and other forms of Islamic charities are distributed. *Zakat* as an individual obligation does not require a third party for its completion. In recent British Muslim 'tradition', it was more common, particularly for followers of Sunnism, to privately and discreetly distribute *zakat* to those they are aware are of need. There are therefore no accurate official national, let alone global, figures to provide the financial flows derived from *zakat*. Nonetheless, it is possible to gather generalized estimates of financial flows. Combined, *zakat* and *sadaqah* are thought to run into the millions across the UK. Fadi Itani estimated in 2012 that worldwide *zakat* and *sadaqah* collections were approximately £130 billion (Itani, 2012). Itani later commented (while Chief Executive Officer of Zakat House in 2013) his own estimate was a 'calculated guess'. A 2015 briefing paper recognized that global annual *zakat* figures have varied enormously from US$200 billion to $1 trillion depending upon the source and year (Stirk, 2015: 11).

Not all Muslim charities cater for the giving of *zakat* as the obligations and constraints are restrictive and many require religious scholars' validation to be considered legitimate. Even then, the charities that do collect *zakat* do not always publish the amounts/percentages that are collected as specifically *zakat* nor are they required to under the Charity Commission's and the Office of the Scottish Charity Regulator's (OSCR) current legislations. Under current charity legislation, registered charities need only separate funds in terms of restricted and unrestricted accounts. As *zakat* can only be legitimately distributed to the eight rightful recipient categories, *zakat* collections fall into the 'restricted' category outlined in British charity legislation.

However, many charities retain their own private records regarding the amount of donations for different funds. From the charities that shared with me their own private records, *zakat* donations tend to amount to anywhere between 10 and 30 per cent of all donations, though notably Interpal stated their *zakat* collections were roughly 60 per cent, which was by far the highest among all respondents. This then means that the vast majority of donated funds from Muslim individuals are not constrained for use on Muslims only nor restricted to 'Muslim' charities. An NPC report indicated, for instance, that Muslim charities may make up around 4.74 per cent of the charitable sector, yet they receive only 3.32 per cent of overall charitable income (Wharton and Las Casas, 2016: 12). This should not be mistaken for Muslim individuals giving less charity than others in society as a 2014 JustGiving report found that Muslims donate on average twice as much as other segments of British society (cited in Muslim Council of Britain, 2015). What this suggests is that far from being isolationists and giving only to fellow Muslims, the British Muslim population are willing to support financially causes that transcend faith boundaries. Monies are therefore donated with the knowledge and intention that they fall into the category of *sadaqah* and will be used for charitable purposes for those in need regardless of faith, nationality or other exclusive categories. Muslim practices of *sadaqah* are therefore largely indistinguishable from non-Muslim charitable donating behaviours and are financially far more significant than annual *zakat* donations.

Differences in Islamic charity

Not all forms or sects associated with Islam follow the same structures of charity. *Zakat* is one of the five pillars of Islam and thus, in theory at least, is applicable to all Muslims who meet the giving criteria regardless of sectarian divisions. However, differences occur between the sects in other forms of charity and the emphasis given to each form. The only participant in this research who admitted to not paying *zakat*, despite being eligible to do so, was a Shia charity worker. The Shia individual asserted that as a member of the Shia community their emphasis was on *khums*. It must be noted that in addition to speaking to Shia lay practitioners the researcher also had lengthy discussions with two Shia scholars and Imams who both asserted that while *khums* was indeed of central importance to the Shia community, it did not eradicate or supersede the obligation of *zakat* in clerical interpretations. Hence, scripture and religious scholarship can give insights on what *should* or *ought* to be done, but as the Shia individual who admitted not paying *zakat* demonstrates, it tells us little of what Muslims *do*.

Shi'i's established the giving of *khums* as an additional mechanism for wealth distribution, towards descendants of the Prophet Muhammad. *Khums* literally means 'one-fifth' or 20 per cent. Shia Islam differs from Sunni Islam in terms of the hierarchical importance of the *'ulama* or Islamic legal specialists (or 'clergy' for want of a better term). Most Shia practitioners, due to the importance of the *'ulama*, will task specific members of the *'ulama* with the distribution of both their *zakat* and *khums* (Marusek, 2019: 17). In the UK, this is most often done via established mosques (run or affiliated by authorized Shia clerics) or charitable institutions – both of which are registered with the Charity Commission or equivalent regulatory bodies within the UK and thus subject to scrutiny and regulation.

In Sunni Islam, there is no official hierarchy within the religious specialists. Like Protestant Christianity, there is assumed to be a direct relationship between the individual and God, thus Imams and religious leaders are subject to scrutiny and critique as much as anyone else. The giving of *zakat* to specific mosques requires the trust of the community, and thus individual acts of giving serve as the initial point of scrutiny for any Muslim institution. While there are some religious leaders and scholars who hold more social sway than others, there are essentially no strict hierarchical figures like popes, bishops, and so forth, in Sunni Islam generally. Twelver Shi'ism, on the other hand, contains within itself a much more hierarchical flow from top to bottom. While many variants of Shi'ism exist, the predominant is Twelver Shi'ism. This hierarchical difference manifests itself (among other differences) to include the rightful distribution of *zakat*. In Shia Islam, it is far more common for believers to donate to mosques and specific Imams than to distribute alms on an individual basis, specifically the obligatory charitable acts of *zakat* and *khums*. A Shia cleric in England explained,

> In Shi'a Islam there is a leader, everyone must choose a leader. All the charities are given to the leader or spent with permission of the leader, so if you have a local problem you write to your leader to explain the problem and ask for permission to use it here. So, the leader has the authority to decide what is the priority so if you give enough reasons to the leader to prioritize your local need you will get the permission to use it . . . . This centre is appointed by a leader. We have five different Imams from different racial backgrounds, and we take care of the different circles in our community . . . . There is a difference of opinion in that some scholars say that every single person has the responsibility of ensuring the money goes to the right people, if it doesn't go to the right person, I am personally responsible. Others say that not everyone has the time to do that so it is better to give to the hands of the experts who have devoted their time for recognizing this problem in the community and once you have given to that leader, of course that leader must be trustworthy, reliable, just, honest . . . then you have done your duty and the leader is responsible.

Unlike in Shi'ism, where the Imam is likely to make decisions on charitable distributions, findings indicate that *zakat* collections in Sunni mosques and other smaller Muslim institutions are redistributed according to consensus from *zakat* committees made up largely from volunteers. The London Central Mosque described its *zakat* committee and decision-making as such:

> The committee who makes decisions regarding *zakat* are all women. This is not intentional, but those that are spending are women. Women are better in this for they have more mercy in their hearts and if a poor woman comes to them, she can feel more comfortable to tell them about her needs. There is nothing in our policy that says it should be like this, but it happened to be like that. Those who spend, we prefer them to be volunteers; they are not paid, they are from the public and

we select people who are reasonable and who are wise and would like to dedicate this time just for the sake of Allah.... Sometimes the women come to me and say 'we gave this man *zakat* but we think he is lying'.... Out of these people coming to you definitely there will be some lying to you, but you do your best to check the papers as best you can but, somethings are beyond your abilities. We have a lot of applicants and we don't give out big money, only small portions.

From the donors and distributers of *zakat*, the problem of misdirection of funds is far more about the funds being received by the correct people for the correct usage rather than fears associated with extremist, let alone violent, activity. As noted earlier, the amounts given to any one individual are small – perhaps enough to pay a week's rent or an electricity bill. Often no monies are given to the individual; instead, the bills are paid directly mitigating against misuse of funds.

The fear of the misuse of funds was echoed in the Shi'a Islamic Centre of England which recalled,

Sometimes we have non-Muslims coming to the centre to ask for charity.... Sometimes we notice they only want to take the charity and go and drink. We have our own kitchen, so we ask: 'are you hungry?' So okay, we give food rather than money because we know the money would be wasted on drink. We have been deceived.

The Imam gave an example of a man who received *zakat* money but then spent it on a gambling addiction. This is the type of deception and fraud that all my respondents were afraid of. In this case, the Imam accepted that the intent was 'sincere' from the side of the donors and that the 'deceiver may be punished by God as misuse of charity is a serious sin'. What should be apparent is that the donors and distributors of Muslim charity have a strong religious incentive to ensure that charitable funds are not misused which is in turn in alignment with current UK legislation. Equally apparent is that the incidences of charitable misuse are relatively minor (though from a religious perspective the consequences for the individual in the afterlife are monumental) and demonstrate misuse as fraud for individual gain not associated with political or religious extremist ideology or funding violence.

From interviews with several mosque directors, Imams and treasurers, most of the *zakat* funds collected in mosques are redistributed into the local community with decisions of distribution made on a case-by-case basis through a *zakat* committee. Such donations may be used for such things as help with student tuition fees, household costs such as electric bills, assistance for tickets to an individual's home country or simply to any person in need with a focus on children and poor women (the reasons again are derived from Qur'anic injunction).

Individual distribution: 'Clandestine' nature of giving?

One aspect of *zakat* that appears to trouble governing agencies and public policy makers is the apparent clandestine nature of *zakat*, which assumedly hinders transparency and accountability which refers back to FATF's initial assertion that charitable and non-profit organizations were 'particularly vulnerable'. However, from interviewees this matter should be interpreted not as an attempt to disguise the 'real' beneficiaries of alms but as an act of dignity, religious intent and a reflection of the rights of recipients. To be truly worthy of spiritual merit, *zakat* must be given in such a way as not to embarrass or hurt the dignity of the recipient. Equally, *zakat* should not be given in an overtly public and boastful manner by the donor, which would weaken the intent of *zakat* and thus reduce the purifying effects of *zakat*. The verse of the Qur'an here was paraphrased by several of my interviewees,

> Void not your charitable deeds by stressing your own benevolence and by hurting [the recipients] like the one who spends his wealth only to show off to people and believes not in God and the Last Day. (Sura al-Baraqah 2: 264)

Schaeublin has posited that the seemingly secretive nature of some forms of *zakat* giving is essentially 'an attempt to acknowledge the fundamental equality of the recipient and herself before God', linking all three elements of the 'triad' of *zakat* practice together (2019: 132). Again according to Schaeublin, 'the challenge in transactions of zakat lies in making them appear *as if* givers and receivers are in a position of fundamental equality before God, despite being divided by their different access to wealth' (2019: 136). If the religious injunction and intent are not reflected upon, and taken seriously in their own terms, assumption reigns as to the reasons for the secretive giving of *zakat*. As one interviewee explained,

> You must not give in public because of the intention. Sometimes the one who receives the money doesn't know where it came from. Sometimes donors ask someone else 'Do you know any poor persons? Are you sure if he or she is *really* deserving?' People try to make this purely for the sake of Allah.

This sentiment was echoed in 2013 by Imam Laiq Ahmad Tahir, then of the Ahmadiyya Association in Bradford, who also explains how seemingly secretive giving can simultaneously be traceable and transparent.

> Due to people's self-respect and dignity, it is prescribed that you should never pay *zakat* directly to your neighbour. This is purely taking into consideration their emotional feelings. You don't want to give anyone the impression that by giving them *zakat* you have performed an act of kindness on them or they owe you or are indebted to you.... In the case of our community we have a very robust and transparent system. We make donations, we pay to the local collective in Bradford and then this is transferred to the central head office which is in London, also the head office globally, and from there they determine who the needy people are. And of course, you can recommend your neighbour without telling your neighbour that they have been recommended... this way you have helped them out but indirectly because you have taken into consideration their feelings, dignity, self-respect and so on. There has to be some transparency, but also in a discreet manner.

It is clear from the above that centralization and bureaucratic processes are not deemed an antithesis to Muslim charitable practice. There are ways to ensure transparency and accountability while simultaneously remaining discreet regarding individual donors and beneficiaries. The above interview was conducted with the Imam's two professional sons present. The Imam and both his sons were keen to show me numerous receipts for charitable donations they had given to the Ahmadiyya community. What my transcripts of this interview cannot portray is the sincerity and willingness these individual practitioners demonstrated to show their record keeping. The Imam, for instance, had pre-prepared an extensive handwritten document recording all the charitable causes that his community donate to. When asked about record keeping, all three individuals began reaching in their pockets and wallets (an act which is itself 'performative') to show me their meticulous handwritten receipts of numerous personal charitable donations ranging from around ten to one hundred pounds sterling. Record keeping in this instance at least was scrupulous.

Islamic charitable practice in the UK: Charity as performativity

Islam as a religion provides instructions on a range of matters and behaviours for everyday life from what is obligatory (*fard*) to what is forbidden (*haram*) and a range of other categories such as desirable, permissible and discouraged. *Zakat* is considered obligatory while additional charitable acts (*sadaqah*) are simply to be encouraged. As *zakat* is applied to social life '*zakat* practice takes on different forms according to changing contexts' (Schaeublin, 2014: 19). It is therefore acknowledged that while charity is an integral aspect to Islam, the ways in which it is practised differ over temporal and geographic contexts. Muslims in Britain have inevitably adapted charitable practices to the conditions of living as a religious minority in the UK's diverse social context. For instance, many Muslim-majority states make institutionalized *zakat* collection and distribution at the national level, an option which is currently not available to Muslims in the UK. Without an official single point for *zakat* collection, Muslims within the UK have developed a variety of methods to collect and distribute their religious alms. Methods of collection and redistribution range from private giving through one individual to another, via mosques, and since the 1980s via specifically Muslim charities that cater for the religious obligations of alms giving.

It is not assumed that the giving of *zakat* and other forms of charity are 'natural' for the Muslim person. The desire to give charity is seen to be cultivated through the very act of giving. For instance, a young married Muslim woman in interview spoke of the difficulty of the sacrifice of giving *zakat* at times when the woman and her husband did not feel particularly financially secure. The young Muslim continued to give *zakat* yet tried to minimize and control her internal reluctance to meet her religious obligations. As Mahmood found in her exploration of the piety movement in Egypt, the desire to give *zakat* 'must be *created* through a set of disciplinary acts' (2005: 126). In other words, Muslim charitable giving is one of the performances that creates a

Muslim person rather than being the consequence of Muslim personhood. It is argued that Muslim charitable practice within the UK can be considered performative not only in the creation of a Muslim person but also in the creation of a *British Muslim* person as charitable practices are constituted by the context in which they are performed.

British Muslim communities are not homogenous and contain within internal discourses and differing interpretations of both the meaning and practice of charitable giving (among an array of other differences). One such way that discourses are articulated is through the retelling of well-known *hadiths* ('sayings and doings' of the Prophet Muhammad). *Hadiths* continue to inform a range of everyday practices and arguments (Mahmood, 2005: 98). As Mahmood found when exploring the piety movement in Egypt, *hadiths* are not simply repeated on rope but are supplemented with commentary, examples and interpretations in their performances in response to the questions and situations discussed thereby imparting contextualized and nuanced understandings.

A common authenticated *hadith* proclaims, 'He is not a believer whose stomach is full while his neighbour is hungry' (Sunan al-Kubra, 19049). Of note is that the saying simply says 'neighbour' not *Muslim* neighbour and all respondents understood it this way. Thus, there is a strong ethos to ensure all in your community, regardless of faith or none, does not go wanting for the most basic of life's necessities. A variant of the above *hadith* was explained to me by a member of a mosque in Scotland who interpreted the *hadith* as

> a Muslim is responsible for forty of his neighbours around him . . . if you sleep at night and your neighbour sleeps hungry God, Allah, will question you on the day of judgement . . . . So, you can't just ignore it – it is not an option for the ideal Muslim it's just not an option . . . the state can do whatever it can but it is the individual responsibility to take care of forty houses around him if he has the means to do that. And I think that's what drives the motive either consciously or unconsciously . . . I think that this is part of the way our culture works and how we've been brought up to know how this has to be done because it is a religious duty that transfers into an action.

Similarly, an employee of Islamic Relief expanded on the same *hadith* saying 'but which neighbour? Black? Muslim? Non-Muslim? *Neighbour*: full stop'. In terms of general charity (*sadaqah*), there is a genuine belief that this encouraged aspect of Islam be employed to benefit all society regardless of faith (or lack of it). In this sense, there can be a broad overlap between Muslim general charity and conceptions of non-Muslim charity held in British societies today.

Bridging differences

Identity politics has been on the rise as an explanatory tool in understanding the presumed failure of multiculturalism and the erosion of social cohesion, yet recent studies have argued that more traditional concepts such as class and local environment still have more explanatory power than other identifiers such as religion and ethnicity

(Laurence, 2009: 70). Laurence's account largely coincides with the findings of the Commission on Integration and Cohesion which states that 'deprivation remains a key influencer of cohesion, but the fact that some areas have high deprivation and high cohesion shows that local action can build resilience to its effects' (CIC, 2007: 20). If this is indeed the case, attempts of poverty alleviation and reductions of wealth gaps have the potential of being a strong instrument to bridge gaps between (and within) communities and assist in the process of social cohesion. Indeed, charitable practices that cross religious, ethnic or cultural boundaries not only contribute in practical assistance to the needy but also potentially create solidarities and community awareness in promotional roles, activities and general negotiations in the third sector irrespective of faith, ethnicity or other identity attributes. Civil society is far from a homogenous unit and diversity exists in all its subsections including the various Muslim communities within the UK. In this sense, even seemingly 'isolationist' practices such as *zakat*, which almost entirely stays within Muslim demographics, can be an important tool for social cohesion in that it can help bridge ties between various Muslim sects, schools of thought (*madhab*), practices and cultures. A young Muslim charity shop manager explained to me the importance of charity in Islam for building common values and perceptions of solidarity:

> It creates brothership – brothers and sisters united – automatically you have been brought up with the belief that you *have* to give to the poor; they need it . . . . They have a right . . . When you give to them you become part of their life to an extent, they become like your brother and this creates a love between you as a human race . . . it creates the bonds of one human race.

Specifying the 'Muslim' charitable sector rather than the charity sector more generally could be perceived as separatist or isolationist practice. When asked why there was a perceived need for specifically 'Muslim' charities, one interviewee working for a leading Muslim charity in the UK responded,

> our ethos, our vision and values are Islamic. Our values are based on the Qur'an, the teachings of the Prophet and the *hadiths* and so on. So that's what underpins us, but our work is humanitarian. So, while we work in predominantly Muslim countries we don't necessarily focus just on Muslim countries and we don't restrict ourselves. . . . So, I think the phrase 'Muslim charities' – you have to be a bit careful because it may give the impression that Muslim charities are only working for Muslims. I think Muslim charities, going back to the religious obligations, have their roots in Islam in that respect they want to help other people because it is a religious obligation, but the actual practical help is not just limited to Muslims – it is to help everybody.

Another respondent asked the same question raised the point of theological (non) understanding as the main reason for the emergence of specifically 'Muslim' charities. As a long-standing employee of an international Muslim relief charity he perceived the reason for Muslim charities in the UK not from an isolationist perspective (the charity works with many non-Muslim secular organizations and distributes aid irrespective of faith or none) but one of religious obligation and legitimacy.

> Muslims may not be comfortable giving their money to non-Muslim charities especially when it is *zakat* . . . how do you expect a non-Muslim who does not believe in your religion to go and do *Qurbani*? . . . Muslim communities would say 'look we need somebody that will understand us' . . . donors want to work with people who can deliver what they want so because of that you will always need a Muslim charity from the Islamic perspective who can deliver and give confidence to the donor.

Therefore, the emergence of Muslim charities should not be regarded as necessarily 'isolationist' or separatist practices but as a mode of facilitating religious obligations in theologically validated ways. It should also be emphasized that even within the British Muslim communities divisions and tensions exist so that charitable work even restricted to this domain can assist in building bridges between diverse, and ethnically mixed, communities. This argument coincides with Barylo's research on Muslim youth charities in Europe. Barylo found 'that the diverse cultural and spiritual backgrounds of their members are no longer sources of division, but a wealth they use to build bridges throughout the Muslim community' (Barylo, 2018: 3–4).

When asked what the purpose of *zakat* is, the potential for social cohesion becomes clear from the view of those interviewed. As a director of a busy mosque in London reported, '*Zakat* is one of the pillars because it is important to guarantee a better society around you; to show your participation to those around you and to do this for the sake of God.' Another interviewee from the Muslim Association of Britain described the consequences of *zakat* as being the 'development of sacrifice, selflessness, to help others. *Zakat* helps combat diseases, aspects of crime, greed or taking advantage of others'. From a scholarly perspective the purpose of *zakat* is said to encourage the development of pious, moral persons in that '*zakat* moulds the individual into responsible caring persons. It inculcates the spirit of good will, cooperation and brotherhood in upholding social solidarity in the society' (Abdullah and Suhaib, 2011: 85). In this sense, Muslim charity can again be considered performative as it is the action, not the belief, that 'moulds the individual into responsible caring persons'. The British Muslim person can therefore be said to be constructed 'by the very expressions that are said to be their results' (Bell, 1999: 43).

Sadaqah is the term used for general charity and is not restricted to the giving of monies alone so that a smile or picking up litter can also be considered an act of *sadaqah*. As a young professional Muslim woman told me, '*Sadaqah* is very flexible: you can give to anything and everybody – Muslim or non-Muslim'. She tells of standing orders the woman and her husband make to non-faith-based charities such as NSPCC, Cancer Research and the Antony Nolan Fund particularly due to the sad loss of her uncle who was struck with pancreas cancer – obviously a disease which transcends secular and faith divides. The practical consequences of this are that Muslims will entrust *sadaqah* to almost any cause they feel worthy and is most often distributed to charities that do not distinguish the Muslim donor from any other charitable actor in society. For instance, the charitable causes respondents purported to give include cancer research, Oxfam, Save the Children, MacMillan Fund, the National Protection of Children and the like. *Zakat* itself, however, has strict injunctions concerning the correct beneficiaries and cannot be used for any need. As such, it is rare (none of my respondents admitted to this) to entrust *zakat* donations to a non-Muslim charity. Muslim charities have arisen in the UK, particularly since the 1980s, in response to the growing need to accommodate religious obligations (specifically *zakat*) in a transparent and accountable way in addition to their broader humanitarian focus. The desire for accountability and transparency is both a product of Muslims wishing to ensure their religious obligations are properly met *and* the wish to coincide with current 'fundamental British values' and rule of law.

Unlike charity as generally understood in Western society, *zakat* is not a 'gift' to the less fortunate but is considered their right (*haqq*). Although there is no mechanism to ensure compliance or punish non-compliance (in this world), it is the fear of Godly punishment that ensures the obligation of *zakat* is fulfilled by believing practitioners. Wealth ultimately belongs to God, and while individuals may be fortunate enough to be granted wealth in this lifetime it is essentially deemed a trust in the hands of some for the benefit of all. '*Zakat* is not a free gift or an act of philanthropy but instead an obligation and act of purification' (Pollard et al., 2015: 88). While the notion of 'gift' is somewhat an antithesis to *zakat*, it relates to Mauss's theoretical work which he points out creates unity as

> it serves to transcend the boundaries of the individual . . . . The gift is not seen as something that is alienated from the giver, or which creates a boundary between the self who gives and the other who receives. Rather, the process of giving incorporates both giver and receiver into a larger self. Giving to the collective is not imagined as impoverishing the individual, but as creating a sum of abundance which is greater than the separate gifts and in which all will share. (cited in Dunn, 1996: 436–7)

Zakat may be the only obligatory alms giving in Sunni Islam but those interviewed considered it merely a trifle in comparison to how much, and how often, most practising Muslims donate and give to charitable causes as *sadaqah*. As one charity employee stated,

> I think, if you have got that core practice of giving *zakat* and you accept it as one of the fundamentals of putting your religion into practice. I think from there will spring other charitable practice and charitable giving and it doesn't have to be monetary either. I think what it does is reinforces your sense of humanity . . . so then you start acting charitably in your general life, like helping the elderly across the road or helping your neighbour all these sorts of things. I think especially for young people it builds up their character and develops them as a human being but also makes them socially aware if you like, by discovering their role in the world.

From the above, the potential for social cohesion therefore lies not only in the practical assistance to the needy but also in helping develop 'human beings' who are socially aware and thus able to become active citizens. Again, the performance of charitable acts can be considered a necessary component of a constructed British Muslim person who discovers 'their role in the world' and the society in which they are embedded.

Summary

Muslim charities emerged as specifically 'Muslim' due to the explicit obligations and rights that are deeply connected to prescriptions regarding charitable giving, with *zakat* as the paramount example. This suggests that Muslim charities did not emerge due to a desire for self-segregation but only to ensure that their religious obligations are carried out in the correct manner. As one interviewee expressed,

> There is a need to make sure that whoever you give your Islamic contribution to is doing it right. Muslims also give to non-Muslim charities, but when it comes to the Islamic duty of giving *zakat* there are restrictions, it *has* to be done with people who understand. Recipients of *zakat* are specific. I will feel comfortable to do my religious duty with someone who will understand it.

This sentiment is also echoed by al-Qaradawi, who stated that *zakat* collectors and distributers must be Muslim: 'it is unreasonable that people that do not believe in *zakah* be entrusted to implement it' (al-Qaradawi, 2000: 26). Despite this, several of my respondents suggested that the norm was now to give general charity (*sadaqah*) to non-Muslim charities such as those designated for cancer research, Oxfam and other major internationally renowned charities, but as one respondent claimed 'they will not give their *zakat* to Oxfam'.

Ultimately the perceived need for specifically Muslim charities does not stem from issues of self-segregation or suspicious intent but from religious injunction and trust in those given authorization to distribute funds according to the obligations and rights of both receiver and donor. None of this can be accurately understood without solemn consideration of the religious character of alms giving. *The 9/11 Commission Report*'s statement that financial origin of violent acts is a question with 'little practical significance' (The 9/11 Commission Report, 2004) not only illuminates the breadth of negligence of the consequences of its speculations surrounding Islamic charitable giving but also demonstrates a misunderstanding of Muslim pious practice and the communities that regularly engage in acts of religiosity. Moreover, the religious conception of *obligation* needs to be earnestly considered to ensure state-centric gazes do not skew our understanding – and policy engagements – with Islamic charitable giving in Britain today.

4

'They keep asking for evidence. We have none . . . Absolutely none'

The Office of the Scottish Charity Regulator (OSCR) gave up considerable time to assist this research. Judith Turbyne, the engagement officer, spoke candidly and rapidly to the author for over two hours in a face-to-face interview in her office in Dundee, Scotland, overlooking the river Tay in 2017. OSCR was upfront and stark in its assessment of the evidence it found in relation to charities (faith-based or secular) dealing with terrorist funding. Ms Turbyne stated,

> we are pushed all the time, and we are trying to make it as evidence based as possible, we have very little evidence. They keep asking for evidence of charities involved with funding terrorism and we have none. We have none, right. We've got absolutely none. We have had no cases that have been raised with us, no concerns raised with us in regard to terrorist financing. Sometimes suspicions from people who go 'Ah, Muslim charity' but no evidence or whatever.

As the chapter title highlights, OSCR has no evidence to support that charities (Muslim or non-Muslim) are connected to violent political action, yet 'they' keep asking for it. But who are 'they'?

This chapter will first answer the question of who 'keep[s] asking for evidence'? It will then provide an example of how the global counter-terror financing (CTF) system pressurizes states and institutions to comply, utilizing the case of the UK-based charity Interpal. The case of Interpal demonstrates the limits of the CTF systems' coercive power on sovereign states. It shall be argued, following the analysis of De Goede (2017a), that the UK can then be considered a 'norm adopter' by modifying global CTF norms to the UK context. Utilizing the idea of 'norm adopters', it will be posited that the devolved powers within the UK also develop their own interpretations of CTF duties due to the differences in context, and nature and size, of their charitable sectors. Both the Charity Commission and OSCR vehemently deny targeting any group within the charitable sector including Muslims. It will be posited that at least part of the perception of disproportionate investigations into Muslim charities is a result not of the charity regulators themselves but the various actors and individuals playing their role as unaccountable and opaque petty-sovereigns.

Who are 'they' who 'keep asking for evidence' from OSCR? 'They' in this instance is the Financial Action Task Force (FATF) which, as an international body, attempts to provide guidance and implementation strategies to global CTF initiatives as outlined in more detail in Chapter 2. OSCR commented that 'we have been involved recently with the Financial Action Task Force, so we have been contributing to that and the number of people hours we have spent on that is ridiculous'. The fact that the engagement officer for OSCR referred to the time spent on FATF as 'ridiculous' gives a fair indication of how high OSCR believes the risk of charities being led into terrorist financing is. FATF while an international body is still largely following the guidelines derived from the United States.

While much of the global CTF system is drawn from the United States, it would be erroneous to believe that American policy guidelines are simply appropriated uncritically and en masse by the rest of the world. While the Financial War on Terror (FWoT) was an aspect of the War on Terror (WoT) that was initially embraced by international states and institutions, in the years following 9/11, the 'evidence' provided by the United States was increasingly scrutinized and often found lacking and insufficient for the burden of proof in European courts. In most cases, where prosecutions have been successful in the United States, the standard of proof required for conviction would not meet the standards of Western European courts (Benthall, 2016: 28).

The Somali remittance organization al-Barakaat (discussed in Chapter 2) and the British-based charity Interpal are cases in point. In the case of al-Barakaat, 'countries ranging from Canada to Sweden, judging the "evidence" furnished by the US unconvincing, refused to comply with requests for further crackdowns against the company and its executives' (Warde, 2007: ix). This suggests that while global states are coerced and persuaded to join the FWoT, they do not necessarily mimic US interpretations and applications entirely.

De Goede (2012b) has argued that current CTF can be viewed as a regime of governmentality which stretches beyond individual states to create a norm of governing and surveillance strategies. Simultaneously, De Goede has warned against assuming that the norms of CTF are applied homogenously globally asserting that

> in practice . . . rather than a pure norm taking, the adoption of US–led security programmes in Europe takes a hybrid shape: initiatives are not copied unchanged or uncritically. Instead, they are appropriated by European institutions, which graft on European checks and balances. (2017b: 255–6)

From this, we can understand CTF initiatives to be part of a wider regime of governmentality which involves a range of state and non-state actors. These state and non-state actors use diverse strategies to not only obtain policy objectives, but 'produce and reproduce' certain types of subjects (Butler, 2006: 52).

Integral to the understanding of how regimes of governmentality operate is Butler's conception of 'petty-sovereigns'. Butler explicates by stating that petty-sovereigns

> reigning in the midst of bureaucratic army institutions mobilized by aims and tactics of power they do not inaugurate or fully control. And yet such figures are delegated with the power to render unilateral decisions accountable to no law and without any legitimate authority. (2006: 56)

To clarify, Butler argues that regimes of governmentality exercise rather than hold power, and thus power is diffused among a range of actors who each individually hold the authority to judge and condemn others without necessarily providing transparency and accountability to their decisions. A range of state, and non-state, actors tasked with the implementation of CTF in charities could be categorized as 'petty-sovereigns'. These petty-sovereigns could include charity regulators, elected MPs, banks and banking staff, media representatives, journalists, bloggers and the public at large (given it is largely the public tasked with reporting 'suspicious behaviour'). Obviously, some of the actors are more accountable than others, but all are 'delegated with the power to render unilateral decisions' (Butler, 2006: 56).

Much of British CTF policy is regulated or designed by the FATF, an international body with expanded powers from anti-money laundering to the inclusion of CTF in 2001 (two weeks after 9/11). In this sense the global and the local are integrally interwoven in counter-terror policies. FATF provides the framework and regulation while the actual procedures and details are left to individual regulators, banks and financial systems allowing for a wide array of CTF practices in a single state with differing consequences. This chapter will uncover the different applications of CTF policies by regulatory and oversight bodies such as the Charity Commission for England and Wales and the OSCR as well as the role of media accusations.

As will be explored, the regime of governmentality operates such that petty-sovereigns have considerable power over another individual's freedom and possess the ability to do violence against another based on judgements of 'suspicion' and 'danger' with little empirical evidence or accountability. It goes without saying that some levels of transparency and accountability are in place in regard to elected MPs and government officials, but what of the media accusations against charities (including personal bloggers), banking decisions that freeze or cancel charity accounts with no obligation to provide detailed reasons or the variety of individual citizens asked to report suspicious activity with little understanding of what counts as 'normal' or 'deviant' behaviour?

The ability to judge someone or something as 'suspicious' or 'dangerous' is classed by Butler as an act of 'deeming' which she explicates as 'they have to be "deemed dangerous", but the "deeming" is not . . . a judgment for which there are rules of evidence' (Butler, 2006: 71). This seems to be implied in Judith Turbyne's (OSCR) analysis when she remarked that there were 'sometimes suspicions from people who go "Ah, Muslim charity", but no evidence'.

Butler expands further, utilizing the case of the United States, claiming,

> The license to brand and categorize and detain on the basis of suspicion alone, expressed in this operation of 'deeming', is potentially enormous. We have already seen it at work in racial profiling. . . . When Rumsfeld has sent the US into periodic panics or 'alerts', he has not told the population what to look out for, but only to have a heightened awareness of suspicious activity. This objectless panic translates too quickly into suspicion of all dark-skinned peoples, especially those who are Arab, or appear to look so to a population not always well versed in making visual distinctions, say, between Sikhs and Muslims or, indeed, Sephardic or Arab Jews

and Pakistani-Americans. Although 'deeming' someone dangerous is considered a state prerogative in these discussions, it is also a potential license for prejudicial perception and a virtual mandate to heighten racialized ways of looking and judging in the name of national security. (2006: 77)

The point being 'petty-sovereigns' wield great and non-accountable power to report and 'deem dangerous' without the necessary expertise and skills to do so in a proportionate and evidence-based manner. The ways in which 'terror', 'Islam', 'Muslim' and, increasingly, 'charity' are interlinked in popular rhetoric and media discourse raise unevidenced perceptions among the population which inevitably feeds into 'profiling' of suspicious and dangerous individuals and activities, resulting in particularly visible 'Muslims' being targeted for 'deeming'. Thus, while the regime of CTF in charities stems from the United States and FATF, in operational terms the implementation is often left to local non-accountable petty-sovereigns.

Charity Commission for England and Wales and the Office of the Scottish Charity Regulator

The UK has demonstrated itself to be a global forerunner in the struggle against terrorist financing, quickly complying and instigating the Special Recommendations provided by FATF. However, arguably, the United Kingdom has not merely implemented the counter-financial rules emanating from the United States but has creatively adapted core components to the context of Britain. Specifically, as Sidel (2011) notes, the United States and the United Kingdom differ substantially, with the United States favouring prosecutions in contrast to the United Kingdom which emphasizes legal compliance and regulation. Instrumental in the UK's adaptation of global financial counter-terror norms has been the role of the Charity Commission and to a lesser extent, the Scottish equivalent OSCR.

As an independent branch of government, the Charity Commission is responsible for regulating and protecting the UK's diverse charitable sector. In theory at least, the Commission 'alone has the authority to investigate an inquiry and to decide on the type of sanction to impose, if any' (Gunning, 2008: 113). Essentially, the Charity Commission has seen its role in regulating charities as to assist, rather than to hinder, organizations to adhere to regulations. As such, the Charity Commission has envisaged the closing down of charities to be a measure of last resort seeking 'rather to identify trustees who were committed to using its resources properly and then to have objectionable trustees removed' (Benthall, 2016: 83).

In February 2006, the then British Chancellor of Exchequer Gordon Brown began the extension of CTF legislation into charity law. The British government announced it would 'use classified intelligence to freeze assets of those suspected of having links to terrorism' (cited Sidel, 2011: 138) in line with the special recommendations outlined by FATF. It was not long after that charities (secular and faith-based) critiqued this approach with a National Council for Voluntary Organizations (NCVQ) report stating that charities should be viewed as allies in the fight against terrorism 'rather than adversaries' (Sidel, 2011: 138). Discomfort in connecting charities, secular or faith-based, with criminal and terrorist activity was quickly made public by the third sector generally. The NCVQ countered that 'by placing a veil of suspicion over all charities, the government is in danger of damaging the trusted reputation of the voluntary sector and making people less likely to donate to good causes' (NCVO cited in Sidel, 2011: 138). Thus, some of the negative consequences of deepening financial counter-terror policies in the voluntary sector were raised from the outset.

In 2014, the Charity Commission powers were extended further following from the Prime Minister's Extremism Taskforce, set up following the murder of serviceman Drummer Lee Rigby in Woolwich in 2013 and also in 2014 by the Home Affairs Committee on Counter-Terrorism which reported that Charity Commission be granted stronger powers to counter abuse of charities by terrorists (Morris, 2016: 970). This saw the implementation of the Charities (Protection and Social Investment) Bill 2015–16 which was passed March 2016 (Morris, 2016: 971). A salient aspect to mention here is that while the murder of Drummer Lee Rigby is reportedly the trigger for extending CTF laws into the charity sector, it is opaque how monitoring charities, or indeed any financial institution, could have prevented this killing. Drummer Lee Rigby was killed on 22 May 2013, in broad daylight in Woolwich, England. His murderers first attacked by hitting him at high speed with their car before descending on the UK soldier with cleavers and knives. What is entirely unclear is how any financial tracking could have prevented this attack given the items used for Rigby's murders were mundane household items purchased at low cost. In this instance at least, it seems that terrorism does not necessarily need to seek additional finances, either overtly or 'by underhand means' (Walker, 2018: 1088). This leads to support for Walker's analysis that states 'the impediments created for the work of charities are alleged to be out of proportion to these risks, giving rise to explanations about official motivations which are less about counter-terrorism and more about the state assertion of control over non-government actors' (2018: 1088).

Anxiety within the sector, and particularly within many Muslim charities, increased with the announcement of William Shawcross as Chairman of the Charity Commission. The decision to appoint Shawcross as Chairman was met with initial controversy not least due to previous negative statements regarding the religion of Islam in its entirety. For example, Shawcross, prior to his appointment as chair of the Commission, is recorded as saying that 'Islam is one of the greatest, most terrifying problems of our future' (cited in Osborne and Delmar-Morgan, 2015). Discomfort over Shawcross's appointment was also due to his former position as board member of the neoconservative think tank The Henry Jackson Society which released several reports alleging links between Muslim charities and extremism (Chang, 2020: 16). The appointment of Shawcross at the same time as expanding the powers of the Charity Commission in line with financial counter-terror initiatives further increased the perception publicly that specifically Muslim charities were perceived to be a threat to national security. The evidence suggests that certainly for some segments of the UK population, the decision to appoint Shawcross as chair verified their perceptions of charities being breeding grounds for terrorist activities as live enquiries grew from 76 in 2013–14 to 135 in 2015–16 (Walker, 2018: 1102).

For some actors within the third sector, these moves undermined the Commission's regulatory role leading Osborne and Delmar-Morgan to pronounce that under chairman William Shawcross 'the Charity Commission seems to have abandoned its previous caution' (Osborne and Delmar-Morgan, 2015). None of my interviewees were willing to go on record regarding their view of the appointment of William Shawcross as they feared negative repercussions to themselves and their charitable works. That being said, off-record many were suspicious of the reasons behind this controversial decision as evidenced in the following from an interviewee who stated, 'the Charity Commission seems more political rather than a body that's neutral and there to do a particular job. And that could be possibly to do with the people who are in the commission, such as the chair'. It should be made clear, however, almost all of those interviewed (whether faith-based or not) made a clear delineation between employees of the Charity Commission they worked directly with and the Commission's board – the former viewed largely favourably while the latter was discussed with apprehension.

Changes to the Charity Commission's regulatory powers were welcome measures according to Nick Donaldson of the Charity Commission who stated that 'we welcome these additional powers, which supplement our existing powers' (in email correspondence with author, 2017). Simultaneously, many within (and without) the sector itself warned against potential counterproductive actions. Primarily, those against the extension of the Charity Commission's powers argued that the voluntary sector should be treated as an ally in the WoT, not a suspect. As Shaw-Hamilton notes, charity could be one of the solutions to political violence, but that potential was being neglected and undermined in the way CTF policies were being developed.

> An effective system of charity regulation can balance the opportunities that charities represent with concerns about misuse, even where that involves terrorism. But to do this, many governments in donor and recipient countries need to take a more creative view of the potential of the charitable sector. Otherwise, there will be a serious risk of criminalizing charitable giving – that is, criminalizing part of the solution to terrorism. (2007: 15)

As the previous discussion suggests, Muslim charities are not alone in their apprehensions of the new regulatory powers of the Charity Commission. The Joseph Rowntree Charitable Trust is on record in saying 'unprecedented regulatory pressure' were neither 'proportionate or warranted' (Osborne and Delmar-Morgan, 2015).

Regarding whether the new regulatory powers were 'proportionate', according to Nick Donaldson of the Charity Commission,

> The Charity Commission has found some evidence of charities' funds being diverted for terrorist financing purposes. We are clear that incidents of abuse of charities for terrorist purposes are rare, but when these do occur significantly threaten public trust and confidence in the sector. (email correspondence with author, 2017)

Unlike OSCR, which stated 'we have none, absolutely none . . . no evidence' (Judith Turbyne in interview, 2017), the Charity Commission believes some evidence has been discovered but 'incidents of abuse . . . are rare' and thus would seem to suggest the media attention, policy initiatives and public funds spent on preventing charities abusing their position for terrorist purposes are indeed disproportionate and 'unwarranted' in terms of the scale of the problem.

In contrast, OSCR, the Scottish equivalent of the Charity Commission, stated,

> Our focus has been (and our board is very, very keen on this), is to be preventative, to be proportionate and positive. So there is no point being a heavy handed regulator in Scotland with the majority of the sector not really doing anything bad, and if they are, it is usually because, they don't have enough capacity, they don't understand, we are not being clear enough . . . we focus on engagement because we really want to stop people from getting things wrong which is really where the focus lies. (Judith Turbyne, Head of Engagement, OSCR in interview with author, 2017)

OSCR was keen to point out the differences in the nature of the charities under the different regulatory bodies. OSCR's Engagement Officer commented,

> I suppose we have a slightly different and increasingly different approach to the Charity Commission in that (although I suspect we will have a different journey and then come back as we have very similar legislation but it is not exactly the same) but the nature of our sector is different.

The differences outlined between the Charity Commission and OSCR coincide with De Goede's concept of the governmentality of CTF policies. De Goede has argued that while global norms exist, the practice and implementation of these norms differ in different national and local contexts. Here, while there is evidence of the differences in emphasis and procedures between the United States and the United Kingdom, there are also differences in practice between the various nations of the United Kingdom. The majority of charities registered in Scotland are extremely small in terms of monies collected and distributed with each and every Girl Guide and Boy Scout club listed individually. Most of the smaller charities are run by volunteers and non-experts who may find the difficulties of traversing the necessary reporting and procedures problematic, not through any suspicious or harmful intent but simply through lack of time and expertise. The larger charities with funds of over £25,000 tend to have premises in both Scotland and England in which case the charity would register with both regulatory bodies. Judith Turbyne of OSCR commented,

> The big charities are very few and far between and most of them . . . are what we would call cross-border charities, so they are registered with us and with the Charity Commission for England and Wales. . . . But the lead regulator for most of these would be the Charity Commission for England and Wales. . . . If they've got

a notifiable (that's what we call it) then they will deal with the Charity Commission and not us. So, the first thing to say is that the sector is highly dominated by very small charities. One of the things we always say is that actually for the number of charities . . . the number of inquiries we actually do over the course of a year is actually very small and most of those are to do with basic governance issues: trustees doing the right thing. The number that are actually nefarious criminal dodgers are tiny, tiny.

OSCR, like the Charity Commission, focuses on regulating rather than prosecuting the charitable sector (Sidel, 2011). OSCR's 2017 report is instructive in understanding the regulators' priorities and assessment of the terror threat. The strategic objectives from 2014 to 2017 include helping the public have more confidence in charities; helping trustees understand and comply with their legal duties; keeping registration procedures straightforward and accessible; and improving efficiency and delivery of services (OSCR, 2017). Of note is that 'terrorism' is not mentioned in OSCR's Annual Report published in 2017 giving a clear indication of the minimum risk that terror-related crimes have in the Scottish sector. Turbyne also notes that 'for the number of charities . . . the number of inquiries . . . over the course of a year is actually very small'. This is also demonstrated in the 2017 Annual Report, which claims that out of roughly 24,000 charities only 349 'concerns' were raised with OSCR between 2016 and 2017 (OSCR, 2017: 5). Of the 349 concerns raised (which were predominantly related to fraud and trustee misuse rather than political violence), none were found guilty of terrorist financing.

OSCR's Head of Engagement elaborated on the evidence of terrorist financing within the Scottish charitable sector stating,

> The conclusion from the work that we have done, which has been fairly in depth, is that we can't give evidence because we don't have any. If we had, we would give them it. The feeling is that the risk profile in Scotland (and this comes up in the prevent meetings as well) is that . . . the main concerns are not really about extremist Muslim terror, but it is more about extremism and sectarian violence at the local level and lone actors of whatever description . . . . if you talk about the actual threat level, not to say that nothing could ever happen, but if you want to deal with the appropriate threat within Scotland, within the charity sector, what you really need to be doing is dealing with government issues overall . . . . The real risk is charity governance because if you have good governance you report fraud and misuse and put in place structures to prevent it happening again. The big risk is not the setting up of sham charities who collect hundreds of thousands and export this.

Of note is that the concerns of charitable abuse highlighted by OSCR are entirely in line with the types of abuses that Muslim charities and donors themselves fear as outlined in the previous chapter.

Instructive is that both regulatory bodies, the Charity Commission and OSCR, accepted that the public at large may have pre-disposed negativity towards Muslim charities, but both denied that their institutions specifically targeted the Muslim charitable sector. The Charity Commission was forceful in stating that

> the Commission totally rejects the accusation of targeting Muslim charities. Our regulatory engagement, including all faith charities, is based on an assessment of risk, in accordance with our published risk framework. Where we find evidence of serious misconduct and mismanagement in charities, we will respond fairly and robustly, regardless of the charity's religion or any other identifying factor. (Nick Donaldson, Charity Commission, email correspondence with author, 2017)

In email correspondence, Nick Donaldson of the Charity Commission instructed the author to view the published records provided by the Charity Commission regarding the number and types of inquiries raised by the regulator, relating to the figures from 1 April 2016 to 31 March 2017 (Charity Commission, 2017). Donaldson stated that 'you will see that Islamic charities are not at all disproportionately represented in these figures in investigations' (email correspondence, 2017). For this period, fourteen investigations were made into 'religious' charities of which two were deemed Islamic which indeed does not indicate a disproportionate amount of inquiries. However, if all the publications available from the Charity Commission are combined a different picture emerges. The following annual publication for the year April 2017–March 2018 (Charity Commission, 2018), for instance, lists a rise in investigations for Muslim charities to seven comprising 43.8 per cent of investigations of religious charities (in comparison six Christian, two Jewish and one Hindu charity were also investigated in the same time frame). Taking statistics published from 2009 to 2018 reveals that approximately one-sixth of all UK-based Muslim charities have undergone some form of inquiry (Imitiaz, 2019: 11). During the same period a total of 296 charities were investigated, 59 of which can be categorized as 'Muslim' which overall does suggest a higher rate of investigation for Muslim charities than other religious denominations. Most investigations were over issues concerning due diligence, trusteeships and annual report publishing. For example, one charity was investigated due to an impersonator falsely claiming to fundraise and another was under inquiry for an event which hosted a speaker who made 'unacceptable comments' (Imtiaz, 2019: 12).

The debate regarding whether Muslim charities are disproportionately targeted by Charity Commission investigations has been ongoing since 2014 and the publication of the controversial Claystone report (Belaon, 2014). This report gathered media attention with reporting of the findings in mainstream national papers such as *The Independent* (Eleftheriou-Smith, 2014), *The Guardian* (Ramesh, 2014) and *The Telegraph* (Gilligan, 2014) and alleged that 38 per cent of Charity Commission inquiries between January 2013 and April 2014 were on Muslim charities (Belaon, 2014). The Charity Commission has consistently and vehemently denied targeting Muslim charities and yet the perception within the subsector remains that they are viewed as a 'suspect sector' (Belaon, 2014). A recent article in the Muslim Charity Forum's journal *The Forum* opens with 'it is a common feeling expressed within the British Muslim charitable sector that the Charity Commission has an Islamophobia or anti-Muslim agenda' (Imtiaz, 2019: 11). So, what are we to make of these two opposing positions?

Given the generally good relationship between Muslim charities and specific people within the Charity Commission, it would be an oversimplification to simply suggest that the Charity Commission has an anti-Muslim agenda. The differing perception is probably correlated to two factors. Firstly, how a 'Muslim charity' is defined and secondly, that investigations are often a result of public notifications to the Charity Commission or media reports. The lack of a robust definition of a 'Muslim' charity arguably is the crux of the issue. There is no uncontested definition of a 'Muslim' charity and as mentioned in Chapter 1, what to include or exclude as 'Muslim' is a methodological quagmire and as such, divergent definitions of what to include and exclude as a 'Muslim charity' will result in very different numbers. In email correspondence, the Charity Commission was keen to emphasize that differing definitions of what constitutes a 'Muslim' charity are in operation with Nick Donaldson commenting,

> I'm aware that there are different interpretations of what constitutes a faith-based charity (i.e. some will be explicitly to advance religion, some will advance other purposes but share a faith perspective, others simply have an underlying faith ethos). Each charity on the Register of Charities self classifies itself according to its charitable purposes, beneficiaries, and objects. In charities' descriptions of charitable purposes in their annual returns, one of the categories is 'advancement of religion' so we can see how many charities have ticked that, and we can also run queries of charities names and objects to look for specific words relating to faith (e.g. Christianity, Judaism, Temple, Quran, Bible, Talmud etc).

Nick Donaldson also wrote that 'the Commission does not hold or record reliable data on how many charities connected with a particular religion there are. The data we hold is based on the information given by charities in their annual return, which does not break down the advancement of religion by a particular faith or identify multi-faith purposes or no particular faith.' While this assists in understanding why the quantitative data is disputed as what counts as a 'Muslim' charity will be different depending on the definition, the last statement by Donaldson does ensure that it is problematic for the Charity Commission to simply dismiss allegations of Muslim targeting if it does not hold the appropriate data to dispute it. However, this does not necessarily mean that the Charity Commission is deliberately, or consciously, focusing on Muslim charities themselves. Again, much of the reporting of suspicious activity is derived from the public and other 'petty sovereigns' which the Charity Commission are obliged to investigate. The second factor concerning public and media allegations and reports fits into De Goede's understanding as practitioners of CTF as 'petty-sovereigns' to be discussed in more detail in a later section of this chapter.

Interpal

Another example that demonstrates the differences between the governmentality of CTF and its practice in the United Kingdom in comparison to the United States is that of the charity Interpal. Interpal is a UK-based charity that was founded in 1994 with the objective of helping Palestinians in the Occupied Territories as well as in refugee camps of Lebanon and Jordan particularly. Its main areas of focus include food provisions, medical services, education and rehabilitation services for the disabled (Keatinge, 2014: 61).

Designated as a terrorist entity in 2003 by the United States and Israel, the US government has repeatedly alleged that Interpal was supporting the armed Palestinian movement Hamas which is also currently designated as a terrorist entity by the United States and the United Kingdom, which resulted in the first investigation from the Charity Commission. Following immense pressure from the United States,

> a further investigation of the charity was instigated in 2003 with President Bush ordering *Interpal's* assets to be frozen pending investigation. The Charity Commission explained that no evidence was forthcoming from the US Treasury other than a selection of newspaper clippings. (Warde, 2007: 145)

As a direct result from allegations from the United States and Israel, Interpal underwent three separate investigations conducted by the Charity Commission with each concluding there was insufficient evidence to suggest Interpal was supporting Hamas or involved in terrorist activities. After American insistence, Interpal's case also went to the European Court of Justice where again no evidence of terrorist activity or affiliation was found. The Charity Commission for England and Wales had asked the United States for evidence to support the allegations which the United States either could not, or would not, provide (Sidel, 2011: 137–8). The Charity Commission reported, after no evidence was forthcoming from the US Treasury, that 'in the absence of any clear evidence showing Interpal had links to Hamas's political or violent militant activities, Interpal's accounts should be unfrozen and the enquiry closed' (cited in De Goede, 2012b: 141).

Over the period of investigation, Interpal's assets and funds were frozen (Keatinge, 2014: 61) which severely hampered its abilities to fulfil its promises to the donors and end recipients which could be constituted as a form of violence by denying rightful recipients of aid the resources required to relieve their physical and emotional suffering. Nonetheless, the case of Interpal again demonstrates the limits of US coercion. In strong support of this argument, the Charity Commission stated that 'as an independent statutory regulator, the Commission will make its own decisions on the law and the facts of the case' (Charity Commission cited in Sidel, 2011: 138).

Continued harassment, allegations and designations from the United States (and Israel) against Interpal, despite the lack of evidence, triggered an Early Day Motion in the House of Commons in November 2013, again signalling a willingness to deviate from US counter-terror norms. The UK House of Commons formally acknowledged,

> the humanitarian work carried out for the people of Palestine by the British charity Interpal; commends the generosity of British donors to the charity; regrets that it has been denied full access to the banking system as a result of an unfounded designation by the US administration in 2003; notes that a US district court in New York saw no evidence that Interpal funded Hamas-supporting charities;

further notes that the court threw out the case against Nat West... and calls on the Government to press the US administration to rescind its damaging designation of Interpal. (Early Day Motion 786, 25 November 2013, House of Commons)

Despite lacking evidence toward terrorism-related offences, select media outlets have consistently repeated false allegations such as the *Daily Mail*, which was later forced to pay £120,000 in damages to Interpal trustees (Weally, 2019), and *The Jewish Chronicle*, which was declared libel and paid £50,000 in damages to Interpal (Whitehead, 2019). In a written apology *The Jewish Chronicle* stated,

> We wish to make clear that Interpal and its trustees have always strongly contested the US designation, and Interpal continues to operate fully lawfully under the aegis of the Charity Commission. We accept that neither Interpal, nor its trustees, have ever been involved with, or provided support for, terrorist activity of any kind. (cited in Whitehead, 2019)

The link between media representations and counter-terror can be further gleamed from the case of Interpal. One of the Charity Commission's investigations against Interpal commenced after the broadcasting of a BBC Panorama programme titled 'Faith, Hate and Charity' broadcast in July 2006 alleging links between Interpal and Hamas. The Charity Commission again found no link to direct terrorist activity but did establish a connection between Interpal and the global organization 'Union for Good' chaired by the controversial figure, Dr Yusuf Qaradawi. This association with the 'Union of Good' was found objectionable by the Charity Commission and Interpal was ordered to cease further and future connections to the organization (Ware, 2009). No evidence was found that Interpal used charitable funds for anything other than which they had declared, yet association was sufficient to cause suspicion. It can thus be considered that media representatives and journalists played their part as 'petty-sovereigns' in the 'deeming' process which in turn affects the perceptions of the general public and their role as 'petty-sovereigns'.

In spite of the initial controversy and anxiety over the broadening of the Charity Commission's regulatory powers, the evidence so far, as indicated in the case of Interpal, suggests that the Charity Commission has dealt fairly and with degrees of transparency to the charities under investigation of terrorist abuses. All the Muslim charities interviewed understood the necessary role of the Charity Commission and most, including Interpal itself, had no specific quarrel with the regulator. Nonetheless, other areas within the UK scene are arguably more detrimental to charities such as media accusations and most deeply banking procedures. Repeatedly, interview participants raised the problem of banking procedures as the main obstacle in the era of CTF, especially for charities whose main operations are overseas. For instance, despite being cleared of financing terrorism and a Charity Commission report verifying that Interpal complied with all requirements of the previous inquiry, the bank Natwest closed Interpal's banking account in 2007 (De Goede, 2012b). Interpal was then forced to switch to the Al-Rayan (previously the Islamic Bank of Britain). However, Al-Rayan is underwritten by Lloyds bank with Lloyds instructing Al-Rayan to close Interpal's accounts in 2008 (Keatinge, 2014: 63).

In the regime of governmentality of CTF, it can be difficult for charities and donors to accurately see where regulations and policies are coming from leading to distrust and sometimes mistaken assertions. For instance, in relation to banking regulations, an employee of a UK-based Muslim charity stated,

> The Charity Commission have affected how to transfer funding and get them to where they are distributing. There is a problem of bringing money in from Middle Eastern countries. Every transaction is processed in each country and processed at each level making it difficult to do in a timely manner. There have been massive delays. It can take four to eight weeks for banks to pass on information and often there are further delays.

In reality, banking procedures are well out with the domain of the Charity Commission but the extension of Charity Commission powers in line with CTF policies and the UK Prevent project has undermined the Charity Commission's independent standing resulting in a number of misconceptions.

The consequences for the charity Interpal of persistent false allegations have been immense yet difficult to quantify and measure. Interpal's own annual report states,

> Interpal works in extremely difficult circumstances in highly volatile and politically charged areas. Aid delivery, by definition, is fraught with obstacles as a result of the local and international political agenda in the area. This is despite the call from international NGOs and human rights organisations to allow the free movement of humanitarian aid and personnel. In addition, the 2003 US designation of the charity continue to create difficulties, especially in the provision of banking facilities, posing a very serious obstacle to Interpal's operations. (Interpal, 2013: 8)

This same report published in 2013 marks a decrease in voluntary donations from the previous year down by a substantial 24 per cent. It is important to note that it is impossible to state with accuracy cause and effect, given the multitude of possible variables and imprecise knowledge of donor motivations. While it is impossible to say with one hundred per cent certainty what caused the dramatic decrease in voluntary donations in 2013 (donor fatigue, global economic downturn, media gaze distracting from Palestinian issues) it does offer some support to the damages being caused by terrorist allegations. The difficulty in determining causation is often the reason for why statistical accounts are rather lacking in explorations of the effect of CTF measures on charitable institutions as the number of potential variables are immense. However, another factor to support the argument that the decline of donations was a direct result of donor scepticism following terror financing accusations is that the following year voluntary donations increased substantially following from the Early Day Motion in the House of Commons distancing the charity from terrorist allegations. It is therefore a possibility that the US designation and negative press of Interpal correlates with the downturn in donations. Equally, the public confidence towards the charity by the signatories of the motion possibly alleviated donor mistrust in the organization resulting in increased donations; however, it is important not to overly determine this argument. While the substantial increase in donations to Interpal in 2014 can be correlated with increased trust, it cannot be currently claimed a causal factor. While 2013 saw the Early Day Motion in the House of Commons in support of the charity Interpal, it must also be understood that 2014 also saw the Israel-Gaza conflict. The war, which heightened media attention to the Palestinian territories and worsened the humanitarian situation in Gaza further, inevitably correlates with increased donations. The complexity of charitable and humanitarian fundraising and distribution makes it extremely difficult to provide quantitative correlation (let alone causation) to increases and decreases in voluntary giving.

Part of the dilemma regarding Interpal is undoubtedly the politically tense context of the Palestinian and Israeli conflict where a perceived alignment for either side of the political debate is read beyond humanitarian efforts to wider political discourses. Conflict areas generally add to mitigating risks for charities, but specific political causes raise the risk analysis considerably. When asked of the challenges for charities working overseas, and specifically territories in politically fragile states, the Head of Engagement from OSCR confirmed the difficulties:

> It's interesting because I used to work for Christian Aid, but they always had a significant programme in Palestine and in a way even back then it was a challenge because people asked 'what are you doing there?' when actually you are trying to work, part of the reason why it is difficult is because it is a political issue. There are lots of movements trying to deal with that internally, but it was tricky even then. You had to be more robust when defending these programmes. You could happily work in Kenya and nobody would ever question, but if you go and work in a place like Palestine you have to be much clearer and be squeaky clean about what you are doing.

In alignment with some of the issues raised by OSCR, in a written correspondence with the author in 2017, Interpal's chair, Ibrahim Hewitt, commented on the politicization of the Palestinian cause alleging Interpal has become collateral damage in the war on public opinion between those sympathetic with the Palestinian struggle and those firmly with the Israeli camp. Ibrahim Hewitt commented,

> Our donor base is usually able to see through the anti-Palestinian propaganda and know that as a charity working solely with Palestinians we are a target for the pro-Israel Lobby. In most cases, this actually boosts our reputation, except amongst those – in the Lobby – for whom Interpal has no reputation to damage in any case. It's perverse, but the trustees and staff believe that we are victims of a political battle of wills.... We have appealed on a number of occasions for the issue of aid to Palestine, Gaza in particular, to be less politicised.

What is interesting from Hewitt's statement is that despite his trust in Interpal's donors, prior to the Early Day Motion in the House of Commons, Interpal's donation base did fall drastically. Evidence for Hewitt's assumption can be gleamed from a statement derived from an interview with a Muslim woman from Glasgow who commented:

> I think that anything that has to do with Palestinians is instantaneously considered a terrorist threat. Of course, I would have concerns if my money was going to ISIS or supporting groups like that, but I think I'd need to see evidence of it and I think if Theresa May was to tell me that then I'd have my suspicions. I mean trying to close down *Interpal* and other charities for example because they support certain groups and I think it's part of a bigger agenda. But if I had genuine concerns I would be supportive of shutting down *any* charity that was committed to supporting any extremist organization whether that is al-Qaeda, ISIS or some other extremist organization like Britain First . . . but I would take things with a pinch of salt if it comes from Theresa May or some kind of politically linked person . . . I'd quite happily overlook Theresa May's concerns unless there was evidence.

From the above, it is evident that there is some traction to Ibrahim Hewitt's comments which asserted a trust in Interpal's donor base to know that allegations of terrorist financing are false and part of a 'political agenda'. What is particularly interesting from the statement from the Glaswegian Muslim is that while trust in Interpal remained intact, trust in the UK government had eroded, with the woman stating she would take statements from the then Prime Minister, Theresa May, with a 'pinch of salt'. It is therefore possible that one of the side effects of current CTF policy, as it pertains to the charity sector, diminishes trust in government and politicians, not necessarily the accused charities. Moreover, the negative effects of restricting or politicizing aid to conflict zones, while perhaps invisible in the short- to medium term in the UK, could have longer term implications. Walker has, for instance, argued that 'the hampering of humanitarian relief in conflict zones is contrary to the public interest because a failure to intervene might worsen the generation of terrorism' (2018: 1103).

The lack of transparent, accountable and robust evidence from both media outlets and certain politicians has added to the perceived feelings of distrust between Muslims and elements within the current British government. This lack of evidence is particularly apparent and visible to Muslim charities (and charities in general) in the contemporary era that has increased surveillance, scrutiny and bureaucracy for the third sector itself while seemingly taking a different approach for policy and government under the guise of 'national security'. The dangers of this perceived duplicity were articulated by one employee of a British Muslim charity who stated,

> A lot of people were saying that there are two different laws here. They are saying 'look, we have tried democracy, we've given it a chance but there are double standards between Muslim and white non-Muslims'. It's why you have people going to the other extreme.

In alignment with De Goede's analysis, 'the post-9/11 pursuit of suspect charities amounts to a regulation of the limits of the sayable and particular types of political discourse' (2012b: 144). As no evidence can suggest that Interpal has any connection whatsoever with political violence or terrorism, it is suggested that sympathy for Palestinians is at (or beyond) the 'limits of the sayable' in contemporary political discourse. The case of Interpal also provides evidence of another challenge to the current CTF norms, which fail to distinguish between transnational de-territorialized movements such as al-Qaeda and essentially anti-colonial nationalist movements such as Hamas in Gaza and Hizbullah in Lebanon. In interview, Interpal stated that it was their work in Gaza (currently controlled by a Hamas government) and not their work in the West Bank (currently controlled by the dominant secular group Fatah) that came under greatest scrutiny. The failure to distinguish between different types of Islamist movements is also a failure in evaluating realistic threat levels. Moreover, the differences between US and European strategies are evident as the European Union has displayed more flexibility towards designating entire groups as 'terrorist' entities with many desiring to differentiate between political and military wings of groups such as Hamas and Hizbullah. Despite greater willingness to differentiate between, and within, movements, global counter-terror norms (prevailing from the United States) prevent more nuanced categorizations from emerging.

MPs and media representatives as 'petty-sovereigns'

One specific example that demonstrates the relationship between 'petty-sovereigns' of media representatives and elected officials is the actions of Eric Pickles in 2014 in the position of Secretary of State for the Department of Communities and Local Government (DCLG) following a publication by *The Telegraph* (Turner, 2014) alleging that the Muslim Charities Forum and associated charities were connected to terrorist activity. Mr Pickles in 2014 publicly made the following statement:

> following a formal review of the project, which included examination of allegations made in the press, ... I have taken the decision to terminate its funding. The Muslim Charities Forum has failed to reassure us that they have robust measures in place to investigate and challenge their members. Concerns have also been raised about events held by member organisations, at which individuals with extremist views have been invited to speak. (Pickles, 2014)

Had any of the charities concerned been found guilty of links to terrorism there would perhaps be a substantially different problem; however, all charities concerned were investigated (after Mr Pickles's public statement and at the behest of the charities concerned) by the Charity Commission and exonerated of links with terrorism and violent activity. The main allegation was not any link to violence or a specific terrorist event but alleged association with 'extremists' including a guest speaker at a fundraising event. A charity worker close to the Muslim sector who agreed to be interviewed on the conditions of strict anonymity stated that the MCF was not directly told who the 'extremist' speaker was and therefore was initially unable to defend against the allegations. It is also relevant to note that there are no government lists of 'extremist' speakers or a checklist of what to avoid when inviting external speakers to an event. With vague legal definitions of what 'extremism' is, it is therefore extremely problematic for charities (or any institution) to know in advance who the government claim are 'extremists' at any given moment in time and therefore who to avoid to ask as a guest speaker. The MCF released a public response to the above allegations emphasizing,

> All MCF members are registered with the Charity Commission of England and Wales, and by default abide by charity law. They also comply with international humanitarian standards and principles and in accordance with this they are signatories to the International Code of Conduct of the International Committee of the Red Cross and Red Crescent Movement. They are purely humanitarian organisations, dedicated to alleviating poverty and promoting sustainable development around the world.

Strikingly the MCF, explicitly mentioned by Mr Pickles, formed in 2007 in an attempt to avoid the exact type of scenario Mr Pickles's allegations placed them in. In interview in 2013, Saif Ullah, then an employee of the MCF, explained the reasons for the establishment of the MCF as 'to promote dialogue and negotiations among Muslim NGOs in the UK. Trying to foster greater collaboration and greater accountability and transparency in their work.' What certainly appears to have occurred is that a published *Telegraph* report (Turner, 2014) was accepted blindly by a government department and acted upon only six days later without an initial investigation from the Charity Commission nor with consultation with the charities concerned. As an employee working within the Muslim charitable sector remarked, the concerned charities were 'charged, convicted and sentenced' without the ability to defend themselves nor be told what exactly the alleged links to 'extremism' were. To restate, all concerned charities were retrospectively investigated by the Charity Commission, cleared of links to 'extremism', issued public statements denying any wrongdoing and are successfully operating to date. What this case demonstrates is the power, lack of transparency and lack of accountability of the decisions taken by the petty-sovereigns tasked with implementing the CTF regime of governmentality. This example coincides with Yasmin and Ghafran's findings which assert that 'the counter-terror narrative in the media was shaping the political decision-making in relation to Muslim NGOs' (2019: 9) demonstrating the power of journalists and media representatives as petty-sovereigns.

Moreover, the actions of Mr Pickles go against the regulatory role of the Charity Commission, which at least theoretically 'alone has the authority to investigate an inquiry and to decide on the type of sanction to impose, if any' (Gunning, 2008: 113). Mr Pickles unilaterally, and without evidence other than that insinuated by *The Telegraph* report, ceased government funding to the organization and publicly associated them with extremism prior to any Charity Commission investigation or legal prosecution. The actions of Mr Pickles also appear to go against the spirit of the Charities Act 2011, which states that 'in the exercise of its functions the Commission is not subject to the direction or control of any minister of the crown or of another department' (Charities Act, 2011b).

Mr Pickles's decision to publicly announce punishment prior to investigation also appears to go against a previous decision to remove the DCLG from the remit of counterterrorism following discussions regarding the implementation of the UK

Prevent policy in 2009 (Thomas, 2014: 482). A Select Committee was created to review the relationship of the DCLG with counter-terror initiatives broadly and the Prevent policy specifically. In conclusion of the Select Committee's investigation they asserted that the 'DCLG should have less of a role in a counter-terrorism agenda and more in the positive work it undertakes in building strong and cohesive communities' (House of Commons, 2010, para 171: 6–7). As criticisms mounted regarding the original Prevent initiative, Prevent underwent an overhaul in 2011 which essentially 'removed DCLG from involvement in Prevent' (Thomas, 2014: 485). Thus, the actions of the then Minister for DCLG, Mr Pickles, not only went against the powers of the Charity Commission but also overextended its authority into counterterrorism which had previously been withdrawn. Again, this demonstrates the uneven application of the regime of governmentality regarding CTF not only between the states of the United States and the United Kingdom but within actors (or petty-sovereigns) within the United Kingdom itself. As Thomas notes, 'the "state" itself has been divided and conflicted over its implementation, primarily on a national/local basis, but also between different departments of national government' (2014: 474).

Media reports evidently have a powerful sway not only on the general public but also on ministerial figures. As Walker notes, 'triggers for investigation about alleged involvement in terrorism has typically arisen from the convictions of trustees, newspaper reports of wrongdoing, or defaults in filing the necessary paperwork' (2018: 1092). When mistrust enters the public sphere, it can have devastating effects for the end-users of those charitable services. Research from the United States has concluded:

> Aggressive prosecutions of Muslim charities and individuals across the country have embittered communities that feel besieged by their government and distrusted by their non-Muslim compatriots . . . . As a consequence, the vibrancy and development of civil society within these communities is at risk of being significantly stunted. (Aziz, 2011)

What is safe to presume is that the very public accusations of linking Muslim charities to extremism will have an effect on the publics' trust in those organizations and perhaps any charitable organization aligned with the faith of Islam. As MP Fiona Bruce noted in the House of Commons in 2017,

> Often, when civil society freedoms are being eroded, it is by creeping incrementalism. The subtle undermining of civil society freedoms is rarely accompanied by great fanfare. A new law may at first seem innocuous, but it might prove to have a devastating effect on civil society – an effect only felt later. (Bruce, 2017)

Summary

This chapter has sought to demonstrate the divergent practices in current CTF initiatives. The case of Interpal illustrates the adaptations and tensions between the

United States and the United Kingdom in their implementation and understanding of global CTF norms. However, the disparages exist not only between states but within them, as the diverse emphasis on the 'terror' risk for charities was understood differently by the Charity Commission for England and Wales and that of the Scottish regulator OSCR. Commonality exists between the charity regulators in that both believe the risk of charitable abuses for terrorist causes are 'rare' and both deny disproportionately targeting Muslim charities. Controversy still pervades whether, or not, Muslim charities have been disproportionately investigated by the Charity Commission with much of the disagreement centring upon what, and who, is considered 'Muslim'. The author's analysis is that sufficient quantitative evidence exists to suggest that Muslim charities have been unduly investigated, but it does not logically follow that this is a consequence of an anti-Muslim agenda by the Charity Commission itself. As was exemplified by the actions of Eric Pickles in 2014, many of the Charity Commission's investigations are instigated by public, media and politicians who act as petty-sovereigns.

Muslim charities most at risk of investigation or public allegations are those working primarily overseas and particularly those working in war-torn or conflict areas. The assumption in public policy is that charitable donations outside of the British state are potential evidence of Muslim disloyalty to Britain. The following two chapters seek to investigate why so many donations made by British Muslims are received overseas and question the logic that giving to Britain necessarily translates as uncritical loyalty to the political and economic system of the UK.

5

'No one starves in Britain'

Tied to the suspicion cast on British Muslims' loyalty to the UK is the dispersal of charitable funds outside of the British state. The general assumption in government policy and media outlets appears to be that charity distributed in the UK is a marker of political loyalty to the British state. In contrast, charity dispersed overseas is deemed to mark the donor as possessing suspicious loyalty to the UK's political system. This prevailing argument is apparent from Kabir who states that 'British Muslims' political activity, charitable fundraising, the delivering of humanitarian relief . . . appear to be a protest against the British government. As a consequence, British Muslims have been perceived by some British people as disloyal' (2010: 10). Overseas charitable donations, particularly those being received in conflict areas, are hampered by banking delays, increased scrutiny and regulation and the politicization of charity and aid generally. The primary purpose of this chapter is to explore the motivations for why Muslims in the UK donate some *zakat* to territories outside of the UK. As shall be discussed, the reasons for overseas charitable giving are predominantly concerned with perceived duties and obligations to kin, the perceived religious requirement to cater for the most needy and concern and solidarity to the global community of Muslims (*ummah*). What is absent from all the interview data is any overt, or covert, support to political entities, parties or regimes outside of the UK. This chapter will primarily draw from transcript material derived from interviews with practising Muslims in the UK in line with Erdal and Borchgrevink whose own research suggested that 'we are not primarily concerned with the theologies and the Islamic teaching underlying each of these ideals and associated practices, but rather with the ways in which the people we interviewed perform, articulate and reinforce Islamic charity through everyday rituals' (2017: 131). Interview quotations provided are thus typical expressions of the views held by interview participants.

The argument presented here is that policy makers have made an error in their reading that overseas charity necessitates lingering loyalties to other political entities. Equally, it is too reductionist to argue that charity donated to the UK necessarily indicates an uncritical stance on the British state, though this in no way infers disloyalty. What shall be argued over the following two chapters is that in many ways charitable donations within Britain could be read as a critique of inequalities resulting from neoliberal economic policies and austerity measures and a growing awareness of relative poverty in the UK. Similarly, charitable donations to sites overseas do not necessarily entail a political loyalty to the state in question but a humanitarian effort and critique of the receiving state's welfare failures. This is not to say that residual identification with 'homelands' is not a factor or that 'belongings' to other identifications other than Britishness have ceased. Neither is it an argument that charitable donations within the UK cannot be read as increased belonging to British society (it is), but simply that the issues surrounding charitable giving are nuanced and contextual. Complex intersections of age, generation of immigration and other factors contribute to forms of identification and community belongings which, while entailing aspects of Britishness, do not reduce all identities to this political nationalist frame. As Miah asserts, 'loyalty to an in-group does not translate into disloyalty to an out-group' (2015: 79).

It shall be argued that transnational charitable giving should not be viewed as a political affiliation to particular states or nations but as religious and social obligations to the global Muslim community (*ummah*) which do not present challenges to concepts of British citizenship per se. In fact, as the following chapter will demonstrate, alterations in charitable giving are occurring which simultaneously present younger Muslim generations as both an expression and constitutive element of contemporary British society. Muslim charitable giving within the UK is therefore specifically British. A strong tradition of charitable giving has existed in British communities generally, and, thus, the secular and religious values associated with charity broadly offer an opportunity where the secular and the religious can inform each other in mutually beneficial ways.

The chapter will first outline Muslim charitable giving in the UK within the frame of migration, transnationalism and diaspora communities before highlighting the period where 'Muslimness' became a primary identity marker for British Muslims. Accentuating 'Muslimness' as a primary identity categorization then facilitates the construction of an imagined global *ummah* which will be discussed briefly before examining the role of Muslim charities. The final sections of this chapter will look to the motivations of overseas charitable giving as explained by interview participants.

Immigration, religion and transnational financial flows

Many Islamic charities and Islamic financial schemes have been highly criticized and frequently associated with funding 'terrorism'. There is a tendency to view such financial flows as unwarranted, uncontrolled, dangerous and a problem with Islam alone as if somehow this is evidence of 'religion gone wrong' as it steps boldly out from its rightful place in the private domestic sphere. However, charitable giving, remittances and philanthropic projects should perhaps better be placed within the wider discourse of migration and immigration financial flows. By discussing Islamic charitable giving in a wider discourse allows similarities to emerge which counter the claim that these transnational flows are evidence of a problem with Islam itself. Remembering that many Muslims living in Britain are permanent migrants and British Muslims are mostly the children, grandchildren and great-grandchildren of migrants helps the picture to become clearer. In terms of migration and immigration, Portes notes that 'migrants do not simply "leave", they maintain intense ties with their families and communities left behind' (2013: 34). Indeed the findings from this research agrees with Portes that the immigrants most likely to take part in transnational philanthropy are not the most recent arrivals but those established immigrants who have managed to obtain a greater degree of security economically in the host country (2013: 34).

Portes own work does not take religious philanthropy into the equation when discussing migrant transnational flows, yet there are remarkable similarities to how migrant communities behave in their host countries regarding charitable donations aimed to benefit their original homeland. Portes refers to the variety of charitable and civic activities aimed at home localities and regions as 'globalization from below' 'through which poor people seek to mitigate the growing inequalities and lack of opportunity foisted on them by capitalist-driven "globalization from above"' (2013: 34). While Muslims in the UK understand their charitable obligations in terms of their Islamic duties, their contributions across states are not necessarily peculiar when compared to other migrant communities.

To restate, British Muslim communities are not a homogenous group though often they are treated as such in European media and policy rhetoric (Nayet, 2017: 6). While British Muslims may share a common faith, how that faith is interpreted differs greatly across communities, cultural backgrounds, class and generation. Drawing from research on transnational and migrating communities can be useful to understand some of the dynamics occurring regarding differences in Muslim charitable giving. Muslim charity, as an obligation for all Muslims wherever they reside, can be considered a transnational activity and as such 'transnational practices among immigrants are highly diverse between and within groups' (Vertovec, 2009: 78).

It is well noted that migrating and diaspora communities carry with them aspects of their previous experiences and perspectives (Nayet, 2017: 2) and as such the constitution of identity is within, and not outside, discourse (Nayet, 2017: 3). As migrants settle in their new homelands, adjustments to previous practices and activities are made within the realm of their new environments in which practice is embedded. As practices evolve and adjust in new environments, they take into consideration the host societies' practices and norms also allowing for a construction of a new British Muslim identity which is neither unified, fixed or homogenous but constantly in flux and negotiation. As Nayet argues, 'identity is about belonging, and is recognition of cultural belonging. It is not a unitary or ever-stable and fixed construct, and thus belonging is also about becoming' (2017: 5). Muslim charitable giving in the UK can arguably be one practice among many that potentially expedites the *becoming* of British Muslimness.

As Benthall has argued, 'charity at its most basic is a bodily act: extending a hand to a stricken traveller or sharing food with a neighbour' (Benthall, 2016: 118). Performativity therefore brings into being British Muslim identities, but this does not mean there is a single homogenous British Muslim identity as 'different socio-political histories resulted in different Muslim performativities for different groups. The process of migrating, conflicting identities, the essence of belonging, and attachment have all been experienced differently by Muslims in the UK' (Nayet, 2017: 46). The current environment in which British Muslims are embedded has altered in the decades since 9/11 and this context shapes the practices of Muslims beyond theological interpretations. The next section will outline the ways in which 'Muslimness' has been raised as an identity marker in the UK.

The rise of 'Muslimness' as a marker of identity

It was not only the events of 9/11 that changed the way British society viewed their Muslim co-citizens. Disturbances in Northern England in 2001 began a series of changes in UK government policy and discourses towards British Muslims (Ahmed, 2019: 581). Public disruptions occurred in cities such as Oldham, Bradford and Burnley by segments of the Muslim communities of these towns. Prior to 9/11, Britain had focused its ideas of citizenship on the concept of multiculturalism which sought to be inclusive of minority groups by defining national identity in 'politico-institutional rather than ethnocultural terms' (Ahmed, 2019: 582). However, after 2001, key members of the UK government began questioning the logic of multiculturalism with David Cameron in 2011 pronouncing its failure (Larsen, 2013: 8).

Consequently, and following the Cantle Report (Home Office, 2001), multiculturalism was replaced by the vaguely defined concept of 'social cohesion' to understand and forge British citizenship (Ahmed, 2019: 582). While vague, social cohesion can be understood as a community which has a shared sense of belonging and a national identity based on 'shared values'. Under the idea of social cohesion, multiculturalism was criticized for failing to produce integration which quickly became seen as the greatest threat to social cohesion. According to Ahmed, 'such a construction dismissed institutional racism and discrimination as barriers to integration, thereby concealing the pervasive and detrimental impact of structural racism in British Muslims' daily lives' (2019: 582). In other words, the logic of social cohesion argues that integration had failed due to the cultural practices of minority communities within the UK and not due to the structural barriers created by the majority of British citizens and governance – it was the minorities' fault. As a consequence of this shift in policy, many minority groups within the UK, and especially Muslim communities following 9/11, began to feel a growing sense of marginalization, isolation and blame which in turn raises concerns for future 'radicalization' or oppositional action. Ahmed posits that it is 'plausible to suggest that the state is in denial about the role of their own policies in isolating British Muslims to such an extent that they no longer feel British' (2019: 592). Though it must be noted that various surveys conducted indicate that Muslims within the UK statistically *do* feel British and often more so than other segments of UK society (MCB, 2015).

The Northern protests in the United Kingdom and attacks on the Twin Towers in 2001 in the United States marked a watershed moment when British Asian communities were transformed overnight from racial categorizations prevalent in the majority society (such as the derogatory slang term 'Paki' which was frequently used not to describe an individual from Pakistan but a catch-all term for those of Asian appearance) to being perceived and identified primarily by their Muslimness. According to Baroness Warsi, 'their Muslimness, not their Britishness became the defining identity – perhaps the only identity they were going to be allowed' (Warsi, 2017: 30). Arguably, the increased visibility and preference given to one aspect of identity facilitated an awareness of a global 'imagined community' of Muslims that spread beyond the borders of the UK while simultaneously the community was imagined from the constructs of British society perceptions of 'Otherness'. Nonetheless, feelings of 'Britishness' still prevail giving further credence to Miah's assertion that 'loyalty to an in-group does not translate into disloyalty to an out-group' (2015: 79). It would be an oversimplification to argue that experiences of racism, Islamophobia and exclusions determine particular responses such as a lack of identification with Britishness as the vast amount of British Muslims have indicated in several surveys that they feel a strong affiliation with the UK. However, as Tehmina and Basit have discussed, 'the perceptions of stereotyping, racism, and harassment prevent them from feeling like British citizens at specific points in time, thus damaging their sense of belonging' (2009: 739). It is not therefore that the majority of Muslims in the UK do not feel British. The challenge is to what extent general British society accepts the Muslim population of Britain as British at any given moment in time.

In 2011, around half (47 per cent) of Muslims were born in the UK and the diversity of ethnicities is wide. Traditionally, the UK attracted Muslims from South Asia, primarily India, Pakistan and Bangladesh coinciding with its colonial history with around 68 per cent of the UK Muslim population being Asian (MCB, 2015: 34). More recently the UK has seen (as elsewhere) a rise in Arab and Afghani Muslims. Interestingly, despite media and political rhetoric suspecting Muslim communities of political disloyalty to the British state, surveys reveal that around 73 per cent of British Muslims self-affirm their sole national identity as 'British' (more than any other community categorization) (MCB, 2015: 34). Therefore, the overwhelming majority of Muslims within the UK see their foremost national identity as 'British' (MCB, 2015: 34), but they also have kinship ties and religious affiliations outside of the British state. All these elements – the national, familial and religious – find expression in the 'tradition of charity giving, both for non-Muslim and Muslim causes' (MCB, 2015: 34). Whether British Muslims distribute their charitable funds locally or transnationally therefore needs to be placed within the context of British residency and global links (familial and religious) which need not be considered as exclusive but mutually reinforcing. Indeed, as Werbner posits, much of Muslim charitable giving in the UK can be considered as another aspect of the dynamics of globalization rather than anything peculiar to the faith of Islam per se. 'The question of exclusive national loyalty or patriotism, self-evident in the age of nationalism has been rendered ambiguous by the globalising thrust of late modernity and its continuous blurring of national boundaries' (Werbner, 2000: 309). In one sense, then, the 'blurring of national boundaries' is less to do with the universal principles of Islam as a religion and more a consequence of the broader condition of advanced globalization. However, the blurring of national boundaries, intertwined with the rise of 'Muslimness' as an identity marker, has facilitated the imagining of a global Muslim community, commonly referred to as the '*ummah*'.

Ummah as 'imagined community'

Zakat can be understood as a performative act or ritual and a constituent aspect of community building. Just as Benedict Anderson argued that the nation is an 'imagined community' (Anderson, 1991) due to the impossibility of meeting each and every fellow national, the global *ummah* is imagined. The imagined *ummah*, like the nation, can be constructed by the knowledge that fellow members, regardless of whether we meet them or not, carry out multiple and simultaneous acts across the community. *Zakat* as an obligatory article of the Islamic faith functions as a performative act carried out by millions of Muslims across the globe all conscious of others performing the same ritual across time and space thus allowing the *ummah* to be imagined and created. As Bell states, 'it is the act. The performance of ritual that each knows the other community member is performing despite the temporal and spatial distances' (1999).

The Quranic term '*ummah*' is widely contested and has at various times been employed to mean the global assemblage of Muslim practitioners, the community of 'believers' incorporating the combined 'people of the book' (*ahl al-kitab*) referring to all adherents of the Abrahamic faiths, or more selectively to connote 'nation' specific to particular political boundaries. Despite the contestation regarding what the *ummah* is, and who belongs to it, the 'imagined' *ummah* is nonetheless a powerful concept that serves to motivate Muslim action and practices that traverse political geographies. According to Roy, 'the space of the umma is no longer a territorial one, implying a political leadership with a nation-state and borders' (Roy, 2011: 246). If Roy is correct, then employing the concept of the *ummah* does not necessarily imply a loyalty or sense of belonging to specific territories or political systems. It does, however, indicate a sense of belonging to a diverse range of peoples and this again stems from Quranic and Prophetic injunctions. As Ayoob states, the concept of the *ummah* ensures that 'Muslims everywhere must, in the view of the Qur'an and Prophetic tradition, strive to be one single body, a worldwide community bound by a common faith that is meant to supersede all other racial, cultural, linguistic ties, or relationships' (Ayoob, 2004: 22). The understanding of *ummah* as espoused by Ayoob was echoed by an interviewee who explained that 'as a Muslim . . . we are taught in our faith that we are all one body so it doesn't matter where you are – we are all one community'.

In addition to facilitating the formation of an imagined and geographically boundless *ummah*, *zakat* also allows the possibility to retain links to places and spaces of origin. This aspect was particularly important to new or first-generation Muslim immigrants in meeting the challenge of how to sustain a sense of community over space and time when the direct contact to lands and people has been acutely disrupted by lack of habitual residence. Retaining linkages to places of origin does not necessarily reduce loyalty to the state of residence though contemporary migration and globalization have contributed to changing notions of the national. As Sassen has argued,

> The fact of global classes that are not necessarily cosmopolitan and that remain partly embedded in localized environments does not diminish the potential for destabilizing the national as historically constructed. Through their daily practices and imaginaries, they partly reconstitute the meaning of the national . . . . One of the crucial dynamics at work here is a process of incipient denationalization, a changed attachment to the national rather than a full exit from it. (Sassen, 2006: 300)

Important in Sassen's position is the emphasis on 'changed attachment to the national rather than a full exit from it'. The national remains important to British Muslim communities, but alterations in what is conceived as 'national' should not be read as a denial or rejection of British attachments. Migrants of whatever nationality of origin, ethnicity or religion remain interested in the social, political and economic developments of their home countries or parental origins. Mustafa indicates this is not unique to Muslim communities and stresses that ethnic minorities have long been involved in the political activities of their home states, for instance, the British Irish, Italian Americans and the Jewish Diaspora (2015: 23). In this respect there is nothing unique about British Muslim communities' retentions of links to home states but is an expected aspect of migration in the age of advanced globalization.

According to Vertovec, transnationalism can be understood as 'a condition in which despite great distances and notwithstanding the presence of international borders . . . certain kinds of relationships have been globally intensified and now take place paradoxically in a planet-spanning yet common . . . area of activity' (2009: 3). In this sense, Islamic charitable giving, and especially the obligation of *zakat*, can be considered a type of common activity that, notwithstanding international political borders, maintains and produces certain kinds of relationships between Muslims globally. Additionally, Bowen posits,

> Islam's transnational character is diffuse but powerful, and it derives its power from the ways in which rituals reproduce, and histories remind Muslims of, the shared duties and practices of Muslims across political boundaries . . . this consciousness first and foremost creates an imagination of an Islamic community transcending specific boundaries and borders. (2011: 202)

It can therefore be understood that the ritual reproduction of charitable giving is a constant reminder to Muslims of their shared practices and obligations to the imagined global Islamic community (*ummah*).

Important in the (re)production of community in the performative sense is the constant potential for disruption and new reproductions. As the practice of *zakat* transforms in the Muslim-minority context of the UK, what is constructed from the 'performance' is likely to differ from that of diverse geographies and temporalities. Charity is one of the many aspects that combine Islamic and British 'values' and British Muslims were not oblivious to this. Especially regarding *sadaqah*, which is voluntary charity and open to any charitable good, there is potential for the performance of Muslim charity to not only help foster Muslim solidarity but also facilitate the emergence of a more plural 'British' community. For instance an Islamic Relief employee in 2013 stated that 'as generations go on we need to define a more British sense of Islam . . . my son for example won't know Pakistan, he will know it through me but . . . we need to define a community in terms of what it means to be British and Muslim'. This participant, alongside all other interviewees, saw no contradiction between their self-identification as both Muslim and British. Charity within the UK, but also beyond, is seen as one way in which to ensure that being both British and Muslim does not constitute identity tensions or contradictions.

Role of Muslim charities

Muslims in the UK use a variety of charitable distribution mechanisms – the specific rules of *zakat* collection and distribution being the subject of endless debate within Islamic scholarship (Benthall, 2016: 6). It is salient to note that there remain controversies regarding the nature and practice of charitable giving *within* Islam and *between* Muslim practitioners. Within *Sunni* Islam, often highly emotional contestations are apparent regarding where *zakat* can be given and to whom. Various *fatwas* have been issued (at times contradictory) stating that it is acceptable (or not) to give *zakat* outside of one's own state when the need is greater. The debate regarding the most deserving has also impacted upon who can receive *zakat* with a division becoming apparent between scholars and lay practitioners regarding if non-Muslims are eligible for *zakat* (May, 2019a).

Some Muslims will distribute their charitable obligations directly to those they know are in need via bank transfers or informal value transfer systems – all of which are heavily scrutinized by political and/or financial bodies as outlined in previous chapters. In addition to this, many Muslims will also contribute to charitable causes in their local mosque and Islamic centres by simply depositing money in collection boxes placed around the institutions. As registered charities, mosques and Islamic institutions are also heavily surveyed in terms of banking procedures but also through regulation from the Charity Commission. A further common way for Muslims to distribute their charitable funds is through established charities either 'Muslim' or secular. Most frequently charitable funds are dispersed through a mixture of all the above mechanisms.

As mentioned previously, Islamic charities in the UK have established themselves in Britain since the mid-1980s. The impetus for Muslim charities began with an explicit transnational and international intention as the 1980s witnessed mass famine in Africa and the 'lost decade' for Latin America. According to Benthall, the Muslim diaspora were additionally conscious of the poor living conditions and economic insecurities of populations in their various countries of origin who 'had no government "safety nets" to fall back on' (2016: 14). Muslim charities began in Britain as a way for the Muslim communities to respond to tragic international events in addition to providing a needed mechanism to distribute Muslim charitable obligations. Charity has a long and resilient history in the British Isles and thus it should not be a surprise that the Islamic sector has proved efficient and resourceful in the British context. In many ways, Muslim charities within the UK have followed the footsteps of their Christian brothers and sisters (such as Christian Aid and CAFOD) by following international charitable norms such as renouncing proselytism and distributing alms non-discriminatorily and transparently (Benthall, 2016: 73). The 1990s saw the expansion and growth of the Muslim charitable sector spurned again by international political events such as the Bosnian crisis. From the beginning, then, the Muslim charitable sector in the UK was international and transnational in scope and sustained a relationship with international political events in terms of providing responses to humanitarian crisis.

Muslim charities essentially began to be both a symbol of and a constituent factor in the building of British Muslim communities and provided facilities to British

Muslims which enabled their ability to fulfil their religious injunctions in addition to their familial duties when living in a Muslim-minority state, geographically separated from other kin and family ties. As Portes states, 'migrants do not simply "leave" they maintain intense ties with their families and communities left behind' (2013: 34).

As Muslim charities began to establish themselves, they initiated strategies that would not only assist those in need but also cater for British Muslim communities' religious obligations by creating *zakat* projects in addition to general *sadaqah*. This step granted the possibility for new *zakat* practices to emerge that, while integrally linked to the past, nevertheless, offered a break from previous practices. The ease of which *zakat* can now be calculated, facilitated by online '*zakat* calculators', is one such innovation as well as the ability to make *zakat* donations quickly and easily online via charity websites.

It was generally accepted by most participants that a substantial percentage of *zakat* donations were received overseas. Most charities interviewed were acutely aware of individuals donating primarily to perceived homelands, particularly for older generations. A Muslim charity shop manager recalled countless encounters of individuals asking for donations to be given to specific villages, homes and persons (an impossible procedure for international charities). However, an employee of Islamic Relief stated that charities are changing this pattern by launching projects that are as 'unrestricted' as possible. For instance, projects may focus on clean water broadly, rather than specify exactly which geographical area will be provided.

Again, by linking British Muslim charitable donation patterns to globalization rather than counter-terror literature, a broader picture emerges that links Muslim experiences to other migrant experiences. It is not their 'Muslimness' that is the challenge per se, but migration generally poses questions to the more historic evaluations of citizenship and political identity. As Sassen argues,

> historically, nationality is linked to the bond of allegiance of the individual to the sovereign ... traditionally this bond was seen as insoluble or at least exclusive. But while the bond of insoluble allegiances was defensible in times of limited mobility, it became difficult in the face of large-scale migration which was part of the new forms of industrial development. Insoluble was gradually replaced by exclusive, hence singular but changeable, allegiance as the basis of nationality. (2006: 279)

Sassen posits that transnational identifications and solidarities arise and are maintained through 'networks, activities, ideologies that span the home and the host society' (2006: 282). The 'host' society, in this case Britain, is therefore as relevant as the 'home' society.

Occasionally charities, both faith-based and secular, are forced to work with what many Western polities would describe as 'undesirable' regimes commonly referred as 'failed' states, simply to gain access to those in need of relief. It is hardly surprising that many of the communities most in need of assistance reside in areas under corrupt governance or in areas of political unrest and conflict. This is particularly true of sites such as Gaza in Palestine run by the political party Hamas considered a terrorist organization by the United States and the UN. As seen in Chapter 4, such geographies can increase the surveillance and scrutiny of the charities working in the area such as the UK-based charity Interpal. However, in terms of the motivations of individuals to disperse their charitable obligations to such territories, it is important to remember that the religious obligation of *zakat* to give to the rightful recipients transcends the political propriety of giving to individuals who happen to reside in states with undesirable governments. Pragmatically any aid or relief agency working in such areas requires permission to do so from 'undesirable' regimes if they are the governing powers of the territory. As Metcalfe-Hough has observed, those most in need are often in areas where all, or large swathes of territory, are under the control of prohibited groups.

> As a result, these INGOs are necessarily engaging with groups such as Hamas and al Shabaab . . . . This engagement does not consist of delivering aid, with, for, or alongside these groups. Rather, it involves essential communication with them for the purpose of gaining access to the civilian population and obtaining guarantees for the safety of an agency's staff and assets, and of intended recipients. (Metcalfe-Hough, 2015: 10)

By default, many individuals who are most in need are those living under corrupt governance and require, by the law of the sovereign nation-state system, permits from national governments to distribute aid and carry out development projects. This kind of accepted modus vivendi is applicable to all relief and charity workers regardless of positions of faith. As one employee of Islamic Relief recalled,

> During the Taliban time in Afghanistan we were one of the few charities allowed to work while others were not. In Sudan, a lot of organisations were expelled but we were allowed to work in those areas – al-Shabaab allowed us to stay. *Islamic Relief* will not interfere with conflict, will not do something which is culturally unacceptable to the community and we will not discriminate in our work and we will do it legally with the cooperation of local authorities' approval.

Muslim charities also have certain practical advantages when working in certain areas or with certain communities. Diaspora populations living in the UK may have direct connections to individuals/communities that charities are distributing to, allowing on the ground reliable accounts of ongoing situations and, importantly, giving a voice to those receiving donations abroad. As one charity employee stated in interview,

> Diasporas have been important for a long time but increasingly vital to connect to areas back home and to act in areas where mainstream NGOs have not successfully accessed in recent times, particularly seen in conflict areas such as Syria. Diasporas accessed areas mainstream NGOs can't . . . . It's knowing communities, knowing people on the ground and ways to get the money to the community that needs it. They have a good understanding of what people need.

Diaspora communities assist in the processes of 'knowing' who is most in need and thus act as mediators for others to fulfil their religious obligation of *zakat* and have become a vital resource for UK charities working overseas.

Injunction to give locally

A wide range of interpretations exist regarding who, where and how to give and disputes between local and transnational charitable givings are no exception. The general accepted understanding of *zakat* in the four leading legal schools of Sunni Islam is that it should be given locally despite the fact that many Muslims in the UK donate their *zakat* overseas (this is in contrast to the voluntary, but encouraged, general charity of *sadaqah* which has less theological restrictions). The injunction to donate within your own locality derives from both Quranic references and the sayings and doings of the Prophet Muhammad (*hadiths*). Numerous versions of the following *hadith* from Muath bin Jabal were given by many of the research participants, 'take from the rich people and give to their poor people'. The important phrase to focus on from this *hadith* is 'their poor people'. 'Their' poor was interpreted as collecting and distributing *zakat*, in and to the same community for the purpose of building 'more communication between people within the society itself' (Mosque director in interview, 2013). The concept of giving back to 'their' poor is echoed in the ethnographic work conducted by Gardner concerning transnational charitable practices among Bangladeshi communities. Gardner found that 'charity is offered to known recipients – "our own poor" – and animated by feelings of obligation and duty as well as compassion' (2016).

The same *hadith* was recalled by a Muslim charity sector worker in London who articulated,

> Allah did not say in the Quran that you must spend it locally, but the Prophet did say we should take it from those who are locally rich and alleviate the suffering of those locally poor, but if there are no poor, some people for example feel uncomfortable giving their contributions here [UK] and I know this from practice. There are some who are really deprived somewhere else, say in Africa or Asia, and they can't see someone here who is really in need. But there are people not covered by the social system here, illegal immigrants, someone who is suddenly going through difficulties and they need some help for a couple of weeks until they sort their own situation. I cannot say to people they must spend their money here or there – I must be flexible. There are causes and cases that need support – you go by coach and I go by train, but we will both meet our target at the end of the day.

Therefore, despite a clear and self-conscious awareness that the Islamic faith advocates donating charity to your own locality or community, many Muslims within the UK felt the overriding factor was not one of geography but need. As the interview extract infers, the UK is perceived to mitigate against some of the worst economic injustices that are perhaps absent in other parts of the global community such as 'Africa or Asia'.

A related debate is regarding who should be considered the 'poor and the needy'? Is poverty understood relatively, in which case *zakat* can be justified to be dispersed within the UK, but if poverty is understood as absolute then many participants could not legitimate giving *zakat* to those cushioned from the extremes of poverty by the British welfare state.

Another aspect of this dilemma goes beyond just perceptions of greatest need but also in interpretations of 'locality', 'family' and 'community'. The challenge arises in the contemporary era of mass migration of where is considered 'local'? Who is considered the 'community'? Should 'closeness' be associated with geographical proximity, or closeness of familial/blood ties, or closeness in terms of religious affiliation? Prior to the rise of globalization and mass migration, geographical and familial closeness were likely to be linked. In the era of mass migration, and in the context of a Muslim-minority state such as the UK, the challenges and contradictions become more apparent. The injunction to donate *zakat* locally is the common understanding of who, and where, to distribute *zakat*, but tensions and challenges arise when practising this article of faith within the British Muslim-minority context. For instance, there may be a contradiction between donating 'locally' and starting with 'your family' if the family is geographically dispersed. In this sense, the research speaks to Fortier who recognized that 'identity is widely understood as lived and imagined in ways that breakdown its contiguousness with a geographically bounded locality' (1999: 41). Equally, 'questions of what it means to speak of "home", "origins", "continuity" and "tradition" are paramount' (Fortier, 1999: 42). According to Mandaville, this has as much, if not more, to do with the conditions of globalization than Islam per se as he argues that

> in globalization, physical presence or proximity is no longer a prerequisite for the practice of community . . . the concept of 'distanciation' is implicated in the ability of certain groups to engage in, sustain, or reproduce particular forms of community across great distances and in the face of competing traditions. (2011: 336)

Particularly for first-generation immigrants, the likelihood is that there will remain a strong sense of attachment to the place of origin; however, as Vertovec states,

> this needn't mean they are not becoming integrated in their places of settlement. Belonging, loyalty, and sense of attachment are not parts of a zero-sum game based on a single place. That is, the 'more transnational' a person is does not automatically mean he or she is 'less integrated'. (2009: 78)

What was considered 'close' was a contentious issue. The challenges raised by globalization and migration were consciously understood by some participants. As the interviewee below indicates, many Muslims regard familial closeness as more important than geographical distance when understanding the need to give 'locally'. As a member of the Muslim Association of Britain understood it,

> Relatives have a right more than people who are more distant . . . not that you are not encouraged to think about people who are more distant, but when you are

limited you prioritize. Family closeness is one aspect, but the geographic is also there.

One participant, a director of a Sunni mosque in London, articulated closeness not as a geographical spatialization but one of familial hierarchy. For him, to start distributing *zakat* closely meant beginning with members of your family you know that are in want. The mosque director articulated,

> It is better to pay your relative who are poor, but of course not your mother or your father, and not your children because your parents and your children, this is your duty. Duty is another thing, but if you have a brother or sister who are poor, they are jobless, they have been unsuccessful in their work, they have debts, then you can pay *zakat*. And it is even better to start with your relative, then from relatives you go to other people.

When asked if there was a contradiction or challenge in giving to geographically local spaces or close family relations the same participant replied,

> It is better to do it locally. You start with your local area, with your family and the neighbours around you, and if you don't find anyone – they are all fine – or you have extra money – then you can now say, 'okay, now we go from Aberdeen to Glasgow or somewhere else.'

This indicates a tension within *zakat* practice regarding geographic local areas and familial local areas. The interviewee seems to assume that the family and the local area will be held in the same locality, but in the era of mass migration family and kin may not be geographically local and donors therefore are forced to choose between the closeness of kin ties and geographic residence. The tension between local and non-local giving here is not, however, within the nation-state framework. 'Local' is not understood as one's 'nation' but one's local community however that is imagined and given meaning. 'Community' need not be imagined as a political entity at all.

Consternation regarding giving within the UK or abroad was evident in many of the participants of this research with the claim to locality being frequently mentioned. For example, a prominent charity sector worker in London commented,

> Each community should sort the poverty which is at home so basically at the moment we all are giving for projects which are overseas. This actually goes against the teaching. Every country has poverty, even England but it is a different level of poverty to somewhere else. So, some collect the money from here as *zakat* and help people who are in a different locality. If the need has disappeared, then you can move to the next and so on. Some scholars say that if the need is greatest somewhere else then okay there is an exception, but some scholars object to this.

Theological differences in interpretation are apparent concerning donating *zakat* locally or to those most in need, but there is a general acceptance that so long as *zakat* is given there is room for negotiation regarding the geographic dispersal. As one charity sector worker commented, 'Islam itself, when you look deeply is flexible.' The participant accepted that there were many different practices and preferences for *zakat* donation. He used the analogy of a journey hypothesizing that it is as if we all need to travel to Edinburgh – some may take a train, others a bus and others may walk. The practice is different, but the end goal is the same. This was related to giving locally or transnationally as either way the intention was perceived to be to alleviate suffering and fulfil an individual's obligations to God. The interviewee stated that all scholars have evidence to support their opinion of giving locally or wherever the need was greatest. For this interviewee, this was not perceived negatively but positively. He stated that 'the difficulty is when people say there is only one way, and they are eliminating all the other solutions because you only believe this is the right one'.

The perception that *zakat* must be received by one of the worthy beneficiaries stated in the Qur'an results in many *zakat* donators preferring to donate individually to retain control and understanding of where their financial sacrifice will be distributed. An Islamic Relief employee understood this dynamic articulating that much of *zakat* is distributed 'to locality more distinctly family linked. Probably sent directly through family or friends rather than through charities'. From this, the suggestion would be family closeness rather than geographic location becomes the forefront of individual donors' motivations. Familial links, rather than state political ties, are the main factor for donating overseas as articulated by the following interviewee.

> *Zakat* is a *haqq* [right], but if we have a poor relative, he has more right to receive *zakat* than a non-relative. So, if we go back to the village not only are you giving *zakat*, you're fulfilling another right which is to give someone close for kinship ties: your intention is definitely rewarded more. For instance, one of my friends was going to Pakistan from Edinburgh. He was from a poor village and he told me about it. So, my wife's *zakat* is due so I can give him the money. Some of the stories he told me . . . people were having operations and they literally hadn't the money to pay and husbands died you know. So, when you hear these stories you think to yourself: why would I give my *zakat* to people who are on job seekers and stuff? We have free health care here. That troubles me. Are there *really needy* here? I don't know.

As the transcript excerpt reveals, the motivations for overseas donations are not necessarily politically linked. The emphasis is on perceived duty to kin, the levels of suffering and poverty outside the UK and the welfare provisions provided by the British state ('we have free health care here'). In many ways the reasons interview participants gave for donating charity overseas coincided with the work conducted by Gardner concerning Bangladeshi communities in the UK. Gardner stated that 'my UK based interlocutors were dismayed at the prospect of donating charity to the poor and homeless in Britain: "real" poverty could not be found in Britain, one man laughed' (2016). This is very similar to the interviewee quoted earlier who remarked, 'Are there *really needy* people here?' and another research participant who proclaimed, 'the British government wouldn't let anyone starve to death.' The perception, therefore, for many individuals who chose to donate outside Britain was that the British state staved off the worst of the suffering associated with poverty and need by providing welfare provisions. Thus, in comparison to the levels of need, want and poverty elsewhere, it was deemed inappropriate by some to donate within the UK.

Transnational giving

Recollecting the religious obligations of Muslim charity helps understand why the dynamics between Islamic charitable giving do not fit entirely with the patterns of other migrant remittances. Migrant remittances remain important as long as ties to a perceived homeland and kin groups remain salient. If, and when, a sense of belonging and identification with a homeland geography wanes, remittances are also likely to diminish. However, Islamic charitable giving, particularly the Quranic injunction of *zakat*, remains a Muslim obligation and thus charitable donations do not cease as links to homelands weaken. Nonetheless, the mechanisms and distributions of Muslim charitable giving can, and do, alter as links to migrant homelands diminish, but importantly, they do not cease. The sustained salience of charitable giving for Muslims links to the perceived heavenly rewards (and punishments) for activating their religious duties. As Erdal and Borchegrevink have posited, 'the link with eternity has an obvious role in maintaining Muslim's focus on the poor, and thus encouraging continued engagements' (2017: 141). There is a noted continued 'salience of religion among immigrants . . . . Although remaining important, the social organization and practice of religion is usually modified nevertheless by a variety of factors involved in movement and resettlement in a new context' (Vertovec, 2009: 137). In fact, in many ways it can be argued that the giving of *zakat* overseas is itself a transformation of *zakat* practices within the conditions of the experience of migration and minority status. As detailed earlier, before the experience of migration most Muslims would have been far more likely to donate their charitable offerings locally or nationally within the context of their country of origin.

The contestation between donating globally and locally can be evidenced in the following extract from an interview with an Islamic scholar based in Glasgow:

> I think our earlier generation that came from Pakistan found life here is of luxury. I mean essentially, they thought a person here can never be poor in the UK as at the end, the state provides for a basic minimum whereas in Pakistan when we say poor, we actually mean *poor*. There is no healthcare and there is literal begging. So, there are those that think *zakat* must go to the right recipients and it was felt that it was needed more there than here . . . . When people travel, they have seen poverty with their own eyes. They've seen people dying. To them you can *never* justify *zakat* being spent in the UK in, essentially, a modern and developed society. I mean the government would never let anyone starve to death. How can you give *zakat* here when you have places like Somalia and Pakistan? It's very difficult to convince people – particularly *zakat* we are talking about, they would happily be giving *sadaqah* and stuff, but when it comes to *zakat* – even me and I am a scholar

> ... I still can't convince myself to give *zakat* here and not back home or Africa, India or wherever.

As the above indicates, the emphasis on the giving of *zakat* was to those most in need. Nothing in this extract would indicate a political loyalty as the reason for overseas donations. What is evident is a critique of the lack of welfare and service provisions in some areas overseas ('there is no health care') and a trust in the British government ('the government would never let anyone starve to death'). Far from overseas donations therefore inferring disloyalty to the British state, trust is placed in the hands of the state and political elites in a way it is not granted to overseas institutions. Collectively, the interview data gained from this research indicates that overseas donations are in fact more correlated to critiques of foreign regimes in their inability, or unwillingness, to provide welfare and social care than of support to such political regimes.

In addition to motivations based on greatest need is of course familial and kinship ties. When need and kinship ties are both perceived to be in the same geographic space, the motivation and obligation to disperse charitable funds are augmented. The following extract is from an interview with a British Muslim doctor who stated,

> I am British but I am Iraqi. Okay? And there is no way you can root me out from that, that is where I come from, that's where the blood and flesh in me come from. However, I don't think there's any clash between the two . . . . See when the recent trouble in Mosul happened three years ago, Daesh went to Mosul and the last of my own immediate family got out before they got victimized . . . From then, the state stopped giving salaries to people. And work is impossible . . . . I have extended family . . . . I am not going to close my eyes and ears and keep my hands tied behind my back and do nothing about it. So as far as I was concerned, and that is one of the things about charity in Islam, you start with the closest and then make a wider circle . . . . If you go and see it, then you will *know* how the scale of the trauma is, you *know*. So, I have family, my nephew lost his house. A rocket went through the roof to the second floor and landed in the living room. Luckily, they got out with his family but now he's homeless . . . . I went to Erbil in the North and made sure I got the money to him. I said: 'go and repair your house, get back to your house, get shelter for your family'. What is wrong with that? This is my connection. I am British. I participate fully here. My life is here. In fact, it's my only identity that's left now. I don't have an Iraqi passport and I don't think it would have any value.

Like the Islamic scholar quoted previously, the British doctor gives no political reasons for distributing his Muslim charity to his previous nation of Iraq (other than the devastating humanitarian consequences caused by the so-called Islamic State Group, Daesh). Rather than display political loyalty to Iraq, the individual provides critique in statements such as 'the state stopped giving salaries' and 'work is impossible'. The main motivations for distributing aid to Iraq were kinship ties and need. Saliently, the above participant saw no tension between his affinity to Iraq as his place of origin and his chosen British citizenship and self-affirmed identity.

Collectively, interview transcripts reveal that the primary reasons for giving overseas were undeniably humanitarian in nature and no evidence was found that donations were in anyway related to support for external regimes. Many Muslim-majority states, such as Pakistan, have state-regulated and controlled *zakat* collection and distribution which none of my interviewees donated to, preferring to circumvent political regimes through charities, international organizations and/or individual donations at kinship/familial levels. This coincides with research by Schaeublin which posited that 'direct giving – circumventing state oversight . . . seems attractive whenever political authorities are perceived to be a source of corruption and political repression' (2020: 130).

Zakat donations are not political acts of loyalty to specific states

For the majority of those interviewed, overt political stances of states and regimes were not the main concern of donors. One interviewee stated that 'I agree one hundred per cent. One hundred and ten percent' that Muslims residing in Britain did not distribute their alms to contribute or show support for political states outside of the UK. No specific political parties or regimes were even mentioned when participants were asked about their motivations for donating overseas. While overt politics was not a motivating factor, theological interpretations and religious authority were an issue. Of particular interest was the question of 'authority' in Islam. Here 'authority' should be understood as religious, not political. For instance, part of the resistance of British Muslim populations to donate *zakat* to states rather than non-profit apolitical charities was the understanding that religious authority is disputed. For example, a charity sector employee stated that 'there is an absence of authority in the implementing of *zakat*. At the moment it is absent even in so called Muslim societies.' This brief statement is interesting for many reasons. First, there is an acknowledgement that there is a lack of consensus on the authority of Islam despite many states claiming to be 'Islamic'. By referring to such states as so-called Muslim societies is to introduce a theological critique of some Muslim-majority states. This is quite the opposite of assumptions by Western policy makers that political loyalty of British Muslims could be torn simply by default of being Muslim. Muslims themselves have agency, reflection and criticisms of states that claim to act in their name.

As one Sunni interviewee based in London stated,

> some people in the Muslim world do not trust the state itself. Okay, I give them the money, but how do I know they are going to spend it on these categories? Maybe they are going to spend it on someone else? And the state, they have their own expenses and administration and when the money is in, you cannot trace it. People say as long as I can meet the poor people myself why give it to the state when I can give myself?

Speaking of state-institutionalized *zakat* the same interviewee responded quite scathingly, 'the problem is when the government came, in the beginning they said they were going to organize it and what happened is they confiscated it'. Again, this ties in with the problem of authority in Islam. Political state authority does not necessarily overlap with religious authority.

Since the 1960s and 1970s a number of Muslim-majority states have created state-run *zakat* organizations and collections, with some states collecting it from citizens as a form of tax. If British Muslims were expressing political loyalty to such states, then it would seem likely and plausible that their *zakat* donations would be aimed at the state-controlled *zakat* institutions: they are not. Not one of this research participants had ever even contemplated donating their *zakat* to state-run *zakat* committees nor knew of anyone who ever had. Overseas *zakat* donations were focused either via charities or by individual and personal donation through family and neighbourhood systems. This was strongly articulated by a charity employee who argued,

> I don't think anybody gives for the government – for the government apparatus. People don't give for that. They give to help other human beings. It's that common humanity. You don't give *zakat* to prop up political machinery and government, political parties and so on. You do it because it is your obligation to help a fellow human being in distress or in need. But those who see *zakat* as political giving – that is incorrect and that is untrue. If there is a social factor then yes, that is true in that you are trying to help other people so you are contributing to society and you are looking to people who share the same values as yourself.

State-initiated *zakat* collections have been met with criticisms and challenges from the onset (Scott, 1987; May, 2013) and in part linked to the contestation over the correct authority in Islam as mentioned above. In fact, there have been ongoing efforts to create an international *zakat* fund, such as that espoused by Prince Hassan of Jordan, but to date this remains a utopian (or 'dystopian' depending on one's point of view) imagining (Benthall, 2016: 16). As such it is generally understood that no *zakat* system functions as it should (according to Quranic interpretations) as the ideal Islamic society does not exist (Benthall, 2016: 59).

It simply cannot be assumed that if someone is Muslim then they will automatically seek the state institutionalization of *zakat*. *Zakat* may be considered a must for most Muslims, and an obligatory article of faith, but the ways in which it is practiced makes coercive standardized donations difficult and open to critique and challenge. For instance, one participant offered the following critique of state-initiated *zakat* collection:

> In some Muslim countries they try to make a center for *zakat*, try to encourage people to pay to a certain account or place. From this the government itself will use its own mechanism to try to distribute use for its own projects but it doesn't work all the time ... people like to pay *zakat* to their relatives first, they don't tell anybody. In Islam it is better to do your charities not in public – secretly – between you and them. You will embarrass them if you give in front of other people ... a center for *zakat* like Malaysia ... and also in Saudi Arabia there is a Ministry for this but the problem is you cannot force people to do this. It is not like a system of taxation.

As stated in Chapter 3, it is not enough to give *zakat* to fulfil an individual's religious obligation. *Zakat* must be received by at least one of the eight worthy recipients. Moreover, relatives are considered to have a higher priority in their 'closeness' than non-relatives. The above infers that states distribute *zakat* according to their own mechanisms and rationales, resulting in some individuals worthy of *zakat* receipts not receiving them and thus for some individual Muslims their religious charitable duties are incomplete.

Summary

It is often assumed in political rhetoric that continued charitable donations outside of Britain are in some way an act of loyalty to an alternative political system. However, while a significant portion of *zakat* donations may still be received overseas, this should not be read as a political belonging to another state but as a critique of the receiving state's ability to provide for its people. It should also be remembered that *zakat* is only one form of Islamic charity and that while *zakat* collections in the UK are often dispersed overseas, *sadaqah*, (general charity) which is financially greater, is largely spent within the UK on non-faith charities (such as Save the Children or Cancer Relief).

Muslim financial charitable flows outside of Britain are generally read by policy makers and mainstream media as suspicion of political loyalty to external states. This chapter has highlighted that transnational giving is not peculiar to British Muslim communities and should be read alongside literature concerning migrant and diaspora philanthropy more generally considering the conditions of advanced globalization. The motivations for transnational charitable giving were not political. Examination of interviewee explanations of giving overseas highlights concerns surrounding obligations to family and kin, religious obligations to the global *ummah* and humanitarian purposes to alleviate suffering and hardship associated with poverty and economic insecurity. Far from being a sign of political loyalty to regimes and institutions outside of Britain, the propensity to donate overseas was far more likely to be a result of trust in the British system to provide welfare and economic cushions for its citizens. Conversely, donations overseas could be read as a critique of receiving states' inability, or unwillingness, to provide basic care provisions for its populations. Importantly for the next chapter, it was highlighted that there is tension in theological interpretations regarding the decision to disperse charity locally or globally. Prior to the experience of migration to a Muslim-minority state, it would have been likely that individual Muslims donated (specifically their *zakat*) to their local communities and areas. However, the experience of migration, minority status and the provision of welfare within Britain led many first-generation British Muslims to donate their religious alms to their places of origin. The next chapter will focus on how patterns of charitable flows are altering with second and subsequent generations of British Muslims regarding both where and how they donate.

6

'Actively awaiting the return'

This chapter will demonstrate that alterations in charitable giving are occurring between Muslim generations which simultaneously present younger Muslim generations as both an expression and constitutive element of contemporary British society. Muslim charitable giving within the UK is therefore specifically British. A strong tradition of charitable giving has existed in British communities generally, and thus the secular and religious values associated with charity broadly offer an opportunity where the secular and the religious can inform each other in mutually beneficial ways. Despite this, following the London 7/7 bombings in 2005, augmented by the flow of British citizens joining the so-called Islamic State Group and accentuated by various 'lone wolf' attacks such as the Manchester Arena bombing and the Tower Bridge attack, scrutiny of 'loyalty' of British Muslims to the British state is at an unprecedented degree. In question is 'the idea of loyalty to the Muslim ummah over loyalty to the nation-state' (Miah, 2015: 51). Rather than assume that transnational charitable giving entails political loyalty or sympathy to external regimes, this research sought to ask Muslim individuals for their own personal motivations of where to distribute their religious alms to. Awareness and solidarity with the abstract conception of *ummah* does not necessarily decrease a sense of belonging to Britain, as shall be explored.

A further dimension to this chapter's analysis is the different geographical donation patterns between older and younger generations within British Muslim communities. The research has found that particularly regarding *zakat* donations, older generations tend to donate to their place (not necessarily state) of origin while younger generations are more likely to distribute their *zakat* either within the UK itself or/and to a wider geographic terrain than their parents and grandparents. This work does not wish to pit older and younger charitable practices as 'traditional' versus 'modern' as both involved innovations based on the experience of migration and then latterly socialization within British society. As Gardner has emphasized,

> it would be incorrect to set up a single cleavage between 'traditional', localized/transnational charity and 'modern' globalized philanthropy. Though arising from different moral economies and theological roots, both 'systems' . . . result from economic change, globalization and (un)development. Rather than transnational charity being in some way traditional or pre-modern, it exists in symbiosis with the global capitalism and high modernity. (2016)

It shall be posited that *zakat*, as both a religious obligation and a means of poverty alleviation, works at contradistinction of evidence of other non-religious forms of transnational giving such as remittances. Portes, for instance, has argued that transnational financial activism is

> by and large a one-generation phenomenon . . . . It strengthens with the consolidation of migrants' economic and legal position in the host society, their off spring cannot be counted on to continue these activities, or at least, carry them on with the same level of fervour. (2013: 37)

This coincides with Maimbo and Ratha who have asserted that 'spending patterns . . . depend on factors such as the strength of the migrant's kinship ties and intent to return to the country of origin . . . remittances may slow as ties weaken with time' adding that 'while the propensity to remit may decline over time it rarely vanishes' (2005: 5). The fundamental difference between immigrant remittances and Islamic charity is the religious obligation which remains a duty even after ties to homelands diminish. What is important for Muslim charitable giving is that the giving continues, but the area of dispersal may change over time and as circumstances alter. This coincides with research conducted by Erdal and Borchgrevink concerning charitable practices among Bangladeshi communities in the UK, which argues that 'although their ties to family in Pakistan have weakened with the passage of time, Islamic charity remains a significant transnational practice' (2017: 142).

In terms of British Muslim *zakat* giving, there are certainly changes in charitable practices between generations, but it would be erroneous to suggest that second and third generations are generally not donating overseas or that they lack the 'fervour' of earlier generations. Certainly, it will be argued that geographic links to 'homeland' based on ideas of 'blood and soil' are generally eroded over time, but other geographies linked to belongings associated with Islam more broadly, and humanitarian issues generally, rise as national 'homelands' fade.

Portes notes that long-term migration (which tends to involve resettling most, if not all, of the family unit) results in fewer kin to send remittances to (2013: 35). However, this does not necessarily result in a decrease of charitable and philanthropic activities but merely a change of destination for redistribution. This is the key differential between transnational charitable works based primarily on loyalty to a home territory and that based on identification with a religious identity.

Identity politics has been on the rise as an explanatory tool in understanding the presumed failure of multiculturalism and the erosion of social cohesion, yet recent studies have argued that more traditional concepts such as class and local environment still have more explanatory power than other identifiers such as religion and ethnicity exemplified by Laurence who has argued that 'importantly, ethnically diverse areas also tend to be more disadvantaged. Disadvantage is posited to heighten perceptions of powerlessness and mistrust, undermining levels of interaction and thus lowering social capital' (Laurence, 2009: 70). Laurence's account largely coincides with the findings of the Commission on Integration and Cohesion (CIC), which states that 'deprivation remains a key influencer of cohesion, but the fact that some areas have high deprivation and high cohesion shows that local action can build resilience to its effects' (CIC, 2007: 20). If this is indeed the case, attempts of poverty alleviation and reductions of wealth gaps have the potential of being a strong instrument to bridge gaps between (and within) communities and assist in the process of social cohesion. Indeed, charitable practices that cross religious, ethnic or cultural boundaries not only contribute in practical assistance to the needy but also potentially create solidarities and community awareness in promotional roles, activities and general negotiations in the third sector irrespective of faith, ethnicity or other identity attributes. Civil society is far from a homogenous unit and diversity exists in all its subsections including within the various Muslim communities in the UK. In this sense, even seemingly isolationist practices such as *zakat*, which almost entirely stays within Muslim demographics, can be seen as an important tool for social cohesion in that it can help bridge ties between various Muslim sects, schools of thought (*madhab*), practices and cultures.

As discussed in the previous chapter, not all Muslim charitable donations are distributed abroad. *Sadaqah*, which is voluntary, is distributed to a variety of charities both national and international, following largely the charitable patterns of the majority of British society with donations being distributed to charities concerned with cancer research, vulnerable children and the elderly (Muderrisoglu and Saxton, 2020: 16). The focus of *zakat*, the third pillar of Islam and thus an obligatory form of charity, is perceived to frequently be distributed overseas. As one charity sector employee stated in interview, 'the norm is now greater to give to non-Muslim charities, especially from new generations and professionals; for instance cancer research, water aid, Oxfam – but they will not give their *zakat* to Oxfam'.

Younger Muslims and second and subsequent generations

The British Muslim community is marked by its youth. In fact, nearly 50 per cent of the UK's estimated 2.7 million Muslims are under twenty-four years of age (Mustafa, 2015: 4). The Muslim charitable sector is reflective of the young age of Muslim British demographics. In stark contrast to many secular charities, the Muslim charitable sector is dominated by young volunteers and employees. The youth and vibrancy of Muslim charitable efforts are the topics of Barylo's research which argues the sector is 'diverse, united, highly skilled and qualified, some of their volunteers are already among the influencers of contemporary European society' (2018: 3).

The first generation of Muslim migrants largely derived from Asia and were marked in British society not for their religion but by ethnicity and racialization as Asians (Mustafa, 2015: 23). Prior to 9/11, and before the Salman Rushdie affair, the categorization of 'Muslim' was not common in the British landscape. Skin colour and racializations were far more prominent than religious orientation. However, what began in the UK from the Rushdie affair and the burning of his books in public demonstrations such as Bradford was augmented with the events of 9/11 and then 7/7 in London. Racializations did not cease but were tied to religious practice with 'Islam' and 'Muslim' becoming the primary markers ascribed upon 'others' by mainstream British society. According to the census data from 2011, around 45 per cent of UK Muslims are British-born, and, thus, the youth constitute second- and third-generation British Muslims who have been socialized in a very different context than their parents and grandparents (Mustafa, 2015: 4). Therefore, particularly since 9/11, British Muslims are more conscious than ever of their 'Muslimness'. One consequence of this has been that younger people in the UK, rather than the older generation, are more likely to identify themselves as Muslims (Mustafa, 2015: 11). Strengthening collective understandings based on 'Muslimness', as opposed to geographical racializations, consequently, creates the conditions in which Kundnani (2014: 38) argues produces a transnational Muslim consciousness 'unbounded by geographical constraints'.

Identification with Islam is strengthening among the younger generations of Muslims both as a reaction to racist hostility and to gain deeper understanding of Islam given heightened awareness of their religiosity (Hussain and Bagguley, 2012; Maurer, 2006: 3). No single 'terrorist' profile exists. From the tiny percentage of Muslims who have engaged in political violence in the UK, they are statistically more likely to be British citizens than recent immigrants (Githens-Mazer, 2012: 559). This has led to increased suspicion and surveillance of British Muslims, particularly Muslim men between the ages of sixteen and forty years old.

In addition to the experiences of British Muslims affected by rising Islamophobia, issues concerning second and subsequent migrant generations are also important. As Vertovec has argued, 'high among questions and criticisms regarding the transnational lens on migration are issues as to how members of second and subsequent generations are affected by transnationalism' (2009: 75). For religious communities, 'issues of religious and cultural reproduction naturally raise questions concerning the maintenance, modification or discarding of religious practices among subsequent generations born and raised in post-migrant settings' (Vertovec, 2009: 139). The process of 'modification or discarding' creates a 'hybrid cultural phenomena', according to Vertovec, particularly

> among transnational youth whose primary socialization has taken place within the cross-currents of differing cultural fields. Among such young people, facets of culture and identity are often self-consciously selected, syncretized and elaborated from more than one heritage. (2009: 7)

Charitable giving has a long and important history within the British Isles, which itself developed from historic Church practices (Benthall, 2016: 30). It is therefore entirely possible that young British Muslims, consciously or unconsciously, employ charitable practices that are in effect a syncretism of Muslim and British charitable actions.

It has been argued that the increased visibility of young British Muslims began in earnest during, and after, the Northern protests of 2001. These protests were as much an internal debate among Muslims of different generations than it was a protest for increased visibility and cooperation with British communities broadly. According to Baroness Warsi, currently in the British House of Lords,

> The riots signalled a generational shift. No longer prepared to engage in passive protest and no longer prepared to carry on being grateful for being 'allowed' to

make Britain their home, Asian youth, becoming increasingly Muslim youth, demanded the political value of equality, had higher expectations of education and the labour market and were increasingly disillusioned in the face of continuing race and religious discrimination and the first generation's compromises with what they viewed as the white power structure. (2017: 29)

Renewed interest in religious charitable giving among British Muslim youth should therefore be read in conjunction with the experiences and socializations that have occurred within the British environment following the last two decades.

The observations made by Vertovec were partially echoed by a Sunni Imam resident in Glasgow who articulated,

I've realized the younger people are very cautious and have interest in *zakat*. Younger Brits, especially London and down South, are more connected to their faith than older people. The age group of around 26-40. A lot of them are professionals but never really found what they wanted. You know the story: you get a good education, a good job, you get married and get a house and a lot of people had that and still didn't feel fulfilled. We are finding a trend regarding the different cultures in Islam. The Islam practiced by the older generation is very different to ours. The older Islam is very austere, very rigid. The younger Islam is that we are Muslims, but we can go to Spain; go to the cinema; enjoy a Nando's and stuff like that. We are very comfortable with our Islam . . . we've seen now a new group of Muslims coming from Britain. Essentially, they live a very British lifestyle, but they are very comfortable with their Islam. And it's these guys who are the game changers cos a lot of them are pharmacists, medics, doctors.

The above interview extract is consistent with the research findings of Barylo (2018) who examined young Muslim charity volunteers across Europe. Barylo argues these Muslim volunteers are 'young, learned and skilled, they break traditional boundaries and redefine society with their own terms and in their own image . . . . These young volunteers build their own tailormade interpretation of Islam in a modern secular society' (2018: 3). The salient point is that Islamic charitable giving cannot be simply considered a continuation of 'traditional' practice passed from one generation unchanging to the next. Like all forms of performativity, the practice of Muslim charitable giving both maintains and transforms as 'traditions' are passed from one generation to another. As the Sunni Imam indicates, Muslim youth do not simply blindly copy the Islam of their parents. Within the context of socialization within the UK, younger Muslims have adapted their faith and practice to the environment in which they live their everyday lives.

Transnational and diaspora lens

Understanding British Muslims as not just migrants but a diaspora community while presenting some theoretical challenges is useful in helping facilitate understandings of transnational practices that do not stem from homeland affiliations or kinship ties. Kabir has argued that factors impacting on the formation of Muslim identity include 'foreign policy, social exclusion and Islamophobia' thus the wider British majority culture can, and does, shape British Muslim identity (2010: 10).

Applying the term 'diaspora' to the global Muslim community is not without problems and can only be of use as long as it is understood that the dispersed nature of Muslim peoples is not necessarily a result of exile from a singular Muslim or 'Islamic' geography. In common usage, diaspora has frequently been associated with Jewish peoples though the term may be (and often has been) invoked to include broader transnational communities beyond the practitioners of Judaism and their descendants. Diaspora in a broad sense could be understood as 'a dispersed people sharing a common religious and cultural heritage' (Vertovec, 2009: 129). Though it is recognized that referring to Muslims as holding a common 'cultural heritage' would be erroneous and imply a homogeneity that lacks empirical support. One way in which the term is useful, however, is that diaspora communities have long created fears in host societies, as historically evidenced by previous Jewish communities in Europe or Catholic communities within Britain. As Vertovec claims, 'for host countries, the dual political loyalties suggested by diasporas raise fears of mobilized fifth columns, "enemies within" and terrorist sleeper cells' (2009: 99–100). The fear of the 'enemy within' is being repeated from historical experiences of Jewish and Catholic minorities within Britain to contemporary demonization of Muslims within the UK (Warsi, 2017).

According to Vertovec, some of the main questions or issues surrounding diaspora and immigrant communities centre around whether, and how, these 'dispersed peoples maintain a sense of self-identity and a measure of communal cohesion. The central question for the diaspora peoples is adaption: how to adapt to the environment faced by the diaspora communities without surrendering group identity' (2009: 131). It is this aspect of diaspora that is most salient to the exploration of Islamic charitable giving in the UK: how to adapt charitable practice to the UK environment without sacrificing an individual's Muslim identity. It is imperative to remember that Muslim identity, within the context of the UK, is a relational concept and is

> shaped by other social dimensions such as gender, class, and lifestyles. Muslims, as actors, occupy different positions in their social settings . . . . They do not engage in a uniform manner, in the construction of Muslim selves. Nor do they reproduce a monolithic Muslim identity. Rather, their engagement in identity construction informs us of the power struggles that are embedded in material local conditions and global processes, and that make use of a multiplicity of registers and frames of reference. (Ismail, 2011: 26)

It is important to not lose sight that while migrating and diaspora communities bring with them their own practices, values, community arrangements and beliefs, they do not bring them to a vacuum but to a space already inhabited with values and practices of its own. Thus, migrants and subsequent generations must adapt to new settings. This is particularly relevant for second and subsequent migrant generations who have a stake and commitment to their residences of birth. Werbner's analysis supports this by stating that

> diaspora communities develop local roots and a stake in the continuity of their relationship to the country of settlement. They are permanent sojourners, in the sense that while they recognise a continued affinity and loyalty to the home country, they increasingly come to participate as active citizens in the country of settlement. (2011: 232)

Therefore, diasporic and migrant practices are as much shaped and constructed through the norms and ideologies of host societies as they are by the values of homelands. Nayet argues that transformations of diasporic practices and identities are particularly vulnerable to 'the host societies' ideologues on race, religion, national origin and culture' (2017: 80). The UK should therefore be mindful that its own policies, rhetoric and hegemonic discourse have as much to do with the ways in which migrants' practices are conducted as the migrants' home countries. Consequently, racisms, Islamophobia, dominations and marginalization all contribute to the ways in which Muslims in the UK are understanding and adapt their practices. As Göle notes, 'acts of performance . . . are not socially neutral concepts; indeed, they are situated in, and produced by, social relations of domination and exclusion' (2011: 225). Again this does not signal that all Muslims will respond to the host societies' ideologies and norms in the same way, and, thus, a plethora of alterations and adaptations to practices are evident as a variety of Muslims-respond to the pressures of a non-Muslim majority environment.

Bourdieu's concept of *habitus* is potentially a useful addition and links to Butler's concept of performativity. *Habitus* can be understood as

> a socially and culturally conditioned set of durable dispositions or propensities for certain kinds of social actions . . . . The dispositions of *habitus* selectively generate everyday social practices immediately and in the context of specific social fields. As a set of neither wholly conscious nor wholly non-conscious perceptions, outlooks or points of reference, *habitus* guides personal goals and social interactions. (Vertovec, 2009: 66)

Drawing from Vertovec, conceptualizing Muslim charitable practices through the understanding of *habitus* grants the opportunity to 'better appreciate how dual orientations arise and are acted upon' (2009: 69). In this sense, not only can Muslim charitable practices in Britain be understood as resulting from continuing practices learnt from homelands within the British context but also to adapt the practices already embedded within British society. *Habitus*, in Bourdieu's account, provides for constant improvisation and continual adjustment (Göle, 2011: 227) while simultaneously allowing for a veneer of continuity and stability. *Habitus* sits with the politics and economics of the 'everyday' in that 'people engage in their everyday activities by selecting certain cultural elements . . . and investing this with particular meanings in concrete life circumstances' (cited in Vertovec, 2009: 72). What meaning is invested depends upon the context in which the practice is embedded.

Giving 'locally' within the UK

The previous chapter argued that Muslims who chose to donate their charitable alms overseas, rather than in Britain, largely do so as they believed that the welfare provisions provided by the UK cushioned the direst effects of poverty and economic insecurity. In contrast, this chapter will argue that often charitable donations, aimed within the UK, are related to the shrinking welfare state and critiques (explicit and inferred) of the dominant neoliberal economic framework. Redirecting charitable flows within the UK itself also signals that second and subsequent generations hold a stake in their local communities and are willing to invest in them for future improvement.

In the early periods of Islamic charities within the UK, the focus of charitable donations was overseas and not within the UK itself – a dynamic which is changing as second and third generations become increasingly ingrained into British society generally, and the social and economic ills of Britain itself become more visible. This can be seen with the emergence, and rapid success, of charities such as the al-Mizan Charitable Trust (registered with the Charity Commission in 2010) and the National Zakat Foundation (registered with the Charity Commission in 2013), which distribute funds solely within the confines of the UK. Interestingly, al-Mizan may derive its ethos from Islam and its members and volunteers are mostly Muslim, but over three-quarters of their beneficiaries are non-Muslim (Benthall, 2016: 14). As one charity worker commented in interview,

> I think a lot of people got interested in tackling poverty in the UK, saying: 'Okay, we need to help people in the same country as us.' Up until that point a lot of the charity organizations within the Muslim charitable sector were concentrating on the Muslim world such as *Muslim Aid*, *Islamic Relief* and *Muslim Hands*.

The interviewee, who worked for a grant-giving charity in London, commented on the success of the National Zakat Foundation stating that 'they've got religious authorities saying *zakat* should be given locally, so that's all helped them quite a lot'. Indeed, the National Zakat Foundation challenges the other *zakat* collecting charities which are largely concentrated on overseas aid and development by emphasizing that *zakat* collections were originally, in Prophetic times, collected and distributed locally (Benthall, 2016: 15). In one sense, the relatively new turn of British Muslims distributing their *zakat* within the UK is a transformation of charitable practice from earlier migrant communities. Simultaneously, the propensity to donate back to one's own locality can additionally be read as a return to more historical practices of local giving. Local giving rises as Muslim communities in the UK become more established and as second and third generations become further embedded and integrated into general British society.

Muslim charities that focus exclusively on the UK are sometimes deemed less suspicious than their international equivalents. Interestingly, while loyalty to the British system is indeed entirely present, there is also a critique of continued neoliberal economics which seeks the private sector to fulfil many of its previous functions of welfare and community services. In one sense, the Muslim charity sector is rising to fill the void while also providing a critique of growing wealth gaps and the shrinking of the welfare state following the years of austerity in the UK after the 2008 global financial crash. Numerous examples of economic critique can be found on the websites of Muslim charities that work predominantly or exclusively within the geography of the UK. The National Zakat Foundation, for instance, provides explicit statements that connect the transformations of *zakat* practices to the broader global economy in the statement 'because the world around us has changed in such extreme and disorientating ways, not least the way it recycles our wealth, this pillar of Islam finds itself confronted by greater challenges' (Shaykh Abdal Halim Murad. Nd. National Zakat Foundation). As the National Zakat Foundation distributes *zakat* solely within the confines of the British state, it justifies its restriction of distribution on economic cleavages within the UK and economic and social marginalization of Muslims specifically, as can be supported by the following quotation found on their website:

> So we have, on the world stage, an accelerating Islamophobia riding on our fears about terrorism, allowing the British state to adopt increasingly illiberal and inquisitorial stance towards Muslim citizens, without there being time to think calmly about the longer term consequences for social integration. And the income disparities continue to grow. (Shaykh Abdal Halim Murad. Nd. National Zakat Foundation)

As opposed to giving charity *either* locally or transnationally, many Muslims within the UK, especially second and subsequent generations, are likely to view their charitable obligations as a both/and choice rather than an either/or. This research suggests that rather than choosing to give *either* internationally *or* domestically, individual Muslims may split their charitable obligations and give transnationally as well as locally. Local charitable dispersal was often understood as a consequence of growing need and economic disparity within the UK. For instance, all the younger Muslims who participated in this research were aware of the growth in food banks across Britain to alleviate food poverty. Dividing charitable donations between causes and geographies is particularly apparent in households which discuss, as a collective group, where their individual *zakat* obligations should be dispersed. This is evident from the following extract:

> I think we have a responsibility to everybody, Globally, locally.... Obviously, there is so much going on globally you think Palestine, Pakistan, there is Yemen, there is Syria, non-Muslim as well, but a lot of Muslim countries that are really disastrous states just now for example Somalia and Sudan.... But sometimes people forget their actual communities require it as well.... We as a family actually sit together, My Dad will give some there, my Mum will say 'okay, I'll give it here – I'll give it to Palestine, you give it to Syria, you give it to Pakistan, etc.'... so we are trying to cover the world.

Research participants discussed how, especially when *zakat* was due, the family would discuss as a collective unit where they would donate to. It was not uncommon for an individual to recount that if one member of their family was already donating their *zakat* to their place of origin, and thus the duty to family and heritage ties was fulfilled, it would allow other members of the family to donate elsewhere such as the UK. Another interviewee from Glasgow explained,

> In the past couple of years, I have been giving to the *National Zakat Foundation*, primarily because . . . my Mum and Dad . . . split theirs and they used to give a lot back home . . . . But for me I felt more that people in our community, in Glasgow, have a stronger . . . right on me. Obviously, you have to look after your family and make sure your extended family are alright but I kinda feel that my parents take care of all that . . . . So, I feel a greater sense of obligation to give to those that are needy in my community i.e. Britain so I tend to give to the *National Zakat Foundation* although I have given to *Islamic Relief*. One of the years I split it between *Islamic Relief*, due to the Syria crisis and things like that – and the *National Zakat Foundation* but I give to *Islamic Relief* anyway in terms of *sadaqah* but the *National Zakat Foundation* is my one for *zakat*.

The extract indicates a disjuncture between the charitable giving of the interviewee's parents and her own charitable giving. Unlike the practice of her parents, this participant emphasized 'the needy' rather than kinship ties. Another aspect to be taken from the interview extract is the changing dynamics of her own charitable donations which reflect the changing global circumstances. Latter donations to Syria and Yemen were based on perceived acute need of the population under the circumstances of civil war and hardship. Noteworthy is the individual's decision to distribute her alms to Syria and Yemen is unlikely to continue if, and when, the situation in these territories improve. Thus, where charitable funds are dispersed they are constantly in flux and transformation. The same participant acknowledged the difficulties and tensions in giving locally or globally in the following dialogue:

> As a Muslim you feel like there are people that are suffering right now, and I think although I want to help my own community right now, you can't lie and pretend . . . . We have an obligation to look after people in our wider communities globally as well . . . . Obviously for me personally, I think you should look after your community as well that is not to deny that there is wider problems out there . . . . I think it would be a bit shady to turn a blind eye to that and say 'Oh you know, I guess the Arab world can look after them.' In my own work we get women off the streets, sometimes homeless and I just think that yes, there are global problems but there are actually people here who are homeless or women who have been through domestic abuse and who are homeless or have no access to public funds and are struggling and things like that. So, I think it's an obligation for both: global and locally but I think that I definitely feel an obligation as well to give globally, especially now.

One female second-generation participant voiced her concern for the tendency to donate *zakat* overseas as opposed to the place of residence when she could see effects of relative poverty around her in her home of Glasgow. She stated,

> It's hard because when you look around you, you can see there is a lot of need in our community as well, not just Muslim communities, I am talking about Glasgow,

you know especially in this sector where I am working right now I see a lot of people coming in with nothing and then you feel that sense of obligation and I think that, not only is it a personal thing but it is dictated by faith that you should be grateful for everything you have and helping and supporting people.

Like the individuals who donated their charities overseas, the above participant did not understand 'local' as a political nation but as her specific community of Glasgow, which included non-Muslims. The above interview transcripts appear to verify Vertovec who has argued,

there appears to be considerable variety of patterns and kinds of transnationalism among different groups of second-generation youth. In each case the interplay is apparent of parent's transnational *habitus*, an array of local conditioning factors, and second-generation youth's own hybrid or multicultural *habitus*. (2009: 76)

Another reason for donating to the community in which an individual resides full time is regarding the process of transparency and accountability. Giving individually to one's own immediate community facilitates the ability to account for the use of the charitable funds as an individual can personally witness the dispersal or benefits of their charitable endeavours. It is therefore important to remember that the initial scrutiny regarding charitable dispersals stems from the individual prior to the inspection from official charity regulators and policy procedures. As one participant voiced, interpreting a *hadith* raised in the previous chapter,

Essentially the Prophet is saying take from the rich to the poor so that the rich will see – it's a transparent process – so the money is not going to the headquarters, Mecca or Medina so they never see the outcome of that donation, They see the direct benefit there and then in their community dealing with their issues. So essentially if every Muslim was to give locally there wouldn't be a local problem – it would lead to no poor around the world because you were dealing with issues locally.

The growing desire to distribute *zakat* locally to ensure transparency and accountability for the donors is also backed by research findings from Benthall who argues 'that once larger institutions become involved, including the state and international NGOs, the effectiveness of zakat, in terms of its capacity to empower the person receiving it is reduced' (Benthall, 2016: 16).

The current perception is that a significant portion of *zakat* is distributed overseas. However, the propensity to look for redistribution within the British context is an interesting and potentially important development. This shift in charitable giving has occurred and developed after the events of 9/11. The environment within British and global society has, since 9/11, accentuated the aspect of 'Muslimness' as discussed in the preceding chapter. Consequently, the shift towards donating *zakat* and other charitable alms within Britain itself has been shaped not only by the experience of second and subsequent generations but also by the post-9/11 environment. It can be argued that the increased saliency of the religious dimension to an individual's identity has facilitated a self-conscious awareness and critique of religious practices. As one interviewee explained,

> 9/11, it was a terrible atrocity. I think one of the positive things to come out of it is that Muslims began to question their own faith. Before they didn't really think other than: 'I'm a Muslim': they wouldn't really query. But now they are being pushed by society that asks: 'What are you? Who are you?' They have gone back and searched their roots and some of them have become a bit more spiritual I would say. And as [President] Trump and as things get worse, I think more Muslims are going to question themselves. No matter how far you move away from religion, even if you drink and stuff like that, you are never really going to be accepted. As long as you have a name like Muhammad, have brown skin, you are always going to be: 'a Muslim' – even if you drink and stuff, people have realized that. Some thought: 'How can we escape from being a Muslim?' but a lot are coming back. Even if we drink a pint we are still going to be seen as 'a Muslim'. Unless we totally give our faith up and convert to a different faith [pause] but even still? Which means for them we kind of turn back to tradition. For a lot of them, their parents were practicing but their parents' Islam didn't attract them in Britain. So, they kind of pushed away from that but what led them back was something that was more modern. You know, young dynamic Imams . . . has brought them back: an Islam with which they feel comfortable.

The rise of religious charitable practices, especially among the youth, was also remarked by another interviewee who stated,

> Donors are becoming more sophisticated because of the information available and because younger generations are more adept at accessing the information. There is an increasing mindset for the younger generation of Muslim people to actually want to contribute to charity services generally. It might be due to the general situation of the Muslim population in the UK today, what's going on around the world, 9/11 that's sparked their interest. It might also be partly due to the economic climate which has less opportunity for full time employment.

Both the interview extracts suggest an increased consciousness and self-awareness of practice and interpretation. The Sunni Imam comments on how the 'Islam' of their parents may not appeal to younger British-born Muslims. Equally, the second interviewee noted that 'donors are becoming more sophisticated' and younger generations 'are more adept at accessing the information'. This suggests a transformation of the practice of younger generations to that of their parents and grandparents residing in the UK. As Amin comments,

> British Muslims who are consciously practicing their faith are neither following traditional religious authoritative figures or institutions blindly . . . Rather they are involved in a complex process of first choosing and self-restricting themselves

to certain scholars and thereafter critically engaging with the scholar in question. (Amin, 2019)

There is therefore growing evidence that 'the power of assimilative forces generally leads to a reorientation of the second generation towards their lives and prospects in what is now their country, to the detriment of the transnational concerns and goals of their parents' (Portes, 2013: 37). However, while indeed a reorientation can be observed in second and subsequent generations to donate within the British state, it is not necessarily at the detriment of transnational giving but often a both/and approach rather than an either/or. While there has certainly been a rise of *zakat* donations within the UK itself, second- and third-generation Muslims still donate overseas. This does not mean that charitable donation patterns mirror that of their parents nor that there is no interest in local giving. Many of the second- and third-generation participants of this research simply partitioned their *zakat* – giving some within the UK and some elsewhere. The 'elsewhere' does not necessarily follow patterns of familial origins, however. Again, this argument coincides with the research findings from Erdal and Borchgrevink who suggest that

> the idea of engaging in development outside one's geographic diasporic homeland is perhaps particularly a 'second generation', or 'first generation Muslim European' phenomena. These young adults pointed out that, for their parents, there were personal obligations to individuals in the family in Pakistan, whereas this is less and less the case for the next generation . . . . The difference between migrant and post-migrant generation is more an openness among the post-migrant generation to contribute beyond Pakistan as well, as opposed to not engaging in Pakistan at all. (2017: 142)

The above sentiment was further echoed by an interviewee in London who stated that 'I used to work for a charity consultancy, and I did some research into Muslim charitable giving. Results of a survey indicated that older generations give abroad while younger generations give to both.'

The following example is an interesting account of an individual's reflections and alterations in charitable dispersals, particularly as they deviate from the charitable patterns of his parents. A relatively young (between twenty and thirty years of age) employee of a charity shop in Bradford altered where he sent *zakat* to over the years he had been *zakat* eligible. He initially sent *zakat* to kin in Pakistan as his parents had done before him. However, after a first visit to Pakistan he discovered that the kin he was sending his annual alms to had a TV and a DVD player. His interpretation of the rightful recipients of *zakat* was the 'most needy' wherever, and whoever, they were. This participant's understanding of poverty did not include possessions of luxury goods such as a television or entertainment system. Shocked that his 'poor' relatives were not necessarily the most deserving of his financial sacrifice he began to search elsewhere for the 'poor and needy'. In one sense, this appears to coincide with Portes's stance that subsequent generations will not provide financial assistance to their kin with the same fervour of previous generations. However, the participant did not cease giving but simply altered where, and to whom, he gave. Thus, Portes is correct that as generations develop ties to kinship erode, but as *zakat* remains a religious obligation the obligations must still be fulfilled despite kinship duties decreasing in salience. This individual continued donating overseas but ceased to give primarily to relations. *Zakat* distributions for this participant were based on who, and where, he thought the need was greatest regardless of homeland or kinship ties.

Increasingly, and facilitated by mass media and information technologies, newer generations do not feel the same constraints to simply give back to perceived 'homelands' but will judge for themselves (often based on media information) who and where are the 'most needy'. Kundnani has observed that while original geographies of migration remain a 'central axes of young Muslim's mental geography', places of origin are also supplemented by

> a growing knowledge of other parts of the world where the ummah was oppressed: Palestine, Chechnya, Kashmir, Bosnia, Kosovo, and Iraq . . . Ultimately, there was no homeland and no diaspora, but a global Islamic consciousness unbounded by geography. This new sense of identity was fundamentally political: it provided a new language for describing injustice and offered a way of filling the void opened up by the decline of the Left. It countered the globalization of capitalism not with a return to local tradition but with a transnationalism of its own. (2014: 38)

Kundnani's observation finds resonance with the conversation had with the charity shop worker who was horrified to find that the kin he had been sending his *zakat* to had a television and DVD player. The participant ceased to give to kin but looked to the media to discover 'the most needy' recalling the same states as Kundnani mentions above (but also included Xinyang and Rohingya Muslims in Myanmar which simply reinforces Kundnani's conception of a 'global Islamic consciousness unbounded by geography'). Kundnani's position is useful as it places transnational giving not in terms of loyalty to political systems, states, regimes or parties but to a global collective of Muslims. By placing Muslim charitable giving in the domain of resistance to globalization and neoliberalism is to distance critiques associated with 'terrorism' and political loyalty/disloyalty. Nonetheless, processes of globalization, mass media, satellite and internet technologies, in addition to growing religious identification, have all contributed to the facilitation of constructing an imagined global community of Muslims: the *ummah*.

Ummah and changing geographies of giving

As the previous chapter posited, the concept of the *ummah* can be considered an 'imagined community' (Anderson, 1991) though one not bound and limited by a defined territory. As previously stated, the ritual act of charitable giving can be considered a performative act that assists in the creation of the imagined *ummah*. With greater identification with Muslimness, renewed interest in core Islamic practices is becoming apparent, specifically in terms of charity for Muslim youth, which in turn helps construct the Muslim person. The affiliation with a global non-territorial Muslim community is felt most acutely by British Muslim youth who lack the sense of belonging to their parental homelands while simultaneously feeling somewhat excluded and marginalized in their own British state (Miah, 2015: 79).

The global Muslim collective can gain consciousness particularly in the contemporary era in which British Muslims find themselves. Both racialized and scrutinized for religious orientations, many British Muslims find themselves having to justify their Muslimness in a period of rising Islamophobia. Hence, Mustafa argues,

> The connection with the ummah is also influenced by the perceived marginalization and disadvantage of Muslims. The international political context that young Muslims of this cohort have experienced leads to a strengthening of these ties and a stronger connection with their religious group and their perceived obligations. A feeling of alienation, together with feelings of discrimination, inequality in political representation and a feeling that their grievances are not being addressed, builds group resentment. (2015: 25)

The alterations in transnational charitable giving cannot be reduced to one variable or simplified easily. Coinciding with diminishing kinship ties, a growing global Muslim consciousness and marginalization in the period of increasing Islamophobia have all contributed to an awareness of the global *ummah* and facilitated its construction. Awareness of the global *ummah* has also been aided by contemporary events, conflicts and tragedies which are disproportionately affecting Muslim populations whether that be famines in Somalia, conflict across the Middle East and North Africa or the forced incarceration of Uighur Muslims in Xingang China. However, concern for the *ummah* (however defined) does not necessarily mean a reduction of loyalty or sense of belonging to Britishness. Again, drawing attention to Miah, 'loyalty to an in-group does not translate into disloyalty to an out-group' (2015: 79).

While the argument is being made that Islamic charitable giving overseas is not a symbol of political loyalty to the receiving state, this is not to suggest that charitable giving is entirely apolitical. Political motivations (widely defined) for charitable giving are tied into concern for human welfare and critique of the receiving states' ability to provide welfare provisions for its citizens, as well as other dimensions particular to specific territories. Younger Muslims, representing second- and third-generation immigrants, were more likely to hold some form of political motivation for giving than older generations as the older generations tend to donate to charitable causes primarily based on kinship ties. As young Muslims begin the process of deciding where to distribute their religious alms to, politics (broadly defined) enters the decision-making process. While an individual action of worship, in practice, *zakat* and *sadaqah* hold important wider social functions, most pertinently the alleviation of suffering associated with poverty and need. As a pious action, *zakat* is fundamentally rooted in obligations to the wider society and thus not simply an expression of religiosity but also a civic duty (May, 2013) As Abdullah and Suhaib explain, 'Islam concentrates on the reform of individuals who are constituents of society. Usually all the Islamic commands start from the individual and travels to the establishment of an ideal society' (2011: 87). The role of religion in welfare provision and charitable purposes is thread through British history and recognized as fulfilling an important role in the emergence of civil society. Thus, Muslim charitable giving is complimentary to the pre-existing civic role of charity generally within the UK but specifically faith-based giving.

> Religions potentially represent an answer to the societal quest for common goals and shared values. Moreover, religions arouse spiritual commitment and charity, motivating individuals to play an active part in the civil society… being structurally independent from the state enables religious institutions and organizations to be legitimate participants in the public discourse of the civil society. (Ziebertz and Riegal, 2010: 299)

Faith-based charitable organizations often rely, at least partially, on teams (and for the larger organizations 'armies') of volunteers marked by their youth. Volunteer initiatives have been seen to hold positive correlations with social cohesion. Heuser emphasizes that 'perhaps just as great as the work they do through their manifest actions is the camaraderie and solidarity they create among their own members and between members of different communities' (2005, 19). The broad sociopolitical motivations were understood in the following way from a London-based charity employee who spoke of the importance of Muslim charitable giving for Muslim youth:

> I think especially for young people, it builds up their character and helps them develop as a human being, but also makes them socially aware if you like, by discovering their role in the world, but also politically as well because they look around they see that maybe governments aren't helping these people, maybe they are being repressed and so on. In a lot of ways, you can use it as a political statement as well. 'I'm going to donate to the Palestinian people because the Palestinian people are under occupation.' So my statement of intent may be that I am not going to go out and shout and scream about it, or I'm not going to go and fight, as these are things I cannot do, and cannot control, but what I will do is express my political opinion by making a donation to help Palestinian people and by doing that you are actually serving several obligations if you like. You are serving your social obligation by helping people who are less fortunate than you, the obligation to help people whose circumstances conspire against them, your religious obligation obviously by helping your fellow brothers and sisters, and of course, there is that political dynamic or political element as well, so I think that it does shape a lot of social and political things – some of them may not be obvious or so blatant. We also try to teach our young people that in this country we have the welfare state, so if all else fails, you will always have something that you won't starve to death, but actually the concept of helping people goes back thousands of years, but has been formalised in Islam by *zakat*, so you are obliged to help those who are less fortunate. So, while people in this country are forced to pay tax to help other people, Islam says to you this is your religious obligation, so we were doing the same thing a millennium ago.

Nothing from the above statement would infer charitable donations are given to be received by political entities, groups or parties. The above interviewee stated 'Palestinian people', not particular political parties or groups. It is the perception of suffering and need which sparks the motivation to make a charitable act. As Fassin observes,

> with the entry of suffering into politics we might say that salvation emanates not through the passion one endures but through the compassion one feels. And this moral sentiment in turn becomes a source of action because we seek to correct the situation that gives rise to the misfortune of others. (cited in Gardner, 2016)

As the above suggests, when politics does enter into the decision-making process it is not necessarily an expression of support to a particular state or political party but more likely a critique of the receiving states' ability to provide for its population and/or the governance of said state. In fact, one of the advantages of faith-based organizations generally has been espoused as their ability to utilize 'ready-made forms of "civil-society" with the potential to bypass corrupt political structures' (Benthall, 2016: 5). This can be observed in the above interviewee extract which states 'maybe governments aren't helping these people, maybe they are being repressed'. Equally, just as the previous chapter argued, reasons for not donating to the UK are not necessarily due to a lack of belonging or loyalty to Britain, but because 'in this country we have the welfare state'. However, there is no escaping the contentious issue of the Palestinian/Israeli debate.

Since the creation of Israel in 1948, Israel has enjoyed overwhelming Western backing, particularly from the United States. Following 9/11, the election of Hamas in 2006 and augmented by the inauguration of President Trump, there has been an increase in the politicization of aid to Palestine seen in the designation of charitable institutions distributing aid to Palestine (the Holy Land Foundation in the United States and Interpal in the United Kingdom) in addition to President Trump's unilateral decision to dramatically decrease US state aid to UNRWA (the UN Relief and Works Agency). Muslim charitable donations to Palestine in particular are read with increased suspicion and scrutiny for fear of funds being misused or misdirected towards 'terrorism'. This suspicion is not reserved for Palestinian territories alone. A report published by the Humanitarian Policy Group, for instance, found that INGOs faced the most severe financial difficulties when attempting to provide emergency relief to areas such as Syria, Afghanistan and Iraq (Metcalfe-Hough, 2015: 6). In the current post-9/11 security environment, expressing concern for certain territories and causes becomes a point of contention of its own. As De Goede has strongly argued, 'the post-9/11 pursuit of charities in effect amounts to a new governing of transnational spaces of donation and political affiliation . . . the key question becomes whether it is legitimate at all to offer aid and humanitarian relief in territories plagued by particular types of violent struggle' (De Goede, 2012b: 127). As Benthall has noted, 'even Islamic Relief, known for its scrupulous administration, found itself under attack towards the end of 2014 by the governments of Israel and the United Arab Emirates because of allegations that its work in the Palestinian Territories had indirectly supported Hamas' (Benthall, 2016: 7). These allegations against Islamic Relief were restated in a Middle East Forum report of 2018 (Middle East Forum, 2018) particularly aimed at Islamic Relief USA. In response, Sharif Aly, CEO of Islamic Relief USA, disseminated a public letter strongly rejecting the allegations referring to them as 'politically motivated attacks' (Aly, 2018). The open letter also infers some of the consequences of such repeated allegations by stating that 'in the last ten years alone, Islamic Relief Worldwide has undergone 500 audits, all of which have demonstrated that the organization and its partners maintain robust systems and processes to safeguard against unauthorised diversion of funds' (Aly, 2018).

One frequently occurring challenge regarding aid to Palestine is the accusation that Palestinian *zakat* committees are merely fronts for Hamas (Benthall, 2016: 7). The connection with Palestinian *zakat* committees and 'terrorism' was made explicit and popularized by Levitt's publication (2006) which argues that Palestinian *zakat* committees are all affiliated with Hamas. The position from the *zakat* committees themselves is that they are independent charitable organizations. Levitt's argument is centred upon the assumption that charitable donations secured by Hamas then free 'fungible' funds for military purposes (Levitt, 2006). The US Material Support Act ensures that any support, even charitable, that is linked to Hamas can be prosecuted as a terrorist act (Benthall, 2016: 61). Notably, Benthall has observed that 'no sentence in Levitt's book . . . acknowledges that Islamic charities in Palestine may be even partly motivated by altruism' (Benthall, 2016: 64). Notably, the work of the Palestinian *zakat* committees began in earnest following the further occupation of Palestinian territories directly after the 1967 Arab-Israeli war. *Zakat* committees emerged as an indigenous response to Israeli occupation as an attempt to meet the growing needs of Palestinians living under occupation. The *zakat* committees organized the collection and distribution of *zakat* funds by supporting orphans, providing medical clinics and hospitals, maintaining schools and educational facilities, creating jobs and providing a wide array of religious services (Schaeublin, 2019: 130).

The risk in increasing obstacles to charitable distribution in conflict areas has been highlighted by a report issued by the independent think tank Overseas Development Institute, which in 2015 warned that frustration caused by increased difficulties in distributing religious charitable obligations contributed towards a select few gaining sympathy for violent political entities (Metcalfe-Hough, Keatinge and Pantuliano, 2015). It should also be acknowledged that Western charity and aid provisions have hardly been historically driven by altruism alone. From the invention of 'development' in the establishment of Bretton Woods and the Marshall Plan directly following the Second World War, 'the Western aid system is deeply connected to national foreign policies and security concerns' (Benthall, 2016: 28). Thus, to argue that Muslim charitable giving (or any form of charitable giving) must be completely void of any political concern is, as Benthall has argued, 'hypocritical' (Benthall, 2016: 28). In turn, the politicization and frequent demonization of aid to specific territories (such as Palestine and latterly Syria) create the impression for some reflective Muslim individuals that Western governments wish 'to monopolise humanitarian action as a political tool to serve their own interests' (Benthall, 2016: 75). It is not a vague sense of belonging or solidarity to the *ummah* which itself is oppositional to a sense of Britishness, but the ways in which 'Britishness' have been constructed in contemporary counter-terror debates that pits the two belongings at odds to one another. The emphasis on 'fundamental British values' appears to view any commitment to values outside of the British frame to be a fundamental threat. This then facilitates the perception that Muslims feel that to be classed as 'moderate' they 'must forget what they know about Palestine, Iraq, and Afghanistan and instead align themselves with the fantasies of the war on terror' (Kundnani, 2014: 110). Similarly, Spalek and Lambert have argued,

> within government rhetoric, those Muslims and community organisations that are viewed as being 'moderate' are seen to be allies in the prevention of terrorism.... Muslim identities that appear to value the ummah over feelings of Britishness, or who appear to isolate themselves from wider society, are negatively judged and seen as a threat to social cohesion. (2008: 261)

Ultimately, Muslim attention to Palestine derives from obligations and solidarity with the *ummah* and the importance of Palestine to the religion (Jerusalem being considered the third holiest site in Islam after Mecca and Medina) and due to the 'consistently high media profile of the Israel-Palestine conflict' (Benthall, 2016: 74).

The influence of media, satellite and internet facilities is not unique to Muslims or the faith of Islam. Sassen has argued,

> the growth of the internet and linked technologies has facilitated, and often enabled, the formation of cross-border networks among individuals and groups with shared interests.... This has engendered or strengthened alternative notions of community membership. These new experiences and orientations of citizenship may not necessarily be new; in some cases they may be the result of long gestations or features that were there since the beginning of the formation of citizenship. (2003: 277)

Sassen argues that the new forms of community membership may not be 'new' but have become enabled due to processes and opportunities of globalization. Therefore, it can be argued that alongside growing awareness of their 'Muslimness', British Muslims are also rediscovering features of Muslim community formation that have been there since the dawn of Islam itself. Arguably, the contested concept of the *ummah* is one such alternative notion of community membership which is not necessarily based on citizenship per se but alternative conceptions of collective and group identity. British Muslims, evidenced by multiple surveys, feel 'British' (Rheault, 2011) but this does not by default negate other forms of community belonging such as obligations to the global *ummah*. These alternative notions of community may not be at odds with Britishness. Britishness expresses belonging to a geographic and political assemblage while other forms of community (whether that be constructed through local communities or through the prism of the *ummah*) can be conceived as complimentary rather than oppositional. Globalization has unlocked the potential of multiple and overlapping identities and belongings to coexist in a both/and manner rather than binary opposites of either/or.

'Knowing' the 'poor' and the 'needy': Media and digital print capitalism

While familial and kinship ties were of high importance in motivations of where and how to distribute *zakat* donations particularly for older Muslim generations, another important factor is the media, particularly for second and subsequent generations within the UK whose ties to their parental place of origin may have weakened. An employee of the Ummah Welfare Trust working in one of their many high street charity shops in England perceived that where charity was donated depended on two main aspects: first, the country of origin/familial ties of the individual donor and, second, the media. He commented that there was not the same need to rely on relatives abroad to tell who were the 'most needy' because now 'we can see with our own eyes' meaning the television or internet.

Further adding to the argument that Muslims scrutinize where their charitable alms go from the outset is the importance of media, satellite and digital print capitalism in providing information regarding those in need. As Chapter 3 demonstrated, for *zakat* to be fully fulfilled it must be donated and *received* by at least one of the eight categories eligible. From those interviewed, the first two categories of the 'poor' and 'the needy' received the most focus for *zakat* distribution. This of course begs the question of how an individual Muslim knows who are the poor and who are the needy? Knowing who was needy was a very important aspect for charitable distribution decision-making for all of my interviewees. For older generations, the tendency was to rely on family and kin from the place of migration to both identify and distribute alms to those in need. However, for younger generations where links to homeland and kin have weakened, the media and other digital forms of information sharing were instrumental in deciding where to donate charitable funds. Attention to disasters, both natural and manmade, in media outlets goes a long way in understanding why charitable alms remains, at least partially, a transnational practice. One charity worker who had vast experience of trying to persuade Muslims to use their charity more locally argued,

> it is difficult to market. People want to see blood unfortunately, but we are working on this. People need to understand that charity belongs at home – an Islamic concept. The Prophet told one of the *zakat* collectors 'take money from the rich people to be distributed to the poor', so back into the community, but if there is enough it goes in the wider society.

Similarly, another charity employee stated,

> People are driven by what they see: good and bad. Some causes are suffering in silence . . . . Syria is in the news every day. If tomorrow Syria disappears from the news the suffering after is even greater than it is now. Burma is an ongoing problem, but it is not on the news . . . the media can dictate the charitable agendas in this way. It is difficult for charities to challenge this. How do you make a charity really deserving, understood and highlighted and made a priority to those who are

giving? This is where regular giving is encouraged: direct debit and standing orders to give some stabilities to those charities and some stable planning.

An employee of a charity based in London when asked which geographies were the most popular destination for charitable dispersals answered,

> Which part of the world you are from, if you have a relationship through kin or friends or whatever I think that is a huge factor. A lot of people will give to a country or countries that they either come from or their family comes from. Again, I think that is something that is common amongst any group. You identify with those people you have some type of tie with. That's one element of it . . . . So in times of, shall we say non-emergencies or when there are no big natural disasters or big civil conflicts, people's attention can be generally diverted to other areas and they do genuinely help and they do give. If a conflict broke out in Gaza tomorrow for instance, you can bet your bottom dollar that a lot of people will give for that because it would be in the news and the media element of it is really, really important. Once people get a wider understanding of an issue, or it is brought to their attention through mainstream media, they are more likely to give. So, if Gaza broke out, or another war broke out tomorrow, and Israel started bombing or whatever . . . a lot of people would give straight away. If there is no news in the media . . . it is a struggle. If Tanzania is not in the news about orphans that are in need, or how the drought was followed by flooding, but none of that was in the mainstream media so people are completely unaware of it so it becomes a battle for us to raise the issue and make people aware of it.

Much of the motivation for overseas giving therefore should not be viewed in terms of political solidarity to states or parties at the expense of Britain but a theological commitment to those in need. What was evident from all the interviews conducted for this research were the levels of awareness of poverty, hardships and sufferings globally by the individual participants. As mentioned earlier, a particularly salient aspect that has facilitated Muslim individuals in 'knowing' who are the most in need are events highlighted in mainstream and social media. While on the one hand, media and social forums assist individual donors in their decision on where to distribute their religious alms the media fetish can at times actually hinder the work of charities (faith-based and secular). The fast 'breaking news' context in late globalization means media attention is skittish – following a news thread for only a short period of time until the next big media event hits. For charitable and development projects this can be harmful, as the effects of specific disasters linger far longer than the cameras and media attention do. Relying on media sources thus means donors may not give consistently and reliably to a single cause resulting in projects losing donation money well before the crisis has been averted or alleviated. This challenge has been met as an opportunity for some charities as the following charity worker insinuated.

> The first thing is them [the donors] coming to us. We are the first point of contact. They come to us saying 'can we give to Syria'? 'Yes of course you can', but then we

can say stuff like 'the stuff that's happening in Syria is dreadful. Have you seen *this*?' China is not a Muslim country so many donors don't know and Burma – these people need help too . . . . People are not aware they just see Syria on the TV so you need them [the donors] to know there are really bad things happening out there. So why are you going to blindly give to Pakistan just because you have some family there? . . . Many will give to different funds – some to family and some to other funds.

In interview with an employee of Islamic Relief in Birmingham, the question was posed what were the most popular appeals: 'anything that comes up in the media. Could be Gaza, Palestine, earthquakes – this seems to take priority'. The same interviewee articulated that the internet has helped donations increase and raise efficiency, but the motivations stem from the media with the interviewee noting that a 'sharp increase [in donations] when an issue is raised and discussed in the media'. Another charity worker echoed the same sentiment in stating that 'the drive is through the media. The Internet is a means to donate, but sharp increase always when an issue is raised and discussed in the media'. For instance, the Tsunami that hit the city of Aceh in 2015 gained unprecedented levels of aid and financial support largely as a consequence of the peculiar natural circumstances and the comprehensive media attention the phenomenal event achieved (Benthall, 2016: 49).

Similarly, a prominent charity sector worker explained that 'people are driven by what they see . . . the media can dictate the charitable agendas in this way. It is difficult for charities to challenge this.' We can therefore see two further motivations for Muslims not to donate their charity to simply their countries of origin. Not only does the media massively drive where donations are given, but charities mitigate the media affect by alerting individuals to an array of tragedies that may not hit the mainstream media regularly. Charities are also advocates of general charitable projects whether that be *zakat* only funds (with no geographic specification) or funds for water projects, poverty, and so on, that are not geographically specified but given to where the need is greatest. Established Muslim charities are therefore both assisting Muslims in fulfilling their religious obligations while simultaneously attempting to direct funds to particular projects and geographies that are in need, but may not be highlighted in the mainstream media and thus bereft of attention and funds. Muslim charities, therefore, are in some ways attempting to direct the collection and dispersal patterns of charitable giving.

The absent Islamic state

Muslim charities, in attempting to direct the patterns of charitable giving, are therefore taking responsibility for many individuals' personal obligations to God. However, what grants Muslim charities the legitimacy and authority in their role of facilitating an individual's religious responsibilities? The following section will focus on the diverse perspectives of the role of the state in distributing alms and the role of British Muslim charities in the absence of an ideal Islamic state.

Research for this monograph began in 2013, prior to the emergence of the so-called 'Islamic State' (Daesh) group which re-territorizalized large swathes of Syria and Iraq. As this research began prior to the infamous use of violence by Daesh references made by interviewees concerning the abstract concept of an 'Islamic state' are not in reference to ISIS/Daesh. The concept of an Islamic state has been the subject of much historical debate with discussions intensifying across the Muslim world following the collapse of the Ottoman Caliphate after the First World War. How an Islamic state should be structured, and indeed if one is necessary at all, has long been an issue of discourse for Muslims globally. It should therefore not be surprising that one of the most contentious issues regarding the distribution of Islamic charity was the role (if any) of the ideal 'Islamic state' or system of governance.

Currently, there is a crisis in authority in Islam (Benthall, 2016: 19). This crisis of authority has bearing on the legitimate collection and redistribution of Islamic alms which have been the focus of debate for many Muslim individuals and Muslim majority states. Diverse sets of opinions were voiced in relation to who, and what, could legitimately collect and distribute *zakat*. Despite differences between Sunni and Shia practitioners, two broad interpretations were apparent that can be categorized as follows:

1) Charity is an individual obligation and a form of worship to Allah alone – the state is redundant at best.
2) Charity includes the above but also sets the economic foundations and social organizational structures of Islamic governance as modelled on the community of the Prophet Muhammad.

The first trend is by far the most common among lay Muslim understandings of their charitable obligations. This perspective reasoned that the Prophet was able to organize the collection and dispersal of *zakat* (and other Islamic charitable donations) precisely because he was the seal of the Prophets. Following the death of the Prophet and the demise of *al-rashidun* (the period of the four rightly guided *Caliphs* succeeding the Prophet Muhammad in Sunni Islam), authority and legitimacy in Muslim leadership have been fraught, thus the possibility of a centralized *zakat* collection for all Muslims in the contemporary era was considered both impossible and undesirable. For most, their charitable obligations, exemplified by *zakat*, were considered an individual obligation to God independent of any organizational or political structure. Some *Sunni* practitioners were emphatic that any form of state collection of *zakat* was illegitimate in the contemporary state system.

In regard to the second broad trend, this should *not* be understood as a violent revolution to forcefully install an Islamic state akin to that of Daesh (also referred to as ISIS or ISIL), but a general articulation aligned with other Abrahamic faiths that the day of judgement will either be preceded or followed by a reign of justice on earth. Discourses concerning the role of *zakat* in the economic system of an ideal Islamic state emerged prominently from an array of Muslim thinkers in the twentieth century such as the Egyptian founder of the Muslim Brotherhood Hasan al-Banna, the executed Egyptian Islamist Sayyid Qutb (in *Social Justice in Islam*, published 1949) and the Indian-born Abul A'la Maududi in his 1969 monograph *First Principles of Islamic Economics* (Schaeublin, 2019: 129). Each of these thinkers and many more considered *zakat* to be a mechanism for state redistribution of wealth that could, and should, be organized centrally by the state (provided the state was 'authentically' Islamic). For a select few of those interviewed, Muslim charities that cater for the collection and distribution of *zakat* are merely temporarily fulfilling the obligations of the absent Islamic state – ensuring the capabilities, structures and administrative facilities are created in advance for the future Islamic state to simply take over.

This sentiment was strongly articulated by a Shia Imam who explained,

> Time is only a product of this world . . . at the end, Jesus and the Mahdi will return together and establish the rule of peace and justice. Until that day we cannot sit idle and let the corruption rule: that is wrong. We believe in correcting society and establishing the rule of justice in society to prepare the platform for the return of Jesus Christ. We should work for that and not sit idle and let the world be taken over by the corrupt rulers. We should oppose and raise objections to the wrong doings. We should be actively awaiting the return.

To be 'actively awaiting the return' is merely understood in the above interview extract to be action to ensure justice in opposition to corruption in the era prior to the return of Jesus Christ and the Mahdi. The Shia scholar did not claim to wish an Islamic state in the UK, nor that one was imminent, but merely that in the absence of legitimate authority (during the occultation of the Hidden Imam) Muslim individuals were not exempt from struggling for economic justice and equitable distributions of wealth.

The concept of an 'Islamic state' is not merely contentious due to the internal debates between Muslims themselves regarding what it is, how it should be structured and if it is desirable at all, but also as a consequence of evolving counter-terror measures which increasingly appear to include what is deemed 'extremist' thought, in addition to 'extremist' action. The UK counter-terror programme was updated in 2009 in what has most commonly been referred to as 'CONTEST II'.

> The emphasis on this new agenda expanded the remit of counter-terror to include not just violent extremism but extremism broadly. The text confirms the emphasis on non-violent extremism in the statement 'views which fall short of supporting violence and are within the law, but which reject and undermine our shared values and jeopardise community cohesion'. (Benthall, 2016)

CONTEST II has effectively ensured that ideas and views which offer an alternative to secular liberalism, even when perfectly legal, are in popular and public discourse regarded as 'reprehensible' (Miah, 2015: 26). Pertinently, under current counter-terror policy such as Chanel in Britain, any 'verbal opposition' to assumed and undefined 'British values' becomes worthy of suspicion and scrutiny. As such, Muslims who verbally discuss the ideal of an Islamic system of governance fall under suspicion for advocating alternative systems and assemblages. As Elshimi has argued, 'Chanel risk indicators correspond to certain behavioural types and patterns by individuals, as well as the articulations of particular views and beliefs associated with religion and politics .... Professing a belief in "sharia" or the "caliphate" ... flag up that individual as a potential terrorist' (2015: 125). Essentially, 'this discourse exceptionalises "Muslim culture" ... which is constructed by political elites and the media as constituting a threat to "traditional British values"' (Githens-Mazer, 2012: 560).

Saliently, few of those interviewed believed there was an authentic Islamic system operating anywhere in the current global environment, despite a handful of states explicitly declaring themselves to be 'Islamic'. It was the perceived absence of an authentic Islamic state that for some of those interviewed was the motivating factor for the rise of Muslim charities in the UK and elsewhere. A CEO of a Muslim charity based in London espoused,

> There is an absence of authority in the implementing *zakat*. At the moment, it is absent even is so-called 'Muslim' societies although they are trying to do it now. In the absence of a system, in the early days in my experience in the Muslim sector, I came across people who believed our priority was to establish the Islamic state first and sort our other problems later. So, they said to Muslim charities they were *haram* [forbidden/prohibited] to exist because they are doing the obligation and duty of the [Islamic] government. I said 'Okay, if the Islamic state is here tomorrow what will they need? The expertise!' If the Islamic state is here tomorrow, I will dissolve as a charity and be at the disposal of the Islamic state.

The CEO, therefore, saw the role of Muslim charities in the UK as fulfilling the function of the Islamic state in absentia. However, he did not necessarily believe that an Islamic state was either possible or desirable in the contemporary era. Similarly, a member of an Islamic institution based in London asserted,

> *Zakat* is a communal activity because traditionally *zakat* should only be collected by the Islamic assigned ruler because it is a system almost like a tax system collected and distributed by the state so that is why there is that communal obligation. [Without an Islamic state in the UK] the charities here set out to fulfil the place of the Islamic state.... They have grown into a professional service with innovative ideas in raising money.

The concept of Islamic charities rising to fill the void of the 'authentic' Islamic state was voiced by the controversial theologian al-Qaradawi in his 1973 PhD thesis which states that 'the Prophet and his successors affirmed this responsibility as part of the state's executive affairs. If the state does not fulfil its responsibility in collecting and distributing zakat, Muslim organisations can make decisions about distributing' (2000: 39). With an ongoing crisis of authority (which arguably arose and has continued since the death of the Prophet Muhammad), Muslim charities have arisen within the discourse of Islamic legitimacy and authority. Benthall has suggested that in many ways the innovations of Muslim charities, their growing bureaucratization and procedure mechanisms 'may be offering complementary alternatives to traditional religious hierarchies and thus subtly changing the balance of internal religious authority' (Benthall, 2016: 35). Equally,

Muslim charities may offer an 'alternative focus of authority for Muslims to traditional religious hierarchies based on the mosque' (Benthall, 2016: 73). As Muslim charities in Britain become further embedded into British society, and as second, third and subsequent Muslim generations affirm themselves in society, there is further future potential for Muslim charitable practices to become increasingly 'British' following new and innovative authorities.

Summary

Motivations for charitable giving are nuanced and complex with an array of mechanisms, practices and destinations. This chapter has sought to explore the changing *zakat* donation patterns between generations to highlight the array of practices and transformations that exist and are still emerging. It has been argued that second and subsequent British Muslim generations will continue to donate *zakat* with much being received overseas. However, this should not be understood as simply a re-appropriation of the charitable practices of the preceding generations. As second and subsequent migrant generations become increasingly embedded and socialized within the British context, charitable performances are re-orientated towards different geographies, including Britain itself.

Evidence appears to suggest that British Muslim youth have increased awareness of social economic problems within the UK and progressively are likely to donate at least part of their charitable obligation within their state of birth. However, this does not negate transnational giving altogether. Rather than being an either/or choice to donate within the UK or elsewhere, younger Muslims are increasingly likely to do both. The continuation of transnational charitable giving is not simply a reproduction of parental practices but will often entail a wider geographical expanse than that of the parental homeland.

It has often been assumed by policy rhetoric and popular media that solidarity to the global *ummah* necessarily results in a lessened sense of belonging to Britain. Arguably, part of the 'pull' factor towards the imagined *ummah* is a consequence of the heightened religious categorization of 'Muslimness' that facilitates an awareness and self-consciousness of other group members. However, concern for the global *ummah* does not necessarily delineate decreased identification with Britain as evidenced by second and subsequent Muslim generations donating to charitable causes both domestically and internationally.

> Far from revealing ambiguous loyalties or unbridgeable cultural chasms.... In the long run, the Muslim diasporic presence in Britain is a potentially enriching one, and particularly so as the state moves to becoming a post-national, multicultural polity. (Werbner, 2000: 307)

Awareness and solidarity with the global *ummah* can be explained by a mix of factors which include theological understandings, but also factors which deviate from the purely religious such as media and internet sources, and the conditions of advanced globalization which have been argued to be changing the nature of the 'nation' and how citizenship is conceived (Sassen, 2003; Werbner, 2000). As previously stated, the UK has a long-standing tradition of supporting charitable causes. Muslims in the UK can, and do, contribute to this shared value of charitable giving. In the performance of charitable giving within the UK context, second and subsequent generations are increasingly likely to donate their charitable obligations within the UK and to non-faith-based causes which in turn contributes to their societal engagement and sense of belonging to UK society.

Like all charitable initiatives, whether secular or faith-based, what is emphasized in the mainstream media goes a long way in explaining the motivations for transnational giving. Events (whether natural or manmade) which find focus in mainstream media tend to receive higher quantities of charitable donations as Muslims can now identify for themselves who are the most in need. This has both helped and hindered the works of both national and international Muslim charities based in the UK. In attempting to mitigate the fickle nature of media attention, charities are using new techniques to encourage charitable giving and in so doing are taking upon themselves the authority to direct the collection and dispersal of charitable obligations. For some, Muslim charities that collect and distribute the religious obligation of *zakat* are taking responsibility in the absence of an Islamic system of governance.

7
'Diamonds are made from that pressure'

By 2019, over fifty Muslim charities had been faced with allegations linking them to 'extremism' or 'radicalism', seventeen of which had subsequently underwent investigations by the Charity Commission since 2013 (Yasmin and Ghafran, 2019: 1). Despite Muslim charities representing less than 5 per cent of the UK charitable sector, between 2005 and 2012, 11 per cent of investigations were conducted on Muslim charities (Yasmin and Ghafran, 2019: 5). This chapter aims to explore the perceived consequences of, and responses to, CTF measures within the Muslim charitable sector. As shall be detailed, a number of negative repercussions have been felt within the charitable sector as a whole and by the Muslim charitable sector specifically. Two main consequences derived from interview participants were reputational damage and challenges from the banking sector. Both consequences felt within the UK have repercussions on charities' ability to carry out their work effectively and efficiently with negative consequences for end-users, particularly the most vulnerable overseas.

Rather than seeking to dismantle new Charity Commission regulations, responding charities have articulated strong working relations with the Charity Commission and guiding frameworks. In contrast, the banking sectors focus on 'de-risking', and implementation of recommendations from the Financial Action Task Force (FATF) has been outlined as one of the major consequences of the extension of counter-terror policy for Muslim charities. Almost all participating charities, including large established charities such as Islamic Relief, faced difficulties finding banks that would accept their custom and received threats and/or actual account freezes and closures. In addition to disruptions to charitable works which potentially risk the lives of the most vulnerable, there is a danger that alternative financial mechanisms will be utilized, or financial flows will be driven underground.

What is clear from the available research is that current challenges and difficulties within the charitable sector are not being met with despondency or withdrawal from the sector (Yasmin and Ghafran, 2019) but with greater resilience and creativity. As the chapter title suggests, many charities who have suffered the worst consequences of current counter-terror policies believe that the current challenges will ultimately make them stronger, more resilient and more effective in the long run. When I asked a founder of one British Muslim charity what the effects of ongoing CTF measures will have on the sector, he replied that 'diamonds are made from that pressure' insinuating that while the burden is intense and often uncomfortable, the consequences will be a tougher and more resilient sector capable of efficient and worthy humanitarian endeavours.

Measuring and establishing cause and effect is incredibly difficult and the wide range of variables factoring into where, how and why donors support specific causes and charities ensures that cause and effect cannot be fully established. Therefore, while consequences of CTF legislation may be felt, and perceived, by many within the charitable sector, it cannot be determined that CTF legislation is deliberately focusing on Muslim actors and charities. However, combined with the media, rises in Islamophobia and the general global environment following 9/11 and the War on Terror (WoT), it seems plausible and likely that at least some of the negative consequences of counter-terror legislation are more real than imagined.

Muslim charities are themselves aware of the difficulty of quantifying the negative effects of CTF measures and public allegations connecting them to extremism and political violence. One charity spokesman, who agreed to be interviewed on the conditions of strict anonymity, stated,

> We have been on the end of things. We have suffered. Financially it has impacted but it is difficult to quantify . . . we can't quantify it, that is the problem . . . it has definitely impacted on the relationship with some donors, with some people, but the converse side is that actually it makes us stronger because it makes us more defiant. We are determined to carry on doing what we are doing and doing it even better if possible.

Like the participant who used the analogy of requiring pressure to create a diamond, the above interviewee also perceived that in the long run the demands and coercions associated with CTF measures will make the Muslim charitable sector stronger and more resilient.

It is certainly true that the charitable and voluntary sectors as a whole (secular and faith-based) have seen rising challenges and costs associated with banking de-risking policies with the added burdens of the global CTF system (Metcalfe-Hough, 2015: 4). The occasionally opaque procedures combined with the unequal application of measures by 'petty-sovereigns' have ensured that accountability and transparency are undermined creating another difficulty in establishing cause and effect. What is certain is that the ever-evolving mix of CTF measures by a range of actors in differing sectors has created the potential environment in which 'counter terrorism laws are inherently vulnerable to mistake and abuse and charities run the risk of irreversible harm on the basis of unsubstantiated evidence without even basic due process protections' (ACLU, 2009).

None of this research is intended to argue that it is only the Muslim charitable sector that is negatively influenced by the global CTF system nor does it insinuate that all Muslim charities are equally affected. As one Muslim charity employee remarked, 'it's not really affected us. I've just personally noticed a lot more investigations into Muslim charities. I think there's been a bit more reporting which is why.'

Muslim charity as a consequence of the post-9/11 British context

As explored in the previous chapters, Muslim charities have arisen in the UK since the 1980s. Over the last two decades, Muslim charities of different sizes, forms and focus have mushroomed within the UK alongside Muslim charitable donations. This blooming of charitable activity can be explained by a number of factors which include the development of neoliberalism that encourages the private sector to fill the void from state withdrawal from welfare and social provisions (Yasmin and Ghafran, 2019: 2), the rise in wealth gap both within and between states, economic crisis stemming from the 2008 economic crash and over a decade of British austerity measures and a renewed consciousness of the Islamic faith and the role of charity within it.

As the last chapter demonstrated, British Muslim demographics are young with over 50 per cent under the age of twenty-four years old (Mustafa, 2015: 4). The Muslim charitable sector in the UK reflects the youth of the demographics with charity employees, volunteers and board trustee's being younger than their secular equivalents. Consequently, many of the individuals involved in the Muslim charity sector, either as full-time paid employees or volunteers, have grown up and experienced their formative years within the context of post-9/11, the securitization of Islam broadly and rises in Islamophobia. Early socialization within this British context inevitably shapes an individual's sense of identity and belonging. Mustafa's research on British Muslims also suggests that the post-9/11 environment has helped shaped British Muslim identity, as she argues that 'perceived alienation from being "British" . . . is pushing them further toward the only group identity they are familiar and comfortable with – their religious one' (2015: 1). It is posited that one repercussion of the post-9/11 environment has been a move away from inherited nominal, 'Muslimness' towards a search for the meaning of Islam for individual practitioners who are self-aware, critical and reflective of what it means to be 'Muslim' within the British context. As one participant explained,

> Starting from the 1990s, especially post 9/11, a lot of people had a spiritual awakening. 9/11 has forced a lot of Muslims to seek their identity or seek who they are and what their place is. There's been a schizophrenic relationship: Are we British? Are we Muslim? Or am I both Muslim *and* proud to be British? These debates have happened, and a lot of the young people have started to become more practising . . . . The 60s and 70s had the first generation come over who were just trying to get their children to go to school and they had a lot of issues trying to adjust, but the generation after are accustomed to their surroundings and their environment. That has a lot to do with why there are a lot of young people involved in the charity sector.

It must be stated that despite this monograph using the concept 'British Muslim', there are tensions in this term which not all those ascribed to this category would self-affirm to. This was highlighted eloquently by one research participant from a leading Muslim charity who argued,

> there is no such thing as a British Muslim. Muslim is a matter of religious identity; it is saying my faith is Islam. Being British means 'I've got a British passport', I may not have been born in Britain, but it is a geographical identifier . . . wherever in the world I go, I am a Muslim. I am not Muslim because of my geographical or national background. We should actually be strong and say we are Muslims when it comes to religion, when it is discussions about religion and, if it is a discussion about identity like, Brexit and leaving the EU, then talk about yourselves as being British. I think eventually people will, but if they can drop this label of British Muslim and be really strong and say we are British and we are equal to the non-Muslim white guy, white woman, black guy, black woman or whatever and under the laws of this country and socially we are your equals and we should be treated as equals and that is how we can actually progress to a better society . . . . A lot of people see themselves as British Muslims and my argument is that the more you do that the more you will actually be seen as being different and you will be treated differently. And because of the way this country still is, you will be seen negatively because of everything that is going on at the moment. It was the Irish, then the blacks now it is your [Muslims] turn.

With Islam hitting the limelight after 9/11, many Muslims globally, but particularly within minority settings, have been forced to contemplate the meaning of their faith. In searching for the meaning of Islam, many Muslims have reconnected with the central five pillars of which obligatory charity is one. This assists in explaining the rise of the Muslim charitable sector in recent years and the youth of its practitioners, experts and volunteers. The proliferation of interest in the voluntary and charitable sectors should be read as a positive outcome of the post-9/11 environment. As another interviewee working within the sector commented, the effects are not always encouraging.

> The response to 9/11 has at times gone really wrong – perhaps to the opposite extreme. Some have said 'I'll push Islam as far away as possible, integrate and try to be like everyone else.' When it has gone *really* wrong is when people have blown things up or have attempted to do so. And then you have people in between who have said, 'I need to study the religion a little more and understand what it is about.' And I think that identity as a Muslim has come up and I think the majority of the population will say that they are not two polar opposites being British and Muslim, we can be both. Most of us say, we are sick and tired of being asked: 'Are you British first or Muslims first?.' I am both and they go side by side.

The above interview extract coincides with the research findings on British Muslims by Mustafa who argues that 'despite . . . identifying as being British, the majority of respondents feel under pressure to justify this identity, even though they know no other national . . . culture' (2015: 184). In contemplating and defending their faith, in addition to their Britishness, many Muslims (in Britain as elsewhere) began the process of distinguishing their own practice and values from those espoused by violent movements such as al-Qaeda and Daesh. One charity worker exclaimed,

> After 9/11, those times did educate and tell people about Islam . . . . It [events of 9/11] did not show Islam at all, that was not Islam. . . . What it did do, the positives . . . it gave Muslims who were just letting life roll by, it gave them a wakeup call to educate ourselves. We are not like these people [the 9/11 perpetrators] who do violent attacks.

With renewed consciousness of the tenets and practices of faith, the performative aspect of charitable giving in facilitating the creation of a pious and civic individual becomes augmented. The performative aspect of Muslim charitable giving was hinted at through the below interview extract:

> I think there has been a bit of a revolution in terms of Muslims discovering their faith and learning what it is to be a Muslim. But non-Muslims are also discovering Islam . . . . People discover Islam through giving . . . giving takes a certain courage and belief . . . by thinking about it and doing it, it kind of resurfaces the individual.

Muslimness is therefore not created simply by declaring oneself a Muslim but by 'thinking about it and doing it'. This aspect of an individual's identity can therefore be argued to be 'constructed by the very expressions that are said to be [their] results' (Butler cited Fortier, 1999: 43). The interview extract above also coincides with Mahmood's position which argues that 'for many pious Muslims, these embodied practices and virtues provide the substrate through which one comes to acquire a devoted and pious disposition' (Mahmood, 2013: 72).

Attempts of Muslims within the UK to showcase the positives of the Islamic faith through charitable practices are undermined by policy and media rhetoric which intertwines Muslim charitable giving with terror and counter-terror discourse. This potentially destabilizes the counter-narratives to violent Islamist ideology that pious charitable practice provides. A senior employee of a Muslim charitable organization commented,

> Muslim charities are doing a lot of great work and they help to provide an alternative understanding of what, and who, Muslims are in the wider world . . . . It is a powerful community building integration opportunity to showcase what Muslim charities do for their local community and for the wider communities around the world. It provides a counter-narrative to the IS [Daesh] narrative.

Despite the humanitarian aims of Muslim charitable giving and the potentially powerful counter-narrative to violent Islamist movements such as al-Qaeda or Daesh (ISIS), Muslim charitable organizations and practising individuals have felt that the Muslim charitable sector has been disproportionately targeted. This perception was voiced by many within the sector, especially those in hierarchically important positions such as trustees, CEOs and others who are potentially in the firing line of CTF measures. The following transcript is a typical representation of the kinds of sentiments expressed by individuals and organizations interviewed:

> The Muslim sector, following September 2001, has really been a victim, been a target because of the names not because of what they do. We have many colleagues and members whose funding, especially transfers through banking systems, when the name 'Islamic' comes the lights start flashing. Even big organisations . . . . The Muslim charity sector has been receiving a lot of this . . . I don't know what to call it? . . . really a campaign which is unfair and unjust which is disabling charities making them less effective when it really should be supportive through official organisations. They should have their flexibility and freedom to work so long as they are known. So, we don't really drive giving underground we want everything on the table and in view. These kinds of measures they are making people who give think that big organisations can't really send their donations or reach those in need, so they find another way.

Muslim charities are potential partners in the so-called WoT, not its adversaries. Pious practices such as charitable giving hold bridging potential between, and within, communities that can assist in social cohesion in addition to alleviating hardships associated with poverty and economic insecurity. Current CTF policies as practised within the UK are undermining the positive capability of Muslim individual actions. Moreover, CTF practices are potentially counterproductive by undermining counter-narratives to violent extremism. As one participant expressed, 'a lot of people were saying that there are two different laws here. They are saying "look, we have tried democracy, we've given it a chance but there are double standards between Muslim and white non-Muslims". It's why you have people going to the other extreme.'

Consequence of CTF measures for charities

Charities and NGOs have as yet been unable to quantify the consequences of CTF measures for end-users for a variety of reasons. First, as this chapter briefly mentioned, scientifically proving cause and effect is extremely difficult with numerous variables. Second, charities and NGOs lack the time, skills and resources to investigate the detrimental outcomes of CTF measures for their intended beneficiaries. Consequently, further research into the effects of CTF measures on end receivers, particularly those overseas, is warranted. However, three broad negative repercussions were perceived by the majority of research participants which were decreased accountability, challenges in finance and banking, and reputational risk to individual charities and the third sector as a whole.

Decreased accountability

One of the most frequently raised and commented upon consequences of current CTF measures from the charitable and third sector is that rather than increasing accountability and transparency, CTF policy is having the perverse and undesirable effect of making monies more difficult to trace (Benthall, 2007: 7). The charity sector, under increased scrutiny by watchdog organizations such as the FATF, national regulators such as the Charity Commission and bank compliance officers, has faced numerous difficulties in receiving and transferring funds from donors to end recipients, with many facing varying degrees of financial exclusion through banking de-risking policies. As such, Aziz has argued that 'the attack on Islamic charities since 9/11 has had the unintended consequence of driving money underground where regulators have no control over it' (Aziz, 2011).

Several individuals who participated in this research noted the danger of funds being driven 'underground' or donors having to find alternative distribution mechanisms. Typical expressions can be demonstrated through the following transcript extract:

> The concern is that donations and distribution are going underground but to confirm this you really need proof. If people can't work through the recognised, registered and official organisations they will have to find another way. This is not a sinister connotation, but people feel there is an obligation to help. This is the basic difference between the Muslim giving and the non-Muslim giving. Muslim giving is based on their belief, *zakat* is an obligation. Generally, when you look at other religions, you are encouraged to do good and give but with us as Muslims it is a *must*.

Similarly, another participant working within the sector stated that 'the money has not stopped going out, but the accountability has disappeared. Now you don't know anything.'

Not only is this profusely against the intended aims of CTF policy, it also highlights the illogical application of anti-money laundering (AML) logic. The high-profile cases in the United States which successfully utilized AML techniques to secure criminal prosecutions for high-level drug traffickers succeeded precisely because bank accounts were left open and fully operable allowing monitoring to take place. Disrupting banking procedures, financial transfers and closing accounts ensures that individuals are highly aware of what monitoring takes place. This fact alone severely diminishes the effectiveness of monitoring back accounts for irregularities as it becomes increasingly unlikely that would-be terrorists would utilize a system that is so knowingly monitored and surveyed. Additionally, when bank accounts are frozen, denied or closed there is nothing left for policy makers and petty-sovereigns to monitor and survey at all, contravening the logic of AML initiatives. As one interviewee expressed, 'five years after 9/11 I had to produce reams of evidence to get a mortgage. It is getting harder for people, not terrorists.'

Banking de-risking

By far the greatest challenge to the charitable sector as a consequence of CTF measures have been banking procedures and de-risking strategies. Banks adopted the 'de-risking' strategy as a combined result of global CTF measures and the 2008 financial crash. One of the special recommendations listed by FATF includes the requirement of financial and banking employees to report Suspicious Financial Transactions when there are 'reasonable grounds' to suspect money laundering of terror financing (Iofolla, 2018: 82). According to Iofolla, 'reasonable grounds' is applied widely by the sector (2018: 82) thus inferring an open interpretation. In this respect, bank employees act as petty-sovereigns, tasked with monitoring and reporting 'suspicious' (deviant) behaviour with little or no accountability themselves. These monitoring activities are 'undertaken by the private sector on behalf of the state' (Iofolla, 2018: 84). As Iofolla argues, 'risk indicators are not used in a vacuum: they are deeply social, and their use intertwines with personal attitudes' (2018: 84). In an era of rising Islamophobia and negative media reporting of Muslims and Muslim charities, it is possible, and likely, that the wider societal context impacts upon bank employees' use of reporting mechanisms. Drawing again from Iofolla, 'determinations of money laundering or terrorism financing are highly contextual and individualised . . . and largely informed by the impressions of the individual(s) conducting the transaction' (2018: 86). The actions and decisions of banking petty-sovereigns are powerful, yet open to wide interpretation and potentially inconsistent with little transparency regarding decision-making. The lack of accountability and transparency has been raised by Levi who argues that 'once categorised, it can be difficult, even impossible for a customer to show that they should be seen as a lower risk, as it is difficult to establish a clear criteria for how this might be done' (2018: 278).

The greatest risk for charities is in banking and financial transfers to territories categorized as 'high risk' such as Somalia, Sudan, Syria, Palestine and Iraq (Metcalfe-Hough, 2015: 7). These are also the geographies of some of the worst human suffering related to conflict, natural disaster and poverty. Delays and denials of funds to these end recipients are potentially a matter of life and death, and thus financial challenges pose a form of violence on the end recipients. As Metcalfe-Hough argues, the UK government has 'a strategic interest in maintaining an effective charitable sector, particularly in relation to overseas aid' (2015: 26). Levi has argued that this strategic interest is potentially undermined by current CTF practices and banking de-risking policies positing that 'there is also a risk of counter-productive regulation by reducing the transparency of financial flows and, to the extent that the policies have the effect of . . . generating greater hostility towards the West' (2018: 274). The counterproductive aspects of current CTF policies and practices 'are damaging Western reputations in Muslim majority states by giving an appearance of a "war on Islam"' (ACLU, 2009: 16). Rather than increasing security, current CTF measures potentially decrease security 'because intensified impoverishment can provide a breeding ground for radicalism and hatred' (De Goede, 2012b: 127). Potentially, therefore, de-risking strategies financially exclude, deny funds to end receivers, increase instability by forcing charitable and financial transactions away from mainstream sectors and increase anti-Western sentiment overseas. The potential decreased security for some is unlikely to be a crude pay-off for increased security for others as Warde has reasoned 'the exponential growth of Suspicious Activities Reports (SARs) has done little to detect crime, and there is no evidence that a single act of terror had been prevented thanks to such reports' (Warde, 2007: 171).

In practice, de-risking policies have slowed financial transactions and frozen, denied and closed bank accounts to reduce a bank's risk (CFG, 2018:1). The negative impact of de-risking strategies by banks on the charitable sector was recognized by the government in 2016, following an inquiry conducted by the Financial Conduct Authority (CFG, 2018: 1). Banks' risk appetites have been reduced, not only as a consequence of the 2008 financial crash but also as a direct consequence of CTF measures that leave banks highly vulnerable to financial and legal sanctions for non-compliance (CFG, 2018: 2). To give evidence of the scale of the problem for charities, a report conducted by the Charity Finance Group published in 2018 found that 32 per cent of charities had financial transfer delays by their own banks (41 per cent faced transfer delays as a result of a correspondents bank), 27 per cent had transfers denied by their own banks, 18 per cent had faced bank account closures, 8 per cent had donations blocked, 8 per cent had funds frozen and 6 per cent were denied bank accounts all together (CFG, 2018: 11). The CFG found that 'overall 79% of respondents had some kind of problem accessing or using mainstream banking channels' (CFG, 2018: 11). Corresponding with the feelings of participants for this research, the CFG argued that problems occurring through mainstream banking 'actually makes charities riskier as they lack access to safer channels for transferring and monitoring funds' (CFG, 2018: 11). All the individuals and institutions interviewed for this research had either directly faced banking difficulties or personally knew someone who had. A typical expression of the difficulties faced can be summarized by the below participant working for a charity registered in England.

> The primary challenges of counter-terror legislation is with banking which is borderline harassment. . . . It is important that there are hoops to jump through but I do feel it is getting a little too much. Rather than being helpful and working to fix the problem there is scaremongering. It is also not fairly based . . . . Ultimately, banking is your life and blood.

The extract again reveals that Muslim charities are not against regulation and procedures illustrated by the words 'it is important that there are hoops to jump through', but the regulations and procedures must be perceived to be warranted, proportionate and just, which is not how procedures are currently viewed, certainly by those who participated in this research. However, perhaps more revealing is the interviewee's comment that 'banking is your life and blood'. Following this analogy, disruptions, freezes and closures of banking procedures would be like freezing or cutting off 'your life and blood'. Therefore, excluding, or threatening to exclude, an individual or organization from formal banking procedures is perceived as a violence, both economically and socially, as it cuts the 'life and blood' from a charity and its intended beneficiaries who are denied the aid/assistance collected to ease sufferings and hardships.

Even if charities and individuals succeed in securing and maintaining an operable bank account this is not achieved without substantial costs. Time, resources and manpower are required to ensure compliance with increased banking procedures and regulations which some charities, especially the smaller ones (in terms of financial resources and manpower), may lack. It may be that irregularities in documentation have nothing to do with terrorism, political violence or extremism, but simply the increased volume of regulation is difficult for some resource bare institutions to carry. As one interviewee explained,

> There is a point where I should be using my time and resources to help the charity but I'm putting my resources into things to simply stop my bank account from being frozen… a lot of people in the humanitarian/volunteer sector don't have the resources. They are not barristers, trained politicians, or financial experts. These are people that just want to do their bit. They are trying to help but are not necessarily experts.

Similarly, an employee from a Muslim charity which had received negative press coverage associated with 'extremism' commented,

> it's difficult for Muslim charities because they want to focus on humanitarian work that we're doing, but we're spending a lot of time responding to these legislations and these accusations based on assumptions that haven't been evidenced. And we're having to respond to that.

The tension between willingness to comply with procedures on the one hand and scepticism of the reasons for increased surveillance on the other was captured by one of my interviewees who stated,

> From the banks we have had regular questions bordering on harassment with no reasons given. And what are they going to do with the answers I give them anyway? And, you don't want to give them the 'wrong' answer because they could close your account.

Several aspects can be deduced from the brief statement above. First, the banks can continuously ask questions and for further documentation without explanation to the client. The increased duty of due diligence on behalf of individuals and charitable organizations stands at sharp contrast to the lack of accountability and explanation required by banks and banking personnel. Poignantly, the interviewee notes, 'what are they going to do with the answers I give them anyway?' indicating at best a scepticism regarding the privacy of information given and the intention of which it is being (or going to be) utilized. This is pertinent as banks often ask charities for information on third persons such as donors, partnering organizations and affiliated networks, often requiring names, addresses, dates of birth and occasionally passports and birth certificates. Despite the discomfort of having to provide banks and financial institutions with such personal and valuable details, charities are forced to comply as providing the 'wrong' answer could result in account closures and expulsion from mainstream financial sectors.

Closures of bank accounts and threats of closure have significant impact on charities and their reputations in the eyes of the donating public. One employee from a Muslim charity who had faced bank account closure commented,

> they're allowed to just do that; they're allowed to close multimillion-pound charity bank accounts who have donors who are regular monthly givers . . . . And they [charities] have to now go through this whole process of getting every single one of

their donors to change their direct debits. . . . the fallout of the charities, and, in terms of losing donors, has a real implication on charity, and then the charity has to contact them [donors] and say that's something has happened. This raises concerns from the donors, they turn out thinking, 'you know, surely big institutions like banks must know what they're talking about, therefore if they've got concerns then we should be concerned as the donors.' So, then there's a reputation risk, as well. . . . one of the other problems is transfers of funds. If you've got a programme, let's say it's in Sudan, for example, and Sudan . . . it's classed as one of those countries where, you know, there's high alert for banks and on their radars and so on, even if the legitimate charity is working for 20 years or 10 years, or however more . . . . You might have to wait many weeks before that payment or that transfer is approved by the banks.

Scepticism of the 'real' reasons for increased monitoring and finance was recognized by a select few of the research participants who inferred that the 'real' reason behind CTF measures was increased government control. One participant commented,

It all boils down to where the finances are – who has it and where is it . . . . No one carries an ID card, but you don't need an ID card now. The government control all the mechanisms – that power, that data, the knowledge of where the money is – there is no getting away.

Current CTF measures are unlikely to prevent or stop violent political activity as argued in Chapter 2, given recent terrorist attacks across Europe have been low cost and did not involve any Muslim charity or Islamic financial organization. However, policies derived from the global CTF system have increased the surveillance mechanisms and powers of the government and associated institutions ensuring that while the purported aim of policy may fail (preventing further terror attacks) the 'side effects' (Ferguson, 1994) of increased government control are realized.

The levels of scrutiny, accountability, transparency and documentation increasingly required by charities are in stark contrast to the opaque and non-accountable decision-making by banking and financial petty-sovereigns. This was expressed by a Muslim charity employee based in London who had frequent difficulties with banking procedures who stated that after closing an account, banks are

giving no further response and you couldn't even inquire. How is that an adequate response from a bank? It should be much more, especially if they ask us for detailed due diligence evidence. Including right down to the name of the person who will be reached, then staff members and offices, and field offices, and all sorts, and their passports . . . . Whatever you can get, you give, and yet their response is so small and a one-line response at that . . . . It's beyond us how's that even possible.

Reputational risk

Another important consequence for the Muslim charitable sector, as well as individual actors, is the reputational risk of association with terrorism, charitable misuse and extremism. In one sense this coincides with the charity regulators who have stated that one of the greatest risks of terrorism to the charity sector is that of trust and confidence in the sector (Charity Commission, 2017). The added burden on Muslim charities is that the association with terror and extremism increases perceptions of Islam and terrorism broadly undermining the efforts and positive goals of the subsector. The threat does not have to be real to be effective but simply perceived, as charity relies fundamentally on donor trust. This sentiment was expressed succinctly by a participant within the Muslim charitable sector who commented,

> there's a reputational risk. The first risk to any charity is their reputation and maintaining the reputation in the eyes of others. Perception is reality. The actual *real* risk is getting your bank account frozen.

Reputations are damaged most severely by negative media coverage which catches the donating public's attention. One Muslim charity that agreed to interview on conditions of anonymity which had been on the receiving end of false media allegations said in interview,

> that impacted on us because it's all over the news and we get phone calls from donors saying: 'You're giving money to extremists'? We say 'no we're not. We're not giving money to any extremists. We're not terrorists, we're not.'

In an effort to maintain reputations and mitigate allegations of criminal and terrorist misuse of funds, Muslim charities are increasingly ensuring their procedures, record keeping, accountability and risk analysis are within the frames of CTF legislation and by default are within the rules and mechanisms of neoliberal rationales.

Neoliberalism and the rise of faith-based organizations

Faith-based organizations (FBOs) broadly have gained increased attention in social science scholarship as they are significant in a range of areas such as development, conflict resolution, migration and social welfare (Wilson, 2014). These positive roles and influences are currently being undermined by associating charities and NGOs with 'vulnerability' to terrorist and criminal abuse. As well as damaging public trust in charities, voluntary services and NGOs, the current CTF assemblage is also hampering the work of charitable organizations by raising costs, increasing demands on time and resources, delaying and occasionally denying international money transfers, and more, all at the final cost of the end receivers who are by default the genuine vulnerable who are not being protected.

With the exception of the unprecedented re-emergence of the state in economic spheres during the global Covid-19 health pandemic, the British state has generally followed neoliberal economic rationales since the mid-1970s. Neoliberal economic frameworks seek the withdrawal of the state from all but key aspects of the economy and charged the private sector to rise to fill the gap (Yasmin and Ghafran, 2019: 2). As Lynch has observed, 'governmentality highlights how contemporary governance mechanisms interpellated by states and international organisations facilitate and even require the expansion of NGOs into issues previously assumed to be the responsibility of government' (2011: 213). The unintended consequence of state withdrawal from welfare and social provisions was that FBOs (as well as secular) rose to meet the challenge. FBOs are not just religious and social entities they can be highly political, engaging actively in campaigning and advocacy work endeavouring to promote an alternative political and ethical paradigm through which politics can be developed and implemented (Wilson, 2014: 222). Active challenges to state policies may be exemplified by the rise of charities that disperse funds solely within the UK to meet the challenges of widening economic cleavages within the UK itself. As Wilson notes, it is not only through violent extremism that groups (religious and secular) can undermine the authority, rationality and sources of power embedded within nation-state and the state system. Most work within the legal system and aim for peaceful change via established political avenues (Wilson, 2014: 224). Consequently, charities (secular and faith-based) are refocusing their governance, internal mechanisms and risk analysis to coincide with CTF measures, increased scrutiny and regulation from charity regulatory bodies and the push towards documentation and data collection in line with mainstream neoliberal economic values and rationales.

For some, this has diluted the alternative potential offered by FBOs and religious economics generally, with Elshurafa claiming that this forces Islamic economic alternatives to develop 'into essentially a Western-based economic system' (2012: 339). Others have reasoned that although the coercion towards neoliberal and Western paradigms is evident, this does not entirely invalidate alternative systems as Nasr writes that 'even a lip-service to Islamic economics is a move away from excessive growth-orientated disequilibria, towards socially-conscious economic change' (1989: 525). Equally Gardner has argued that 'in analysing the relationship between moralities of giving, the politics of suffering to which they adhere, and economic change we thus cannot assume a straightforward, Weberian transition into rational or utilitarian systems' (2016).

To re-emphasize, British Muslims are not a homogenous whole in terms of religious interpretation, practice, levels of piety or any other aspect. Obviously, therefore, the range of political and economic persuasions is as wide and varied as other segments of British society. This monograph certainly does not wish to argue that *all* Muslims are critical of neoliberal economics or that they all favour increased 'Islamization' of economic and financial systems. Opinions and arguments are varied with many Muslims adhering to neoliberal rationales, while others seek to critique, reform or revise the dominant economic system (May, 2019b).

De Goede reasons that within the global CTF system 'the core assimilation model, then, is the drive to *formalize the informal*' (2012b: 107). It is this drive, within the UK context and beyond, that has seen a deliberate attempt to 'neo-liberalize' Muslim charitable giving with increased bureaucracy, regulation and transparency in line with Mahmood's argument that states have endorsed policies which seek to regulate 'Islamic principles to ensure that they take a particular form' (2005: 74). What Atia calls the 'melding' of piety and neoliberalism in Egypt (2012), when transcribed to the context of the UK, is less of a natural 'melding' and more of an enforced set of criteria which charities have had to accept in order to operate successfully in the UK environment. This is despite a report published by the CFG stating 'the perception that charities are "unregulated" or "less regulated" than the private sector is a myth' (CFG, 2018: 4).

Muslim charities response: Rationalizing Muslim charities

The WoT and ever-evolving global CTF measures are increasingly influencing and shaping the discourse of charities and NGOs, especially 'Muslim humanitarian NGO activists who seek validation and funding from Western donors' (Lynch, 2011: 205). In order to function effectively in a global, as well as domestic, environment charities (of all types and denominations) must adhere to neoliberal frameworks in order to access mainstream financial services and in attempt to avoid allegations of 'extremism' or 'radicalism'. On the surface at least, this diminishes the alternative frameworks potentially inherent in some charitable institutions and organizations. As Lynch argues, 'liberal market economic practices also condition how religious actors conceptualise their work, as well as which issues, they prioritise' (2011: 205). What is behind much of the assumptions of CTF measures is that non-mainstream financial flows are vulnerable resulting in Western, neoliberal frames acting as the 'norm' and the standard to which all else is evaluated. De Goede has argued, for instance, that 'the suspicion cast on Muslim practices of aid and charity through the securitisation of zakat simultaneously stabilises Western networks of aid as the cultural standard against which money flows are to be judged' (De Goede, 2012b: 131–2).

From 9/11 onwards, charities and organizations have been undergoing an extensive bureaucratization process to increase transparency, accountability and donor and state trust. As Chapter 1 stated, a hidden aspect of current CTF measures is to distinguish between 'normal' and 'deviant' behaviour. As was argued, what is considered 'normal' is largely derived from how the majority of any given population act, behave and what values they hold. 'Deviant' ('radical'/'extreme') is understood as anything that is not 'normal' but often falling short of criminality or illegality. As such, alternative or seemingly 'abnormal' financial practices, mechanisms and institutions are monitored and coerced to comply to 'normal' behaviours or risk the label of 'extremist' or 'radical'. Consequently, charities are coerced and pressurized to conform to dominant neoliberal values and performance measures. As Lynch has put forward,

> According to the governmentality paradigm, however such influence by NGOs does not translate into independence for civil-society actors, who must constantly demonstrate their worthiness to assume the functions previously allocated to the state, by carrying out their tasks in accordance with the appropriate (or approved) model of action. Approved models of action include results-orientated market discourses that value and prioritise accountability, efficiency, and sustainability. States, international organisations, and NGOs, including FBOs, reproduce these discourses through their programming, marketing techniques and annual reports. (2011: 214)

Muslim charities were fully conscious of the push for bureaucratization, documentation, reporting and rationalization within the sector, which has proven to be especially significant for the Muslim sector.

> Authorities and regulatory bodies increasingly emphasise documentation, transparency, and the creation of a paper trail as the basis on which trustworthiness and neutrality can be attested by aid organisations. The levels of scrutiny and record keeping demanded under the new guidelines of the Charity Commission are, according to interviewees from one faith-based Islamic charity, 'very extensive to the point of being unrealistic'. (De Goede, 2012b: 151)

Yasmin and Ghafran have argued that Muslim NGOs have become 'exposed' organizations to such an extent that 'fulfilling their formal reporting obligations no longer serves to remove suspicion and secure their legitimacy' (2019: 2). One charity employee interviewed feared that if compliance was not transparent to the penny, that 'they will find any reason to close us down' but was equally aware that bad practice within the sector was unhelpful, required a proactive response and damaged the reputation of Muslim charities as a whole. The interviewee commented,

> We know that some have said that they will go after specifically Islamic charities and look to the penny where that money is being utilised. We are very aware of that – they will find any reason to close us down, so we have to be very transparent. There is another issue to it as well. A lot of Muslim charities, the majority of them, have never submitted their reports on time. So, if you go on the Charity Commission website you will see 'delayed by 30 days'; 'delayed by 60 days' and that causes a problem. If you are not working to target, if you are never on time and there are discrepancies . . . these two-fold issues make it very difficult for Muslim charities.

As the interview extract reveals, Muslim charities are not against regulation and monitoring per se and wish to limit damaging practices by some charities that potentially harm the reputation of all within the sector. However, increased bureaucratization and rationalization do not necessarily lead to a 'disenchantment' as Weber envisaged (2001). Capitalism and neoliberalism do not hold the monopoly on concepts such as transparency and accountability. Chapter 3 took seriously the religious intent of Muslim charitable giving and particularly that of *zakat*. Charity in Islam is deemed a worship to God and a way to secure a good afterlife – to abuse this dimension of faith is thought to invoke Godly punishment and is no laughing matter. The seriousness of accepting the charge of an individual's religious donations and obligations was well understood by those working within the sector. Taking the religious injunctive to give seriously helps to understand the efforts Muslims make (at both an individual and institutional level) to ensure monies and charities are not abused and are accountable to their donors. It can therefore be considered that transparency and accountability are inherent in the practice of *zakat* from the start and thus the increased rationalization of the charity sector is not fundamentally oppositional to *zakat* and charitable practices.

For instance, a Muslim charity that has arisen within the UK over the last decade commented,

> We don't just do normal or emergency donations, we also do faith-based donations, so we look after people's *zakat*. It is extremely important that we care for that so that *zakat* is received as *zakat* and distributed as *zakat*. It is discussed in panels of imams and scholars to ensure we are *Sharia* compliant and so on and so forth. That's a responsibility on our shoulders and we have to make sure we execute this in the best possible way.

The same interviewee then reconciled the religious responsibility with modern mechanisms and neoliberal values in commenting that 'we pride ourselves on being up there and tech savvy, good visuals, good feedback, being transparent and that kind of relationship with our donors'.

Similarly, another UK-based Muslim charity employee stated,

> Donation money is taken really seriously. It is given to us as a trust and abuse of that trust, well, there are various verses in the Quran and Hadiths that say if you abuse that trust you will be in major sin. Ideally, every Muslim charity dealing with donations has to be very rigorous right down to the penny. It should be accountable to every penny so if someone asks how much you are spending on each project, we have to make that information available.

While FATF amended its special recommendations, withdrawing the statement that charities and NGOs are 'particularly vulnerable' (FATF, 2010) to terrorist abuse, the perception of vulnerability lingers and has resulted in a sustained and powerful push for increased documentation and neoliberal mechanisms in all financial transactions and institutions (Yasmin and Ghafran, 2019). To remain operable, charities (of all categorizations) have been forced to comply with increased bureaucratization, documentation and transparency. This is all within an environment in which the state itself is withdrawing from the same processes of accountability and transparency. As De Goede has observed, 'in sharp contrast to the call to complete accounting, transparency, and record keeping by charities ... governments themselves are increasingly willing to act on the basis of invisible and unaccountable grounds' (2012b: 175).

It can be argued that the call to normalizing financial procedures, mechanisms and transfers alongside mainstream financial and banking systems is a form of rationalization and bureaucratization as theorized by Weber (2001) and others preceding him with the potential result of a 'disenchantment' and movement away from religious ethos and values. However, as Rudnyckyi has claimed, 'both Weber and Foucault investigated rationalization, the reflexive application of knowledge to human practice to achieve optimal standards of efficiency and productivity' (Rudnyckyi, 2010: 12). Both focused on ethics and practices rather than 'ideas or mental states' (Rudnyckyi, 2010: 13). This is the opposite of what global and national CTF policies are doing. The global CTF system is not focused on increasing efficiency and productivity of charitable organizations and institutions but on their 'ideas and mental states'.

An exemplary example of the kinds of rationalizing and bureaucratizing moves that Muslim charities have made since 9/11 and the evolution of CTF system is the creation of the Muslim Charity Forum (MCF). The MCF was established in 2007 as an umbrella hub for small and emerging charitable organizations. The brainchild of Dr El-Banna, founder of Islamic Relief Worldwide, the MCF began as an effort to coordinate and provide guidance and regulation to new and evolving Muslim charities to militate against allegations and charges of financial wrongdoing. According to Itani in an interview in 2013, the MCF aimed to promote dialogue, negotiation and best practice among British Muslim NGOs and charities. Then employee of the MCF, Saif Ullah in 2013 stated that the MCF was an attempt to 'foster greater collaboration and greater accountability and transparency'. The MCF aims to provide training and advice for start-up agencies and identify areas of weakness in governance of charities, trusteeships and general practice to safeguard against problems arising further down the chain (Yasmin and Ghafran, 2019). In addition to obviously being a response to CTF initiatives and increased scrutiny of the sector in general, the MCF also recognizes the potential within the subsector of Muslim charities in trying to reduce duplications of work and sharing links and distributions. In this way, the increased bureaucratization, rationalization and documentation resonate with Weber's historical understanding of 'rationalization' as improving efficiency and productivity but does not involve a disenchantment per se.

Despite enormous efforts to comply with CTF guidance and provide efficiency and accountability, the MCF and associated charities have not avoided false allegations and negative media attention. The public allegations cast by MP Eric Pickles in 2014 discussed in Chapter 4, six days after the release of a *Telegraph* article (Turner, 2014), embroiled the MCF in investigations by the Charity Commission at the behest of the MCF itself in an effort to clear its name and comply fully with Charity Commission regulations. The *Daily Telegraph* was forced to offer a correction after restating links between the MCF and extremism acknowledging that 'The Forum has asked us to make clear that it is not extremist and abides by the principles of democracy and interfaith tolerance' (*The Daily Telegraph*, 2014). These allegations were restated in 2015 in another *Telegraph* article that focused largely on the charity Human Appeal, a member of the MCF (Gilligan, 2015). The Charity Commission found no evidence on the back of these media allegations that the MCF or associated charities had misused funds for terrorist use. This has lead Yasmin and Ghafran to assert that 'right-wing media' are 'influencing the accountability demands upon Muslim NGOs' (2019: 11). Rather than investigations of charities deriving from evidence, or the designated regulators, frequently charities are publicly accused by media representatives and journalists in their role as petty-sovereigns who are neither fully accountable nor required to have the same levels of evidence as compulsory by law courts or Charity Commission investigations.

Much of the work of the MCF and other like-minded organizations is related to due process, staff training, trusteeship, guidance and documentation. However, a large part of the rationalization and increased documentation of charitable and aid services is concerned with transparency for their own donors. Providing accountability and transparency for donors sits comfortably with both the neoliberal and Islamic frames of reference and thus the secular and religious rationales are mutually compatible. The need, or desire, to be accountable to donors assists in donors feeling comfortable that they have met their religious obligations as well as mitigating against allegations of charitable financial misuse. With wide negative media attention on the Muslim charitable sector, most charities are keen to mitigate any donor mistrust by increasing accountability. As one charity employee exclaimed in interview, 'I think from the donor's perspective they should know that their money is going to a worthy cause that we're not going to use it for anything particularly extravagant . . .: we've done all the checks and things like that and checked references.' The same charity employee stressed that 'we've always been quite strict on processes and procedures. We are generally strict that people follow best practice.' What is considered 'best practice' falls in line with regulations and financial organization associated with mainstream neoliberal paradigms.

Creating and maintaining 'best practice' seems an obvious path for charities to follow but as the following charity sector employee relates, this procedure is time consuming and involves levels of expertise that perhaps very small and voluntary-led charities find difficult to manage. Yasmin and Ghafran have argued that 'conventional accountability requirements hinder rather than advance the social change agenda' of charities and humanitarian organizations (2019: 3). One charity employee explained the processes of beginning their charitable organization in 2009 which from the outset spent considerable time and resources focusing on ensuring financial scrutiny, best practice, practical efficiency and transparency.

> Once we got a group of people together that were interested in working with us we then in a short period of time met and consulted with grant giving institutions, learnt best practices, how to streamline the process, how do we make sure the monies spent on what it was granted for in the first place – how to make sure it goes to those who genuinely need it. It was about a year to eighteen months just developing the process and doing research.

Despite ongoing efforts by many Muslim charities, large and small, to comply with increased regulation and documentation, Muslim charities have struggled to de-link the sector from association with 'terrorist' financing. This has led scholars such as Yasmin and Ghafran to conclude that 'Muslim NGOs, operating within the current socio-political discourse, which views their Islamic identity with suspicion', ensure that the 'normal routines of accountability no longer serve to satisfy or appease the regulator, or reassure the public' (2019: 11). Yasmin and Ghafran's observation pertinently link to one interviewee working for a Muslim charity who stated,

> we are asked a variety of different compliance questions, and having answered all those compliance questions, and even then, there's no guarantee that they will even accept it, no matter how much evidence you might give, if they wanted, they could just stop that payment.

Many Muslim charities and humanitarian organizations thus feel that no matter how compliant they are, and regardless of how much documentation and evidence is provided, they are unable to calm suspicions of charitable misuse.

Charity as 'shared values'

Yasmin and Ghafran's (2019) research on Muslim charities and NGOs argues that the Muslim charitable sector is undergoing alterations in response to CTF measures. They argue on the one hand that Muslim charities are complying tactically to increased accountability due to the external pressures of state and international policies (2019: 9) while on the other hand Muslim charities are also engaging in 'anticipatory accountability' (2019: 4). Anticipatory accountability 'refers to organisations proactively formulating standards in anticipation of changing legislation. It also refers to attempts made by organisations to shape these standards that may eventually be imposed' (Yasmin and Ghafran, 2019: 4). As 'anticipatory accountability' is concerned with future potential legislation and procedures, this too could be argued as 'speculative' as De Goede has termed the CTF system. Concurring with Yasmin and Ghafran's analysis, Muslim charities participating in this research were eager to demonstrate and engage with compliance and regulatory mechanisms, but were also keen to develop proactive stances to facilitate the management of external perceptions of the Muslim charitable sector (2019: 9). As 'anticipatory' measures, Muslim charities have been advancing inter-faith work, strengthening relations with the charitable sector as a whole and moving into 'advocacy-related areas' (Yasmin and Ghafran, 2019: 14).

One aspect of the anticipatory nature of Muslim charitable work is their eagerness to be viewed in line with other charitable organizations and institutions and to expand their donor base beyond Muslim communities. As one Muslim charity employee stated regarding his own charity,

> The inspiration is from Islamic visions and Islamic values. I think once these charities grow, they will start to encompass a larger section of the community ... like Cafod or Christian Aid or Islamic Relief. As the donors expand, probably the vision of the charity will expand as well.

A component of the advocacy-related areas that Muslim charities are moving towards is being a voice for the sector. Interview participants all felt that the Muslim charitable sector was ignored, or side-stepped, by politicians and policy makers rendering them voiceless and their concerns and fears unheard. An employee from a Muslim charitable institution stated,

> We want to enable Muslim charities to have a voice on the various platforms ... not for the sake of it but because they have a meaningful role to play. For example, Muslim charities tend to be some of the first responders in crises that happen overseas ... they have key learning experiences that can be shared with the wider sector but that sharing has to happen by claiming we have a legitimate role to play and an opinion to give in the wider sector. If we don't get recognised, we are at the receiving end of wisdom ... we are not part of the conversations when they happen.

The transcript extract relates to Yasmin and Ghafran's concept of anticipatory accountability in that 'it refers to attempts made by organisations to shape the standards that may eventually be imposed' (2019: 4). The interviewee argued that Muslim charities 'have key learning experiences that can be shared with the wider sector' and thus are keen not to simply be end receivers of 'wisdom' but wish to proactively be involved in knowledge accumulation and dissemination.

Another aspect of Muslim charities is that many are negotiating a difficult path of attempting to be accepted by mainstream society and the charitable sector while still retaining their core Muslim donor base. In order to traverse this difficult terrain, Muslim charities are stressing the shared British values of charitable giving in line with CONTEST II's focus on 'British values'. A Muslim charity employee optimistically expressed that 'I think the next generation, people born in the UK, the question will not necessarily be about faith, but about "what is charity"? Even in the Islamic context – I don't help you because you're a Muslim, I help you because you are human.' This sentiment was echoed by a spokesperson for a Muslim charitable institution who commented that 'Muslim charities, like all other charities have set themselves up to respond to humanitarian need and the needs of all human beings across the world and that is what we need to remember. Our work is there to serve humanity.'

The humanitarian aspect of Muslim charity, and the shared charitable values across British faith communities, was expressed by a charity founder who articulated that 'I think maybe because I am old fashioned or have old fashioned Muslim values, or Christian/Judaic values, quite biblical, you know: work hard, graft, make sure you tidy up, make sure you welcome people, listen to your elders, be caring – all of those values'.

These anticipatory measures, in conjunction with tactical compliance, are resulting in a stronger and more robust Muslim charitable sector in the UK which is both Muslim and British. Many of the research participants were keen to demonstrate not only their Muslim credentials but also their ties to Britain. One charity founder expressed that 'we are able to influence and affect the lives of millions, if not several millions globally, all because we were willing to help people. Every charity takes its form and character from its board of trustees and ours are all British born and mostly Muslim.' There is therefore a conscious move within the British Muslim charitable sector to emphasize the shared 'British values' of charitable giving.

Summary

This chapter has demonstrated that there have been various negative repercussions on the charitable sector resulting from CTF measures and practices. It cannot, however, be determined that CTF measures *deliberately* target Muslim charities and organizations. Nonetheless, there is clear *perception* of targeting Muslim organizations and practitioners which affects the reputation and donor trust of charitable organizations. It is undeniable that increased scrutiny and regulation of the charitable sector as a whole has negatively impacted upon efficiency and increased costs to charities both financially and through other resources, such as time.

Nonetheless, charities and NGOs, like many other economic sectors, hold the possibility (albeit minimal) of abuse. None of the charitable institutions interviewed for this research believed that charities should not be regulated or held to account. In fact, most welcomed increased scrutiny and perceived a problem in the sector especially regarding charities not meeting financial publication deadlines, thus they accept some of the increased powers of the Charity Commission. What Muslim charities are specifically concerned about is the perception that Muslim charities in particular are being disproportionately affected and that the risk of funds being diverted to terrorist causes or groups is massively overdetermined. Charities, secular and faith-based, welcome regulation but resist increased politicization of charity and ties to 'terrorism' and encroaching CTF measures which are viewed as disproportionate, unwarranted and potentially counter-effective.

Perhaps surprisingly, Muslim charities have, on the whole, responded positively to changes in regulation and increased bureaucratization. Charities that had been investigated by the Charity Commission, and cleared of allegations of terrorist financing, ultimately felt that consultation with the Charity Commission improved organizational practice, due diligence and risk analysis (Yasmin and Ghafran, 2019: 10). As the title of this chapter suggests, it takes pressure to create a diamond. Muslim charities are, however, not only responding to the external pressures for increased accountability and documentation but are proactively seeking further improvements by 'anticipatory accountability' as Muslim charities increasingly emphasize the humanitarian nature of their work that crosses faith and non-faith communities, in addition to advocating 'shared British values'. The positivity of the sector, in spite of current CTF measures, is largely a tactical response to ensure their humanitarian and relief efforts remain operable and sustainable in the evolving global CTF system. The resilience of the Muslim charitable sector should not, however, distract from the various violences the CTF system evokes, whether that be financial exclusions for charitable practitioners and organizations, reputational damage or restrictions and delays for end receivers. The suffering, endurance and resilience of the sector can be summed up by the following transcript extract from a Muslim charity that had been faced with false and spurious allegations.

> We have suffered as an organisation. We have suffered because of the direct action and direct consequences of government and their authority and instruction. However, we are determined that that will not deter us from our work, and we will carry on. We are looking at the regulations under the Charity Commission, working on their legislation of this country and also the countries we deliver projects in. (Anonymous Muslim Charity, in interview with author, 2017)

Conclusion

Counter-terror or counterproductive?

Beginning immediately after 9/11 and augmented by the publication of *The 9/11 Commission Report*, states and policy makers have closely scrutinized Islamic charities and the obligation of *zakat* globally. The *Commission* report states that the 9/11 hijackers 'moved, stored, and spent their money in ordinary ways . . . . The origin of the funds remains unknown' (US government, 2004: 169). Yet this did not prevent the authors from speculating that 'Al Qaeda . . . took advantage of Islam's strong calls for charitable giving, *zakat* . . . . Charities were a source of money and also provided significant cover, which enabled operatives to travel undetected under the guise of working for a humanitarian organization' (US government, 2004: 170–1). Following 9/11, a number of financial measures were taken as a consequence of the above speculation including the closure of all the largest Muslim charities within the United States and the expansion of the Charity Commission's regulations in line with the UK's anti-terrorism policy strand of Prevent. This is despite the concluding remarks of *The 9/11 Commission Report* stating that 'to date, the U.S. government has not been able to determine the origin of the money used for the 9/11 attacks. Ultimately the question is of little practical significance' (US government, 2004: 172). However, the question has had widespread 'practical significance' globally as international humanitarian NGOs have been closed, had assets frozen, individuals arrested and charged (Keatinge, 2014; Aziz, 2011; Sidel, 2011; Warde, 2007) and, importantly, suspicion cast upon large swathes of Muslim communities attempting to fulfil their charitable and spiritual obligations (Delmare-Morgan, 2015).

While this research found no evidence to suggest that charities (Muslim or otherwise) were particularly vulnerable to terrorist or criminal abuse, this is not to suggest that abuses cannot occur. Of the small number of Muslim charities in the UK that have allegedly been involved with 'terrorist' entities and have been investigated, no evidence has been found that the charities have actively, or directly, engaged with any specific violent act. The allegations are most frequently associated with individual employee associations with other bodies and persons associated with 'extremism', not violence. Hence, the attention on trustees and their personal association with 'designated' individuals and or entities becomes the focus of investigation rather than direct links to violent actions or illegality.

None of this research has argued that charitable misuse is impossible but concurs with Benthall that 'the attack on Islamic charities since 9/11 . . . was an overreaction' (Benthall, 2007: 2). The Office of the Scottish Charity Regulator in interview stated they had no evidence or any concerns raised with them regarding terrorist financing. The Charity Commission for England and Wales (in email correspondence) referred to charitable misuses as 'rare' with the largest risk being the charities' reputation (Charity Commission, 2017). While rhetoric concerning counter-terror initiatives in the UK stress 'proportionality' in prevention and response to terrorist activities, the undocumented and unanalysed consequences of current initiatives counter such claims. Scant attention to the consequences of counter-terror legislation on charities renders invisible the societal and economic violences which outweigh the positive perceptions of prevention policies where the risk to the general public is more marginal than policy rhetoric would suggest.

This research has found several shortcomings of the current CTF system. These shortcomings include inappropriate and illogical assumptions within policies; increased instability for charitable practitioners, institutions and end recipients; and violence on individuals and users as reputations are damaged and social and financial exclusions endured.

Inappropriate and illogical assumptions within the CTF assemblage

As Chapter 2 detailed, the arguments for the inappropriateness and illogical assumptions of the current CTF system are multiple. Assumptions that terrorist financing and criminality operate on the same logic enabled the re-appropriation of anti-monetary laundering techniques into CTF measures. In truth, anti-money laundering (AML) and terrorist financing operate on reverse logic. The former begins with 'dirty' money and uses banking and financial services to 'clean' the money, while the latter is usually 'clean' to begin with only becoming 'dirty' with the act of terror itself (Warde, 2007: xxii). As the monies are 'clean' prior to the act of terror there is rarely anything for banks and financial petty-sovereigns to suspect. Moreover, with banking de-risking policies and 'know your customer' regulations the logic of AML is circumvented. Highly publicized convictions in the United States, resulting from AML techniques, were successful precisely because bank accounts were left open and operable allowing surveillance to take place. As current banking procedures associated with de-risking strategies often freeze, close or deny bank accounts, there is nothing left for governments, petty-sovereigns and others to monitor at all, and thus the entire raison d'être of the CTF system is undermined. What is particularly damning, and raises scepticism regarding the true intent of such policies, is that the ability to freeze criminal assets was ingrained in previous UK CT legislation but rarely utilized as it was understood that terror attacks do not necessarily require large sums of finance (De Goede, 2012b: 40). What is even more unflattering is that the CTF system has now been in place for almost two decades yet there does not appear to be any evidence that it has succeeded in preventing a single violent act from occurring. While the purported aim to stop, or prevent, terrorism has so far failed, it has not prevented creeping encroachment of surveillance and data mining of British citizens' everyday financial practices. As Iofolla has stated, 'private citizens may never know that their transactions ... have been subject to increased investigations and in many cases disclosed to government agencies' (2018: 101).

Extending existing legislation to CTF procedures adds additional challenges. In the United States, CTF legislation largely derives from previous AML legislation, while the United Kingdom has adapted pre-existing counter-terror acts originally designed to tackle instances of political violence as a result of the Troubles in Northern Ireland (Ryder, Thomas and Webb, 2018: 784). This reveals that CTF measures assume a connection between terrorism and criminality, and further assumes that all forms of political violence can be tackled with the same legislation despite differing motives, aims, ideologies and operational strategies (Keatinge, 2014: 40). To assume that criminality and terrorism are necessarily interlinked and both 'for profit' is an argumentative leap that is not supported by evidence in all cases of political violence. There is little indication that the terror attacks across Europe in the last decade have been 'for profit' or linked to organized crime. Importantly, the violent attacks that have occurred in the UK, as elsewhere, did not cost much (De Goede, 2012b: 40). There is little to suggest that any form of financial monitoring would have detected the attacks prior to the events themselves or that the freezing of financial assets would have prevented the attacks due to lack of finance. No large funds were accumulated, most cost considerably less than £300 (Neumann, 2017: 96) and none were connected to 'dirty' moneys. Most pertinent to this research is that none of the attacks that have occurred within the UK in recent decades can be connected to Islamic charities.

Proclaimed as the 'soft' power of the War on Terror, the CTF system claims that if an individual and institution have nothing to hide, there is nothing to fear. Yet, individuals and organizations have been embroiled in spurious allegations of terrorist financing that have no connection whatsoever to terrorism or criminal activity. Much of the surveillance of current CTF norms is focused upon establishing and identifying deviant economic behaviour as opposed to criminality. However, detecting deviant economic behaviour necessitates the ability to establish normalcy. What is, or is not, considered 'normal' is in fact entirely reliant on the beliefs, practices and values held by the majority of a population at any given time (Dudenhoefer, 2018: 159). 'Normalcy' is not a static entity and what it is, or is not, is constantly in flux, open to interpretation and dependent upon the categories in which it is compared. As Iofolla warns, 'it is imperative for understanding what kinds of transactions are unusual, and thus worthy of reporting' (2018: 87). As 'normal', in the UK context, is largely considered currently as that which fits into the secular neoliberal framework, Islamic charities become susceptible to being deemed radical or extreme (read also as 'deviant').

Government and non-government actors, including general citizens, are asked to engage with CTF procedures by raising Suspicious Activity Reports. Given that no single terrorist profile exists, and that 'normalcy' is essentially what the dominant group in a society value and practice, non-dominant behaviour becomes an act of suspicion itself, despite being well within the confines of legality. As De Goede has forcefully argued,

> there is no longer any meaningful relationship between the moment of criminalization and the act of violence. In other words, the abnormal transaction,

the 'inappropriate' political support and the suspect association themselves become cause for criminalisation or intervention regardless of their relationship to any (planned or potential) act of violence. (De Goede, 2012b: 192)

Following from De Goede's appropriation of Butler's concept, this work has understood the numerous individuals involved in CTF monitoring and compliance to be 'petty-sovereigns'. Non-accountable, petty-sovereigns are asked to identify and act on 'suspicious' or 'deviant' activity despite having no firm criteria to do so. This results in decision-making by petty-sovereigns being highly contextual, open to multiple interpretations 'and largely informed by the impressions of the individual(s) conducting the transaction' (Iofolla, 2018: 86). It was therefore posited that disproportionate numbers of allegations and investigations into Muslim charities were likely to be a result of the context of rising Islamophobia and public media allegations which feed into who, and what, petty-sovereigns deem suspicious and risky.

CTF, alongside other non-financial CT measures, assumes at its core 'vulnerability'. Charities, NGOs and humanitarian organizations, particularly those that work transnationally, have been deemed especially 'vulnerable' and thus in need of increased regulation, bureaucratization and surveillance. It is assumed that financial and economic practices that lay outside the secular neoliberal framework are vulnerable and susceptible to misuse. This monograph has argued that contrary to public opinion, the charitable sector is heavily regulated and monitored and thus not as 'vulnerable' as is often assumed. According to a recent Charity Finance Group report, 'the perception that charities are "unregulated" or "less regulated" than the private sector is a myth' (CFG, 2018: 4). The report continues by arguing 'unlike businesses, which are designed and regulated in order to generate profit, charities are *specifically designed to ensure that money goes to its intended destination*' (CFG, 2018: 7 emphasis in the original). *The 9/11 Commission Report*'s statement that the financial origin of violent acts is a question with 'little practical significance' demonstrates a misunderstanding (and/or neglect) of Muslim pious practice and the communities that regularly engage in acts of religiosity. It was therefore argued that incomplete and insufficient understanding of the sectors being embroiled into the CTF system has allowed for inaccuracies, errors and counterproductive practices.

The religion of Islam has been 'securitized' in that there is said to be a threat and the dominant national audience has accepted there is such a threat. Once securitization is successfully accepted by an audience this then allows for circumvention or breaks from established norms of law and conduct in the name of 'national security'. Breaks from 'normal' legal procedures are evidenced in policies which allow 'the freezing of assets even before conviction' (Warde, 2007: 25). As the legal burden of proof is reversed, the securitization of charity is complete as it breaks and circumvents 'normal' legal and political procedures. Successful securitization of the Muslim charitable sector makes critique of the current CTF system problematic. As the securitization rhetoric focuses on the protection against harm for the nation, breaches of law and rights for the few become tolerated to ensure the safety of the many. Thus, critique becomes associated with complicity with the threat or political naivety at best. By presenting financial and everyday securitization as both necessary and unavoidable, securitization of the mundane is portrayed as apolitical: simply a technical tool to map and scrutinize those with criminal intent but with no effect on those who have nothing to fear. To portray financial counter-terror measures this way is to deny the political and dislocate agency, leaving the effects (both intended and unintended) opaque.

Arguably, much of the societal and policy apprehension concerning Muslim charities is the covert secular bias in both society and politics following from the still dominant, though heavily critiqued, secularization thesis which assumes that religion in the public sphere is a security threat in and of itself and a risk to the secular liberal underpinnings of society (Mavelli, 2011: 179). In essence, the research concurred with Barzegov and Karhill who argued that 'policy makers should become better acquainted with the Muslim humanitarian landscape. Not only with Muslim institutions and NGOs but also the religious injunction to give and the individual practices of giving' (2017: 8). Equally the work coincided with El-Fath's basic premise that 'policies based on inappropriate understanding are bound to be counter-productive' (2009: 20). Consequently, a large element of this research therefore was to explore the meaning of charitable giving as expressed by practitioners themselves to unearth the errors and misconceptions which in turn feed into policy such as the Center for Security Policy which claimed that Muslims gave charity to terrorists because 'shariah mandates it' (Holton, 2009). Exploration of the theological injunction to give, especially how that obligation was operationalized and practised, demonstrated that the Center for Security Policy's analysis was entirely at odds with the views expressed by the interlocutors of this research and thus simply demonstrated insufficient understanding of both Islamic theology and Muslim pious practice.

Allowing religious actors and practitioners to explicate how charity is understood and practised in their everyday lives contributes to our understandings of the effects and unintended consequences of CTF measures that cannot possibly be legible if the practice is misunderstood to begin with. This is evident with the practice of both *zakat* and *sadaqah*. Practices of *sadaqah* reveal that Muslims respond and donate to the same charities and causes as their non-Muslim counterparts (Muderrisoglu and Saxton, 2020). Therefore, this aspect of Muslim charitable giving is entirely consistent with dominant British values of charity and humanitarian assistance and a potentially strong bridging tie between various British communities. Explorations of *zakat* on the other hand cannot be understood without taking into account a number of complexities and factors such as the experience of migration, generation, theological injunctions, relations with kin/family and media attention on specific events and tragedies. Taking the theological understandings of *zakat* seriously renders visible the sincere efforts Muslim practitioners themselves make to ensure their religious and financial sacrifices are received by the truly deserving, thus mitigating against charitable misuse from the outset.

Moreover, placing the practice of *zakat* within the context of advanced globalization and migrant philanthropic activity facilitates understanding of why significant amounts of *zakat* donations are received outside of the British state. The theological injunction to distribute *zakat* to close relatives, alongside the charitable practices of migrants generally, assists in understanding that transnational charitable donations are humanitarian and devolve from theological and moral considerations towards familiar relations. This was found to be particularly prominent for first-generation Muslim migrants who altered their 'traditional' *zakat* practices with the experience of migration to a non-Muslim-majority state. Attachments and residual belongings to 'home countries' (Portes, 2013) were found to be an aspect of migration broadly and not specific to practitioners of Islam.

The difference between migrant philanthropy generally and Muslim charitable giving broadly is that the obligation to donate charity does not cease as ties to 'homelands' fade. This does not mean that 'homelands' will necessarily remain the focus of Muslim charitable giving for second and subsequent generations. Research revealed that many second and subsequent generation British Muslims simply split their *zakat* contributions to different causes and projects both within the UK and to a wider geographic terrain than their parents and grandparents (Erdal and Borchgrevink, 2017: 142). This adaptation of charitable practices between generations is considered to be a result of socialization within the British context, awareness of increased economic wealth disparities within the UK itself and a growing self-consciousness of Muslim identity in the era of increased Islamophobia, which in turn helps construct the abstract concept of the Islamic community: *ummah*. Concern and attachment for the abstract *ummah* was argued to be a sense of belonging to a geographically dispersed religious community rather than specific political states, regimes or parties. Thus, religious identification with one group does not necessarily diminish civic senses of belonging and loyalty to the British state.

What the earlier discussion reveals is that policy assumptions which read Muslim charitable donations within Britain as a political act of loyalty, while transnational charitable giving is read as potential disloyalty to the UK, is problematic. First-generation Muslims residing in Britain effectively altered their *zakat* practices upon the experience of migration because they understood the UK to be affluent and to serve and protect its citizens via state welfare and service provisions. Trust in the UK's ability to meet the needs of her population led most first-generation Muslims to donate to their place (not necessarily state) of origin with the view that their religious obligations should be received by the 'poor' and the 'needy'. As one interviewee commented, 'Are there *really* poor in Britain?' Rather than display loyalty to political entities and systems, such charitable practices demonstrate a critique of states of origin in their inability, or unwillingness, to provide adequate levels of care for its citizens.

Conversely, Muslim charities have arisen in the past decade which distribute *zakat* collections solely within the UK. The fact that such charities have developed in the aftermath of 9/11, and in the post-2008 financial crash context, means that such charities have arisen due to the specific context of the contemporary UK. To focus charitable giving, especially that of *zakat* within the UK, is to implicitly declare state failures in welfare and service provisions for poorer segments of society. Far from indicating an uncritical stance on the UK, these charities are implicitly critiquing the UK's ability to meet the needs and demands of its people. Critique, however, does not infer disloyalty, but a desire to improve the society in which one lives inferring British Muslims have a stake in the communities in which they reside.

Concern for the global *ummah* does not necessarily delineate decreased identification with Britain as evidenced by second and subsequent Muslim generations donating to charitable causes both domestically and internationally. In the performance of charitable giving within the UK context, second and subsequent generations are increasingly likely to donate their charitable obligations within the UK, and to non-faith-based causes, which in turn contributes to their societal engagement and sense of belonging to UK society. The work drew from Butler and Mahmood's use of 'performativity' in creating personhood. It was argued that charitable giving was the performance that did not so much express, as create, the Muslim person. As performances change and adapt to the context, British Muslim charitable giving arguably creates a sense of British Muslim identity. The performance of Muslim charitable giving within the UK is therefore explicitly British and facilitates the construction of British as well as Muslim belongings. To undermine, or destabilize, Muslim charitable practices therefore threatens the production of British Muslims derived from the 'performance' of charity within the UK context.

Augmenting the powers of the Charity Commission has not in itself been viewed as undesirable nor unnecessary. It was noted several times by many participants that there is strong sector backing for increased regulation and monitoring of charities for correct conduct. What is debated is the reasoning behind the extensions of the Charity Commission's powers. Many participants were sceptical about the increased politicization of the regulatory body which in turn renders suspicion for the true motives and 'agendas' behind the extenuated powers of the Charity Commission. A typical expression of this sentiment can be gleamed from the below interview extract from a Muslim charity based in London.

> if charity is made something political, then it takes away something functional that you're trying to achieve. Charities are there to respond and help society, to respond to gaps in society that perhaps the government is not responding to, and help to enhance the services that the government is already providing. Or to respond to a need that has not been yet identified.... And when you're trying to do all that, you need a body that would help you to be the best that you can be.... the powers that the Commission has got... I think that's quite good.... I don't see charities having any issues with that because there's a need for that. Because there are charities out there... taking money from donors and are not being accountable for it, not upholding their responsibilities for every pound and penny that comes in. And, for such individuals, the commission needs to have some sort of power to act and respond, and not just be there to just give advice. So, that's a good thing, and that's needed... and we need that from the Charity Commission. And, it means that everybody, all charities, not just Muslim charities, can be that ideal charity that we all set out to be.... But we do have issues... when they use those powers, or whatever, unfairly... targeting Muslim charities, for example. That's what the charities have issues with because we think these things should be there, but they should be there with a purpose, not with a political agenda behind it. Targeting specific groups of individuals. Then, it no longer becomes, you know, a tool for the commission to do its job properly. It becomes someone else's tool to further a particular narrative which, we don't know what that is.

None of the charities interviewed for this research were against the Charity Commission's reformed powers per se. In agreement with Warde, all participants felt that 'reforming the Islamic charities system was long overdue' (2007: 147). What is being critiqued is the assumptions of links between charities and 'terrorism' of which there is little substantiating evidence and particularly the perception of disproportionate investigations and treatment of Muslim charities. To draw again from Warde, 'most significantly, the relentless attacks against Islamic charities provided considerable ammunition to all those who argued that the war on terror was above all a war against Islam' (Warde, 2007: 147). Warde's analysis finds echo in a report of CTF consequences in the United States which found that financial counter-terror policies aimed at charities and humanitarian NGOs are damaging Western reputations in Muslim-majority states by giving an appearance of a 'war on Islam' (ACLU, 2009: 16).

Counterproductive and violent

The non-violent rhetoric of the FWoT has been exposed as a veneer for the real violence occurring which is hidden and obscured in mainstream British society. As noted in Chapter 1, how violence is defined and understood is highly contested. This research drew from a broad definition of violence that includes financial and social exclusions. Particularly relevant was Jackman's observation that 'when violence is motivated by positive intentions or is the incidental by-product of other goals . . . it escapes our attention' (2002: 388). As a result of CTF measures, individuals and institutions have been unnecessarily and unwarrantedly accused, causing negative social repercussions and potentially devastating financial consequences as accounts and assets are frozen, closed and denied. In addition to the personal individual reputational damage, the damage to a charity's brand is potentially irrevocable when allegations are cast, even when proven false. The efficiency and ability of charities to carry on their humanitarian work are severely hampered by intrusive documentation and banking de-risking strategies. In addition to the social, economic and institutional violence occurring are the life and death consequences for end recipients of aid, especially those in 'vulnerable' territories overseas. Any attempt of shrouding current CTF practices in the rhetoric of 'soft power' is instantly undermined by the effects and violent results of CTF policies for overseas end-users. It would be advisable for global state actors to revise and amend the current CTF system as 'it is a measure of human callousness when social actors, despite the absence of a deliberative intent to harm, fail to be deterred from a course of action by the knowledge that injuries may, or will, be the by-product' (Jackson, 2002: 402). Essentially, in an attempt to limit or prevent violent harm in our own state, we risk inducing disproportionate harm on others who already suffer physically and economically in high risk areas. Violence is thus not prevented but simply geographically relocated beyond Western audiences' visions.

Unintended consequences such as detrimental global perceptions and pushing monies underground (Benthall, 2007: 7) may have increased insecurities rather than lessened them. The restriction of aid and religious practice is also likely to increase feelings of grievance and injustice, which in turn feeds into further insecurities. As

Gunning has argued, 'the delegitimization of social welfare activities in particular, especially accompanied by the freezing of charitable assets is likely to contribute to human suffering... which similarly may increase the attractiveness of unconventional forms of warfare' (2008: 112). In terms of global perceptions, current policies risk denting 'the image' of the UK in 'the Muslim world' (El-Fath, 2009: 1). El-Fath continues by arguing that a real potential consequence of those harmed by the CTF system, who have nothing to do with terrorism or criminality, could endanger national interests and 'the security of the world in the long term' (2009a: 7). El-Fath argues, as does this research, that not only are current CTF policies inefficient and unlikely to decrease terrorist activity, they are in fact counterproductive, adding to perceptions of harm, grievance and marginalization thought to be correlating variables in violent action 'which is likely to increase recruitment and support, including financial, for terrorism' (2009a: 20). In agreement, Walker has argued that hindering the work of charities, especially humanitarian overseas engagement, is 'contrary to the public interest because a failure to intervene might worsen the generation of terrorism' (2018: 1104).

In terms of diplomatic soft power, charities and faith-based NGOs can be successful in a range of ways but not least in promoting democracy and human rights (Sheikh, 2012: 379). Charitable donations and the ease in which they can be distributed can create positive perceptions of both a state and its people that in turn can assist in the efficiency of soft power being deemed 'legitimate'. Conversely, if actions are deemed illegitimate (such as the withdrawal, restriction or curtailment of aid and charity) a nation's soft power may be drastically reduced internationally. The positive aspects of Muslim charitable giving are currently in danger of being curtailed by negative press, societal suspicion and the damaging consequences for end-users and recipients. The detrimental consequences of current counter-terror initiatives that have penetrated the charitable sector, therefore, risk more than just the financial and social security of those actively involved in charity, but also the effectiveness and success of British diplomatic initiatives, especially in countries with sizeable Muslim populations.

Current CTF practices do more than undermine the UK's international standing as they are potentially disrupting the fabric of British society and efforts towards social cohesion and shared 'values'. Kundnani has argued that rather than undermining the positives of Muslim charitable giving, what is needed is 'a strong, active, and confident Muslim community enjoying its civil rights to the full' which in turn is posited as 'the best way of preventing violence' (Kundnani, 2014: 199). Agreeing with Kundnani, governments and institutions would be best to support the opportunities presented by charitable practitioners rather than focusing on the (minimal) risks that charitable misuse could potentially uncover (Shaw-Hamilton, 2007: 21–2). As Smith and Felipiak have argued, Muslim charities across Europe have provided an important 'secondary role of providing Muslim communities in Europe with integration assistance.... They can also serve as a bridge between Muslim and non-Muslim communities by promoting dialogue and partnering Christian organisations on joint projects' (Smith and Felipiak, 2007: 82). Undermining Muslim charities simultaneously destabilizes their important civil function for social cohesion, risking further alienation, marginalization and isolation for Muslim communities and practitioners – variables thought to be correlating factors in motivations for political violence (Gunning, 2008: 107). Current CTF policies therefore potentially increase, rather than decrease, our long-term security. As Alam and Husband have suggested,

> At the level of policy, this post-9/11 development of Britain's counter-terrorism approach has significantly nurtured the growth of anti-Muslim sentiment in Britain, at the level of practise, it has also significantly increased the sense of marginalisation and stereotyping felt by Britain's Muslim population. (2013: 247)

Insecurity is increased as speculation and suspicion intensify, and measures are put in place that deepen the challenges of charitable donations with consequences at national and international levels. The intended goal of reducing or preventing violent political action may not succeed, but the 'side effects' (Ferguson, 1994) of increased state control are deepening. In the name of counter-terror initiatives and national protection, our use of ATMs, which banks we service, what charities we give to and what direct debits are made are all collected and mapped by government initiatives. Little evidence currently exists that would point to the effectiveness of such policies in thwarting violent political action or terrorist activities, but where such initiatives do succeed is in their extension and deepening of state power and control into our mundane activities and everyday lives.

References

Abdullah, Muhammad and Suhaib, Abdul Quddus. 2011. 'The Impact of Zakat on Social Life of Muslim Society', *Pakistan Journal of Islamic Research*, 11, http://www.bzu.edu.pk/PJIR/eng8Abdullah&AbdulQuddusSuhaib.pdf (Accessed 03/09/2017).

ACLU. 2009. *Blocking Faith, Freezing Charity: Chilling Muslim Charitable Giving in the 'War on Terrorism Financing'* (New York; American Civil Liberties Union).

Ahmed, Shamila. 2019. 'British Muslims Perceptions of Social Cohesion: From Multi-Culturalism to Community Cohesion and the "War on Terror"', *Crime, Law and Social Change*, 71: 581–95.

Ainsworth, David. 2013. 'Muslim Donors Give More on Average than Other Religious Groups in the UK', *The Third Sector*, https://www.thirdsector.co.uk/muslim-donors-give-average-religious-groups-uk/fundraising/article/1192969 (Accessed 12/06/2020).

Aisenberg, Eugene et al. 2011. 'Defining Violence', in Todd et al. (eds), *Violence in Context: Current Evidence on Risk, Protection and Prevention* (Oxford; Oxford University Press).

Alam, Yunis and Husband, Charles. 2013. 'Islamophobia, Community Cohesion and Counter-Terrorism Policies in Britain', *Patterns of Prejudice*, 47 (3): 235–52.

Al-Mizan Charitable Trust. 2019. 'Al-Mizan: Annual Report and Accounts 2018–19', http://apps.charitycommission.gov.uk/Accounts/Ends52/0001135752_AC_20190331_E_C.PDF (Accessed 14/06/2020).

Al-Qaradawi, 2000. *Fiqh al Zakah*, II, https://iei.kau.edu.sa/Files/121/Files/152672_34-A-FiqhAlZakah-Vol-I.pdf

Alterman, Jon B. 2009. 'Saudi Charities and Support for Terrorism', pp. 64–80, in Alterman, Jon B. and von Hippel, Karen (eds), *Understanding Islamic Charities* (Washington, DC; Center for Strategic and International Studies).

Aly, Sharif. 2018. 'Letter to Congress', *Islamic Relief USA*, http://irusa.org/wp-content/uploads/2018/07/2018.7.19-IRUSA-Congressional-Response-to-MEF-Cover-Letter-FINAL.docx.pdf (Accessed 04/05/2020).

Amin, Hira. 2019. 'British Muslims Navigating Between Individualism and Traditional Authority', *Religions*, 10: 354.

Ammermon, Nancy T. 2014. 'Finding Religion in Everyday Life', *Sociology of Religion*, 75 (2): 189–207.

Anderson, Benedict. 1991. *Imagined Communities* (London; Verso).

Atia, Mona. 2012. '"A Way to Paradise": Pious Neoliberalism, Islam, and Faith-Based Development', *Annals of the Association of American Geographers*, 10 (4): 808–27.

Ayoub, 2004. *Islam: Faith and History* (London; Oneworld Publications).

Azim, Abdul. 2005. *Zakah: A Bibliography* (Jeddah; King Abdulaziz University).

Aziz, Sahar F. 2011. 'Countering Religion or Terrorism? Selective Enforcement of Material Support Laws Against Muslim Charities', *Institute for Social Policy and Understanding*, Policy Brief Number 47, https://papers.ssrn.com/sol3/papers.cfm?abstract_id=2022748 (Accessed 05/06/2020).

Azmi, Sabahuddin. 2004. *Islamic Economics: Public Finance in Early Islamic Thought* (New Delhi; Goodword Books).

Barnett, Michael and Stein, Janice. 2012. 'The Secularization and Sanctification of Humanitarianism', in Barnett and Stein (eds), *Sacred Aid: Faith and Humanitarianism* (Oxford; Oxford University Press).

Barylo, William. 2018. *Young Muslim Change-Makers: Grassroots Charities, Rethinking Modern Society* (Abington; Routledge).

Barzegar, Abbas and El Karhili, Nagham. 2017. 'The Muslim Humanitarian Sector: A Review for Policy Makers and NGO Practitioners', *Georgia State University and the British Council*, https://www.britishcouncil.us/sites/default/files/final_report_-_the_muslim_humanitarian_sector.pdf

Belaon, Adam. 2014. *Muslim Charities: A Suspect Sector* (London; Claystone).

Belew, Wendell. 2014. 'The Impact of US Laws, Regulations, and Policies on Gulf Charities', pp. 231-58, in Lacey, Robert and Benthall, Jonathan (eds), *Gulf Charities and Islamic Philanthropy in the 'Age of Terror' and Beyond* (Berlin; Gerlack Press).

Bell, Vikki (ed.). 1999. *Performativity and Belonging* (London; Sage).

Benthall, Jonathon. 1999. 'Financial Worship: The Quranic Injunction to Almsgiving', *The Journal of the Royal Anthropological Institute*, 5 (1): 27–42.

Benthall, Jonathan. 2007. 'The Overreaction Against Islamic Charities', *ISIM Review*, 20: 6–7.

Benthall, Jonathan. 2012. '"Cultural Proximity" and the Conjuncture of Islam with Modern Humanitarianism', in Barnett and Stein (eds), *Sacred Aid: Faith and Humanitarianism* (Oxford; Oxford University Press).

Benthall, Jonathan. 2016. *Islamic Charities and Islamic Humanism in Troubled Times* (Manchester; Manchester University Press).

Benthall, Jonathan. 2018. 'The Rise and Decline of Saudi Overseas Humanitarian Charities', *Centre for International and Regional Studies, Georgetown University in Qatar*, Occasional Working Paper Number 20, https://repository.library.georgetown.edu/bitstream/handle/10822/1051628/CIRSOccasionalPaper20JonathanBenthall2018.pdf (Accessed 14/08/2020).

Benthall, Jonathan and Bellion-Joudan, Jérôme. 2009. *The Charitable Crescent: Politics of Aid in the Muslim World* (London; I.B. Tauris).

Biersteker, Thomas and Eckert, Sue. 2008. 'Introduction: The Challenge of Terrorist Financing', pp. 1–16, in Biersteker and Eckert (eds), *Countering the Financing of Terrorism* (London and New York; Routledge).

Bishop, Ryan and Philips, John. 2006. 'Violence', *Theory, Culture and Society*, 23 (2–3): 377–85.

Bokhari, Yusra, Chowdhury, Nasim and Lacey, Robert. 2014. 'A Good Day to Bury a Bad Charity: The Rise and Fall of the Al-Haramain Islamic Foundation', pp. 199–230, in Lacey, Robert and Benthall, Jonathan (eds), *Gulf Charities and Islamic Philanthropy in the 'Age of Terror' and Beyond* (Berlin; Gerlach Press).

Bolleyer, Nicole and Gaiya, Anika. 2017. 'Combating Terrorism by Constraining Charities? Charity and Counter-Terrorism Legislation Before and After 9/11', *Public Administration*, 95 (3): 654–69.

Bosco, Robert. 2014. *Securing the Sacred: Religion, National Security and the Western State* (Michigan; University of Michigan State).

Bowen, John R. 2011. 'Beyond Migration: Islam as a Transnational Public Space', pp. 199–209, in Volpi, Frederic (ed.), *Political Islam: A Critical Reader* (Abington; Routledge).

Brown, Gordon. 2001. 'Action Against Financing Terrorism', Commons Debate, Parliament UK, https://publications.parliament.uk/pa/cm200102/cmhansrd/vo011015/debtext/11015-11.htm (Accessed 02/10/2019).

Bruce, Fiona (MP). 2017. 'Civil Society Space', House of Commons, UK Parliament, *Hansard*, https://hansard.parliament.uk/Commons/2017-01-26/debates/1CD71CEA-045B-4C93-9558-97BB416EDD6C/CivilSocietySpace (Accessed 23/05/2020).

Bush, George W. 2001. The White House, 'Terrorist Financial Network Factsheet', https://georgewbush-whitehouse.archives.gov/news/releases/2001/11/20011107-6.html

Butler, Judith. 1988. 'Performative Acts and Gender Constitution: An Essay in Phenomenology and Feminist Theory', *Theatre Journal*, 40 (4): 519–31.

Butler, Judith. 2006. *Precarious Life: The Powers of Mourning and Violence* (London and New York; Verso).

Butler, Judith. 2009. 'Performativity, Precarity and Sexual Politics', *AIBR*, 4 (3), https://www.aibr.org/antropologia/04v03/criticos/040301b.pdf (Accessed 20/07/2019).

Casanova, Jose. 1994. *Public Religions in the Modern World* (Chicago and London; The University of Chicago Press).

Cesari, Jocelyne. 2012. 'Securitization of Islam in Europe', *Die Welt Des Islams*, 52 (3–4): 430–49.

CFG. 2018. 'Impact of Money Laundering and Counter-Terrorism Regulations on Charities', *Charity Finance Group*, https://cfg.org.uk/userfiles/documents/Policy%20documents/Impact%20of%20money%20laundering%20and%20counter-terrorism%20regulations%20on%20charities.pdf (Accessed 05/06/2020).

Chang, Agnes. 2020. '(Self) Regulation of Muslim Charitable Sectors in the US and the UK in the Post-9/11 Era', *Journal of Muslim Society and Civil Society*, 4 (1): 180–205.

Charity Commission. 2008. 'Counter-Terrorism Strategy', https://assets.publishing.service.gov.uk/government/uploads/system/uploads/attachment_data/file/465994/counter-terrorism_strategy.pdf (Accessed 08/10/2019).

Charity Commission. 2017. https://ogs.charitycommission.gov.uk/g410a001.aspx#tab2 (Accessed 17/05/2020).

Charity Commission. 2018. 'Charity Commission Inquiry Statistics: Cases opened 1 April 2017 to 31 March 2018', https://www.gov.uk/government/publications/inquiry-case-statistics-1-april-2017-to-30-june-2017 (Accessed 07/03/2021).

Charity Commission. 2019a. 'Over Half of Charities Hit by Fraud Knew Perpetrator, According to New Research', *Charity Commission for England and Wales*, https://www.gov.uk/government/news/over-half-of-charities-hit-by-fraud-knew-the-perpetrator-according-to-new-research (Accessed 24/07/2020).

Charity Commission. 2019b. 'Preventing Charity Fraud: Insights and Action', *Charity Commission for England and Wales*, https://assets.publishing.service.gov.uk/government/uploads/system/uploads/attachment_data/file/841403/Web_CC_Fraud.pdf (Accessed 24/07/2020).

Charity and Security Network. 2010. 'Holder V. Humanitarian Law Project: Addressing the Impact of Material Support Laws on Peacebuilding Programs', *Charity and Security Network*, https://charityandsecurity.org/litigation/hlp/ (Accessed 16/08/2020).

Charity and Security Network. 2016. 'World-Check: The Dangers of Privatising Terrorist Lists', *Charity and Security Network*, https://charityandsecurity.org/financial-access/worldcheck_private_databases_raise_concerns/ (Accessed 17/08/2020).

Charity and Security Network. 2019. 'Material Support Definitions', *Charity and Security Network*, https://charityandsecurity.org/material-support/material_support_definitions/ (Accessed 14/08/2020).

Charity and Security Network. 2020. 'Civil Society Organisations Issue Joint-Statement on the 10th Anniversary of Holder Vs. Humanitarian Law', *Charity and Security Network*, https://charityandsecurity.org/news/civil-society-organizations-issue-joint-statement-at-the-10th-anniversary-of-holder-vs-humanitarian-law/ (Accessed 16/08/2020).

CIC (Commission on Integration and Cohesion). 2007. *Our Shared Values*, http://image.guardian.co.uk/sys-files/Education/documents/2007/06/14/oursharedfuture.pdf (Accessed 20/05/2020).

Cooney, Rebecca. 2019. 'Charity Commission Accused of "Undue Scrutiny" of Muslim Charities', *Third Sector*, https://www.thirdsector.co.uk/charity-commission-accused-undue-scrutiny-muslim-charities/governance/article/1660369 (Accessed 14/05/2020).

Crowe. 2017. 'Annual Fraud Indicator 2017: Identifying the Cost of Fraud to the UK Economy', Centre for Counter Fraud Studies, https://www.crowe.com/uk/croweuk/-/media/Crowe/Firms/Europe/uk/CroweUK/PDF-publications/Annual-Fraud-Indicator-report-2017 (Accessed 12/02/2021).

De Goede, Marieke, 2012a. 'The SWIFT Affair and the Global Politics of European Security', *JCMS*, 50 (2): 214–30.

De Goede, Marieke. 2012b. *Speculative Security: 'The Politics of Pursuing Terrorist Monies'* (Minneapolis; University of Minnesota Press).

De Goede, Marieke. 2016 'The Politics of Security Lists', *Economy and Space*, 34 (1): 67–88.

De Goede, Marieke. 2017a. 'Chains of Securitization', *Finance and Security*, 3 (2): 197–207.

De Goede, Marieke. 2017b. 'Secrecy and Security in Transatlantic Terrorism Finance Tracking', *Journal of European Integration*, 39 (3): 253–69.

De Goede, Marieke. 2018. 'Proscription's Futures', *Terrorism and Political Violence*, 30 (2): 336–55.

Delmar-Morgan, Alex. 2015. 'Islamic Charities in UK Fear They Are Being Unfairly Targeted over Extremism', *The Guardian*, last modified 22 July 2015, https://www.theguardian.com/society/2015/jul/22/muslim-charities-uk-targeted-extremism-fears (Accessed 01/05/2018).

Downs, Stephen and Manley, Kathy. 2013. 'Why All Americans Should Care About the Holy Land Foundation Case', *Washington Report on Middle Eastern Affairs*, https://www.wrmea.org/013-january-february/why-all-americans-should-care-about-the-holy-land-foundation-case.html (Accessed 08/10/2019).

Doyle, Charles. 2016. 'Terrorist Material Support: An Overview of 18 USC S32339A and S2339B', *Congressional Research Service*, https://fas.org/sgp/crs/natsec/R41333.pdf (Accessed 08/10/2019).

Dudenhoefer, Anne-Lynn. 2018. 'Resisting Radicalisation: A Critical Analysis of the UK Prevent Duty', *Journal for Deradicalisation*, 14: 153.

Dunn, Elizabeth. 1996. 'Money, Morality and Modes of Civil Society Among American Mormons', pp. 27–49, in Dunn and Hann (eds), *Civil Society: Challenging Western Models* (London and New York; Routledge).

El-Fath, A. Adel Salam. 2009. 'War on Terror: Fantasy and Fiction Behind the Mythology of Terrorist Financing', *Intellectual Discourse*, 17 (1): 1–23.

Eliftheriou-Smith, Loulla-Mae. 2014. 'Charities Investigated for Radicalisation and Extremism Links', *The Independent*, 17 November, https://www.independent.co.uk/news/uk/home-news/charities-investigated-for-radicalisation-and-extremist-links-9865169.html (Accessed 14/05/2020).

Elshimi, Mohammed. 2015. 'De-Radicalisation Interventions as Technologies of the Self: A Foucauldian Analysis', *Critical Studies on Terrorism*, 8 (1): 110–29.

Elshurafa, D. 2012. 'Islamic Capitalism – An Imminent Reality or A Hopeful Possibility for Islamic Finance?', *Arab Law Quarterly*, 26 (3): 339–60.

Erdal, Bivand Marta and Borchgrevink, Kaja. 2017. 'Transnational Islamic Charity as Everyday Rituals', *Global Networks*, 17 (1): 130–46.

FATF. 2008. 'Terrorist Financing', *Financial Action Task Force*, https://www.fatf-gafi.org/media/fatf/documents/reports/FATF%20Terrorist%20Financing%20Typologies%20Report.pdf (Accessed 08/05/2020).

FATF. 2010. 'FATF – Special Recommendations', https://www.fatf-gafi.org/media/fatf/doc uments/reports/FATF%20Standards%20-%20IX%20Special%20Recommendations%2 0and%20IN%20rc.pdf
FATF. 2014. *Risk of Terrorist Abuse in Non-Profit Organisations*, FATF, https://www.fatf -gafi.org/media/fatf/documents/reports/Risk-of-terrorist-abuse-in-non-profit-organis ations.pdf (Accessed 17/05/2020).
FATF. 2017. *Anti-Money Laundering and Terrorist Financing Measures and Financial Inclusion*, http://www.fatf-gafi.org/media/fatf/content/images/Updated-2017-FATF-2 013-Guidance.pdf (Accessed 03/10/2019).
FATF. 2019. 'International Standards on Combating Money Laundering and the Financing of Terrorism and Proliferation: FATF Recommendations', http://www.fatf-gafi.org/ media/fatf/documents/recommendations/pdfs/FATF%20Recommendations%202012 .pdf (Accessed 08/10/2019).
Faure, Lucas. 2020. 'Muslim NGOs Facing Covid-19 in France #MUHUM', *Allegralab*, https://allegralaboratory.net/muslim-ngos-facing-covid-19-in-france-muhum/ (Accessed 23/07/2020).
Ferguson, James. 1994. *The Anti-Politics Machine: Development, Depoliticisation and Bureaucratic Power in Lesotho* (Minneapolis; University of Minnesota Press).
Fitzgibbon, Francis. 2015. 'Low Hanging Fruit: Francis Fitzgibbon on the Show Trial of the Holy Land Foundation', *London Review of Books*, 37 (2), https://www.lrb.co.uk/the -paper/v37/n02/francis-fitzgibbon/low-hanging-fruit (Accessed 14/08/2020).
Fortier, Anne-Marie. 1999. 'Remembering Places and Performance of Belonging(s)', *Theory, Culture and Society*, 16 (2): 41–64.
Freedman, Michael G. 2011. 'Prosecuting Terrorism: The Material Support Statute and Muslim Charities', *Hasting Constitutional Law Quarterly*, 38 (4): 1113–50.
Frith, Maxine. 2004. 'US Deports Yussuf Islam Over Claims He Supports Terrorist Groups', *The Independent*, https://www.independent.co.uk/news/world/americas/us -deports-yusuf-islam-over-claims-that-he-supports-terrorist-groups-547332.html (Accessed 15/08/2020).
Gardner, Katy. 2016. '"Our Own Poor": Transnational Charity, Development Gifts and the Politics of Suffering in Sylhet and the UK', *Modern Asian Studies*, https://eprints.lse.ac .uk/68086/1/Gardner_Our_own_poor.pdf (Accessed 14/06/2020).
Gilligan, Andrew. 2014. '"Terror Link" Charities Get British Millions in Gift Aid', *The Telegraph*, 29 November, https://www.telegraph.co.uk/news/uknews/terrorism-in-the -uk/11263309/Terror-link-charities-get-British-millions-in-Gift-Aid.html (Accessed 14/05/2020).
Gilligan, Andrew. 2015. 'Human Appeal and Hamas: The Evidence', *The Telegraph*, 19 October 2015, https://www.telegraph.co.uk/news/uknews/terrorism-in-the-uk/ 11940489/Human-Appeal-and-Hamas-the-evidence.html (Accessed 30/05/2020).
Githens-Mazer. 2012. 'The Rhetoric and Reality: Radicalisation and Political Discourse', *International Political Science Review*, 33 (5): 556–67.
Glass. 2018. 'The Unjust Prosecution of the Holy Land Foundation Five', *The Intercept*, https://theintercept.com/2018/08/05/holy-land-foundation-trial-palestine-israel/ (Accessed 08/10/2019).
Global Freedom of Expression. 2020. 'Holder V. Humanitarian Law Project', *Global Freedom of Expression*, Columbia University, https://globalfreedomofexpression.c olumbia.edu/cases/holder-v-humanitarian-law-project/ (Accessed 16/08/2020).
Global Terrorism Index. 2019. 'Global Terrorism Index 2019: Measuring the Impact of Terrorism', Institute for Terrorism and Peace, http://visionofhumanity.org/app/uploads/ 2019/11/GTI-2019web.pdf (Accessed 14/08/2020).

Göle, N. 2011. 'Islam in Public: New Visibilities and New Imaginaries', pp. 220–30, in Volpi, Frederic (ed.), *Political Islam: A Critical Reader* (Abington; Routledge).

Gronemeyer, Marianne. 1995. 'Helping', pp. 53–69, in Sachs, Wolfgang (ed.), *The Development Dictionary: A Guide to Knowledge and Power* (London; Zed Books).

Gunning, Jeroen. 2008. 'Terrorism, Charities and Diasporas: Contrasting the Fundraising Practices of Hamas and Al-Qaeda among Muslims in Europe', pp. 94–125, in Biersteker and Eckert (eds), *Countering the Financing of Terrorism* (London and New York; Routledge).

Gunning, Jeroen and Jackson, Richard. 2011. 'What Is So "Religious" about "Religious Terrorism"?', *Critical Studies on Terrorism*, 4 (3): 369–88.

Hayes, Ben. 2013. 'How International Rules on Countering the Financing of Terrorism Impact Civil Society', Policy Briefing, *The Transnational Institute (TNI)*, https://www.tni.org/my/node/1452 (Accessed 17/08/2020).

Heuser, Brian L. 2005. 'Social Cohesion and Voluntary Associations', *Peabody Journal of Education*, 80 (4): 16–29.

HM Government. 2011a. '*Prevent* Strategy', https://assets.publishing.service.gov.uk/government/uploads/system/uploads/attachment_data/file/97976/prevent-strategy-review.pdf

HM Government. 2011b. 'Charities Act', http://www.legislation.gov.uk/ukpga/2011/25/contents

HM Government. 2015. 'Revised *Prevent* Duty Guidance: For England and Wales', https://assets.publishing.service.gov.uk/government/uploads/system/uploads/attachment_data/file/445977/3799_Revised_Prevent_Duty_Guidance__England_Wales_V2-Interactive.pdf

HM Government. 2018. Contest: The United Kingdom's *Strategy of Countering Terrorism*, https://assets.publishing.service.gov.uk/government/uploads/system/uploads/attachment_data/file/716907/140618_CCS207_CCS0218929798-1_CONTEST_3.0_WEB.pdf

HM Treasury. 2018. 'Anti-Money Laundering and Counter-Terrorist Financing: Supervision Report 2015–17', https://assets.publishing.service.gov.uk/government/uploads/system/uploads/attachment_data/file/685248/PU2146_AML_web.pdf (Accessed 03/10/2019).

Hoffman, Bruce. 2010. 'Today's Highly Educated Terrorists', *The National Interest*, https://nationalinterest.org/blog/bruce-hoffman/todays-highly-educated-terrorists-4080 (Accessed 02/10/2019).

Holton, Christopher. 2009. 'Obama, Zakat and Islamic Charities', *Centre for Security Policy*, https://www.centerforsecuritypolicy.org/2009/06/08/obama-zakat-and-islamic-charities-2/ (Accessed 01/05/2018).

Home Office. 2018. 'Individuals Referred to and Supported through the *Prevent* Programme, April 2017 to March 2018', https://assets.publishing.service.gov.uk/government/uploads/system/uploads/attachment_data/file/763254/individuals-referred-supported-prevent-programme-apr2017-mar2018-hosb3118.pdf (Accessed 08/10/2018).

House of Commons. 2010. 'Preventing Violent Extremism, Sixth Report of Session 2009–10', House of Commons Communities and Local Government Committee, https://publications.parliament.uk/pa/cm200910/cmselect/cmcomloc/65/65.pdf (Accessed 07/03/2021).

House of Commons. 2013. 'Early Day Motion 786 25 November, "Interpal"', https://edm.parliament.uk/early-day-motion/46282/interpal

House of Commons Library. 2020. 'Terrorism in Britain: The Statistics', Briefing Paper Number CBP7613, House of Commons Library, https://researchbriefings.files.parliament.uk/documents/CBP-7613/CBP-7613.pdf (Accessed 11/08/2020).

Hudson, P. 1999. *The Sociology and Psychology of Terrorism: Who Becomes a Terrorist and Why?* (Library Congress).

Huntington, Samuel. 1993. 'The Clash of Civilizations?', *Foreign Affairs*, 72 (3): 22–49.

Hurd, Elizabeth. 2012. 'International Politics After Secularism', *Review of International Studies*, 38 (5): 943–61.

Hussain, Y. and Bagguley, P. 2012. '"Securitised Citizens": Islamophobia, Racism and the 7/7 London Bombing', *The Sociological Review*, 60 (4): 715–34.

Ibn-Khaldun, 1958. *The Muqaddimah: An Introduction to History* (New York; Pantheon Books).

Imtiaz, Atif. 2019. 'An Examination of the Inquiries Conducted on British Muslim Charities by the Charity Commission', *The Forum*, 2, https://www.muslimcharitiesforum.org.uk/wp-content/uploads/2020/01/MCF_JOURNAL_1920_WebSinglePage_FINAL.pdf (Accessed 14/05/2020).

Interpal. 2013. Annual Report, https://www.interpal.org/wp-content/uploads/2018/03/AnnualReview:2013.pdf (Accessed 25/01/2020).

Iofolla, Vanessa. 2018. 'The Production of Suspicion in Retail Banking: An Examination of Unusual Transaction Reporting', pp. 81–107, in King, Colin, Walker, Clive and Gurele, Jimmy (eds), *The Palgrave Handbook of Criminal and Terrorism Financing Laws* (Cham; Palgrave MacMillan).

Islamic Relief. 2020. 'About Us', *Islamic Relief UK. org*, https://www.islamic-relief.org.uk/about-us/ (Accessed 14/08/2020).

Islamic Relief Worldwide. 2019. 'Annual Report and Financial Statements, 2019', *Islamic Relief*, https://www.islamic-relief.org.uk/wp-content/uploads/2020/09/IRW-Annual-Report-2019-140920-min.pdf (Accessed 12/02/2021).

Ismail, Salwa. 2011. 'Being Muslim: Islam, Islamism and Identity Politics', pp. 16–29, in Volpi, Frederic (ed.), *Political Islam: A Critical Reader* (Abington; Routledge).

Itani, Fadi. 2012. 'Can Charitable Donations From Muslims Compensate for an Uncertain Giving Environment?', *The Huffington Post*, 20 July 2012, http://www.huffingtonpost.co.uk/fadi-itani/can-charitable-donations-_b_1686963.html (Accessed 04/01/2017).

Jackman, Mary R. 2002. 'Violence in Social Life', *Annual Review of Sociology*, 28: 387–415.

Jackson, Richard. 2007. 'Constructing Enemies: Islamic Terrorism in Political and Academic Discourse', *Government and Opposition*, 42 (3): 394–426.

Jodicke, Ansgar. 2018. *Religion and Soft Power in the South Caucasus* (London; Routledge).

Jonsson, M. 2007. 'Countering Terrorist Financing: Lessons from Europe', *Georgetown Journal of International Affairs*, 8 (1): 69–78.

Kabir, Nahid A. 2010. *Young British Muslims: Identity, Culture, Politics, and the Media*, (Edinburgh; Edinburgh University Press).

Keatinge, Tom. 2014. 'Uncharitable Behaviour', Demos, https://www.demos.co.uk/files/DEMOSuncharitablebehaviourREPORT.pdf (Accessed 17/05/2020).

Kepel, Gilles. 2003. *Jihad: The Trail of Political Islam* (London; I.B. Tauris).

Khan, Ajaz Ahmed. 2012. 'Religious Obligation or Alturistic Giving? Muslims and Charitable Donations', in Barnett and Stein (eds), *Sacred Aid: Faith and Humanitarianism* (Oxford; Oxford University Press).

Khimji, Ali. 2014. 'A Survey of Charitable Giving in the British Muslim Community', Cause4, https://www.cause4.co.uk/home/wp-content/uploads/2014/12/Cause4-A-Surv

ey-of-Charitable-Giving-in-the-British-Muslim-Community-December-2014.pdf (Accessed 14/08/2020).

Kroessin, Mohammed Ralf. 2009. 'Mapping UK Muslim Development NGOs', Religions and Development Research Programme, Working Paper, https://assets.publi shing.service.gov.uk/media/57a08b5bed915d622c000c41/wp_30.pdf (Accessed 14/08/2020).

Kundnani, Arun. 2009. 'Spooked! How Not to Prevent Violent Extremism', Institute of Race Relations, London, http://www.kundnani.org/wp-content/uploads/spooked.pdf (Accessed 24/05/2019).

Kundnani, Arun. 2014. *The Muslims Are Coming!: Islamophobia, Extremism and the Domestic War on Terror* (London and New York; Verso).

Lambek, Michael. 2013. 'The Value of (performative) Acts', *Journal of Ethnographic Theory*, 3 (2): 141–60.

Larsen, C. A. 2013. *The Rise and Fall of Social Cohesion: The Construction and Deconstruction of Social Trust in the US, UK, Sweden and Denmark* (Oxford: Oxford University Press).

Laurence, James. 2009. 'The Effect of Ethnic Diversity and Community Disadvantage on Social Cohesion: A Multi-Level Analysis of Social Capital and Interethnic Relations in the UK', *European Sociological Review*, 27 (1): 70–89.

Levi, Michael. 2018. 'Punishing Banks, Their Clients, and Their Clients' Clients', pp. 273–91, in King, Colin, Walker, Clive and Gurele, Jimmy (eds), *The Palgrave Handbook of Criminal and Terrorism Financing Laws* (Cham; Palgrave MacMillan).

Levitt, Matthew. 2006. *Hamas: Politics, Charity, and Terrorism in the Service of Jihad* (New Haven and London; Yale University Press).

Lipka, M. 2017. 'Muslims and Islam: Key Findings in the US and Around the World', Pew Research Centre, http://www.hopelutheranfresno.org/wp-content/uploads/2019/11/Muslims-and-Islam-Pew-Research-Center-2017-002.pdf (Accessed 14/08/2020).

Lynch, Cecelia. 2011. 'Religious Humanitarianism and the Global Politics of Secularism', pp. 204–24, in Craig Calhoun et al. (eds), *Rethinking Secularism* (Oxford; Oxford University Press).

MacDonald, Malcolm and John O'Regan, Duncan Hunter. 2013. 'Citizenship, Community and Counter-Terrorism: UK Security Discourse 2001–2011', *Journal of Language and Politics*, 12 (3): 445–73.

Mahmood, Saba. 2005. *Politics of Piety: The Islamic Revival and the Feminist Subject* (Princeton; Princeton University Press).

Mahmood, Saba. 2013. 'Religious Reason and Secular Affect: An Incommensurable Divide?', pp. 58–94, in Asad, Talal, Brown, Wendy, Butler, Judith and Mahmood, Saba (eds), *Is Critique Secular? Blasphemy, Injury and Free Speech* (New York; Fordham University Press).

Maimbo, Samuel Munzele and Ratha, Dilip. 2005. 'Remittances: Development Impact and Future Prospects', (Washington, DC; World Bank Group), http://documents.worldban k.org/curated/en/435901468139206629/Remittances-development-impact-and-future-prospects (Accessed 05/07/2020).

Manchanda, Rita, 2010. 'Media-Mediated Public Discourse on "Terrorism" and Suspect Communities', *Economic and Political Weekly*, 45 (15): 43–50.

Mandaville, Peter. 2011. 'Reimagining the Ummah? Information Technology and the Changing Boundaries of Political Islam', pp. 331–54, in Volpi, Frederic (ed.), *Political Islam: A Critical Reader* (Abingdon; Routledge).

Marusek, Sarah. 2019. *Faith and Resistance: The Politics of Love and War in Lebanon* (London; Pluto Press).

Maurer, Bill. 2006. *Pious Property: Islamic Mortgages in the United States* (New York; Russel Sage Foundation).

Mavelli, Luca. 2011. 'Security and Secularisation in International Relations', *European Journal of International Relations*, 18 (1): 177–99.

May, Samantha. 2013. 'Political Piety: The Politicization of Zakat', *Middle East Critique*, 22 (2): 146–64.

May, Samantha. 2019a. '"The Best of Deeds": The Practice of Zakat in the UK', *Journal of Church and State*, 61 (2): 200–21.

May, Samantha. 2019b. 'Islamic Charitable Giving in the UK: A "Radical" Economic Alternative?', *New Political Economy*, https://doi.org/10.1080/13563467.2019.1664445

May, Samantha, Wilson, Erin K., Sheikh, Faiz and Baumgart-Ochse, Claudia. 2014. 'The Religious as Political and the Political as Religious: Globalisation, Post Secularism and the Shifting Boundaries of the Sacred', *Journal of Religion, Politics, and Ideology*, 15 (3): 331–46.

Metcalfe-Hough, Victoria, Keatinge, Tom and Pantuliano, Sara. 2015. 'UK Humanitarian Aid in the Age of Counter-Terrorism: Perceptions and Reality', *Humanitarian Policy Group Working Paper* (Overseas Development Institute, London), https://www.odi.org/sites/odi.org.uk/files/odi-assets/publications-opinion-files/9479.pdf (Accessed 03/05/2020).

Miah, Shamim. 2015. *Muslims, Schooling and the Question of Self-Segregation* (Basingstoke; Palgrave Macmillan).

Middle East Forum. 2018. 'Islamic Relief: Charity/Extremism/Terror, Middle East Forum', https://www.meforum.org/MiddleEastForum/media/MEFLibrary/pdf/Islamic-Relief-Dossier-v3.pdf (Accessed 04/05/2020).

Milton-Edwards, Beverley. 2017. 'Securitizing Charity: The Case of Palestine Zakat Committees', *Global Change, Peace and Security*, 29 (2): 161–77.

Morris, Debra. 2016. 'The Charity Commission for England and Wales: A Fine Example or Another Fine Mess?', *Chicago and Kent Law Review*, 91 (3): 965–90.

Muderrisoglu, Secil and Saxton, Joe. 2020. 'How Do BAME Audiences Engage with Charities', *nfpSynergy*, https://nfpsynergy.net/sites/default/files/hosted-downloads/BAME%20charity%20engagement%20April%202020.pdf?utm_source=Newsletter+Mailing+list&utm_campaign=63bbeb4f3f-EMAIL_CAMPAIGN_2020_04_16_09_57&utm_medium=email&utm_term=0_8fefd36561-63bbeb4f3f-74728017&mc_cid=63bbeb4f3f&mc_eid=21bd03de19 (Accessed 04/05/2020).

Muslim Aid. 2019. 'Muslim Aid: Trustee's Report and Financial Statements: For the Year Ended 31 December 2018', *Muslim Aid*, https://muslimaid.storage.googleapis.com/upload/www.muslimaid.org/about-us/Muslim%20Aid%20-%20Signed%20accounts%202018.pdf (Accessed 15/08/2020).

Muslim Aid. 2019. 'Trustee's Report and Financial Statements for the year ended 31 December 2018', *Muslim Aid*, https://muslimaid.storage.googleapis.com/upload/www.muslimaid.org/about-us/Muslim%20Aid%20-%20Signed%20accounts%202018.pdf (Accessed 12/02/2021).

Muslim Aid. 2020. '35 Years of Muslim Aid', *Muslim Aid Centre*, https://www.muslimaid.org/media-centre/news/35-years/ (Accessed 15/08/2020).

Muslim Charities Forum. 2014. 'MCF's Response to Allegations in *The Daily Telegraph* 23/09/2014', https://www.muslimcharitiesforum.org.uk/mcfs-response-to-allegations-in-the-daily-telegraph-23-09-2014/ (Accessed 20/08/2020).

Muslim Council of Britain. 2015. 'British Muslims in Numbers: A Demographic, Socio-Economic and Health Profile of Muslims in Britain Drawing on the 2011 Census', www.mcb.org.uk/wp-content/uploads/2015/02/mcbCensusReport_2015.pdf (Accessed 04/04/2017).

Mustafa, Asma. 2015. *Identity and Political Participation Among Young British Muslims: Believing and Belonging* (Basingstoke; Palgrave Macmillan).

Nasr, Seyyed Vali Reza. 1989. 'Islamic Economics: Novel Perspectives', *Middle East Studies*, 24 (4): 516–30.

National Commission on Terrorist Attacks Upon the United States. N.d. 'Monograph on Terrorist Financing', https://govinfo.library.unt.edu/911/staff_statements/911_TerrFin_Monograph.pdf (Accessed 08/10/2019).

National Zakat Foundation. 2019. 'National Zakat Foundation: Annual Report and Financial Statements for the Year Ending 31 December 2019', https://nzf.org.uk/wp-content/uploads/2020/08/Annual-Report-2019-1.pdf (Accessed 14/08/2020).

Nayet, Amina Alrasheed. 2017. *Alternative Performativity of Muslimness: The Intersection of Race, Religion and Migration* (Beirut and Leeds; Palgrave Macmillan).

NCP. 2014. 'Thinking Through Faith: More Research Needed', *New Philanthropy Capitol*, https://www.thinknpc.org/blog/thinking-through-faith-more-research-needed/ (Accessed 12/06/2020).

Neumann, Peter R. 2017. 'Don't Follow the Money: The Problem with the War on Terrorist Financing', *Foreign Affairs*, 96 (4): 93–102.

Nye, Joseph. 2004. *Soft Power: The Means to Success in World Politics* (New York; Public Affairs).

Obama, Barak. 'Text: Cairo Speech', *New York Times*, 4 June 2009, http://www.nytimes.com/2009/06/04/us/politics/04obama.text.html (Accessed 31/05/2017).

Osborne, Peter and Delmar-Morgan, Alex. 2015. 'Uncaging the Charity Commission', OpenDemocracy, https://www.opendemocracy.net/en/opendemocracyuk/uncaging-charity-commission/

OSCR, The Office of the Scottish Charity Regulator. 2017. 'Annual Report and Accounts for the Year Ended 31 March 2017', https://www.oscr.org.uk/media/2837/oscr-annual-report-and-accounts-2016-17-signed.pdf (Accessed 27/03/2021).

OSCR, The Office of the Scottish Charity Regulator. 2018. 'Annual Report and Accounts for the Year Ended 31 March 2017', https://www.publicinformationonline.com/download/148606 (Accessed 09/01/2020).

Osella, Filippo. 2019. 'Islam, Humanitarianism, and Everyday Religion', *AllegraLab*, https://allegralaboratory.net/islam-humanitarianism-and-everyday-religion-muhum/ (Accessed 14/08/2020).

Penny Appeal. 2019. 'Penny Appeal: Annual Report and Financial Statements for the Year Ended 30 April 2019', http://apps.charitycommission.gov.uk/Accounts/Ends41/0001128341_AC_20190430_E_C.PDF (Accessed 14/08/2020).

Petersen, Marie Juul. 2015. *For Humanity or for the Ummah?: Aid and Islam in Transnational Muslim NGOs* (London; C Hurst & Co.).

Philpott, Daniel. 2000. 'The Religious Roots of Modern International Relations', *World Politics*, 52 (2): 206–45.

Pickles, Eric (MP). 2014. 'Integration Update: Written Statement -HCW5154', https://www.parliament.uk/business/publications/written-questions-answers-statements/written-statement/Commons/2014-12-18/HCWS154/ (Accessed 23/05/2020).

Pollard, Jane S., Datta, Kavita, James, Al and Akli, Quman. 2015. 'Islamic Charitable Infrastructure and Giving in East London: Everyday Economic-Development Geographies in Practice', *Journal of Economic Geography*, 16 (4): 871–96.

Portes, Alejandro. 2013. 'Migration and Development: Reconciling Opposite Views', pp. 30–51, in Eckstein, Susan and Najam, Adil (eds), *How Immigrants Impact Their Homelands* (Durham; Duke University Press).

Qurashi, Fahid. 2018. 'The Prevent Strategy and the UK "War on Terror": Embedding Infrastructures of Surveillance in Muslim Communities', *Palgrave Communications*, 4 (7): 1–13.

Ramesh, Randeep. 2014. 'Quarter of Charity Commission Inquiries Target Muslim Groups', *The Guardian*, November, https://www.theguardian.com/society/2014/nov/16/charity-commission-inquiries-muslim-groups (Accessed 14/05/2020).

Rheault, Magali. 2011. 'British Muslims Feel, Well, British', *Gallup*, https://news.gallup.com/opinion/queue/173222/british-muslims-feel-british.aspx (Accessed 05/06/2020).

Roth, John, Greenburg, Douglas and Wille, Serena. 2003. 'Monograph of Terrorist Financing', *National Commission on Terrorist Attacks Upon the United States*, https://govinfo.library.unt.edu/911/staff_statements/911_TerrFin_Monograph.pdf (Accessed 17/05/2020).

Roy, Olivier. 2011. 'Islamism in the West or Western Islam?', pp. 244–9, in Volpi, Frederic (ed.), *Political Islam: A Critical Reader* (Abington; Routledge).

Roy, Olivier. 2017. *Jihad and Death: The Global Appeal of Islamic State* (London; Hurst & Company).

Rudnyckyi, Daromir. 2010. *Spiritual Economies: Islam, Globalization, and the Afterlife of Development* (Ithaca; Cornell University Press).

Rumaniuk, Peter. 2008. 'International Initiatives to Combat the Financing of Terrorism', pp. 234–59, in Biersteker and Eckert (eds), *Countering the Financing of Terrorism* (London and New York; Routledge).

Ryder, Nicholas, Thomas, Rachel and Webb, Georgina. 2018. 'The Financial War on Terrorism: A Critical Review of the United Kindom's Counter-Terrorist Financing Strategies', pp. 781–806, in King, Colin, Walker, Clive and Gurule, Jimmy (eds), *The Palgrave Handbook of Criminal and Terrorism Financing Law* (Cham; Palgrave Macmillan).

Salgado-Pottier. 2008. 'A Modern Moral Panic: The Representation of British Bangledeshi and Pakistani Youth in Relation to Violence and Religion', *Anthropology Matters*, 10 (1), https://doi.org/10.22582/am.v10i1.44

Sassen, Saskia. 2003. 'Towards Post-National and De-Nationalised Citizenship', pp. 277–91, in Isin, Engin F. and Turner, Bryan S. (eds), *Handbook of Citizenship Studies* (New York; Sage).

Sassen, Saskia. 2006. *Territory, Authority and Rights: From Medieval to Global Assemblages* (Princeton; Princeton University Press).

Schaeublin, Emanuel. 2014. 'Zakat Practice in the Islamic Tradition and Its Recent History in the Context of Palestine', pp. 19–26, in Davey, Eleanor and Svoboda, Eva (eds), *Histories of Humanitarian Action in the Middle East and North Africa*, HGP Working Paper, https://www.odi.org/sites/odi.org.uk/files/odi-assets/publications-opinion-files/9141.pdf (Accessed 17/07/2019).

Schaeublin, Emanuel. 2019. 'Islam in Face-to-Face Interaction: Direct Zakat Giving in Nabulus (Palestine)', *Contemporary Levant*, 4 (2): 122–40.

Scott, James C. 1987. 'Resistance Without Protest and Without Organisation: Peasant Opposition to the Islamic Zakat and the Christian Tithe', *Comparative Studies in Society and History*, 29 (3): 417–52.

Shaw-Hamilton, James. 2007. 'Recognizing the Umma in Humanitarianism: International Regulation of Islamic Charities', pp. 15–31, in Alterman, Jon B. and Von Hippel, Karin (eds), *Understanding Islamic Charities* (Washington, DC; Center for Strategic and International Studies).

Shaykh Abdal Hakim Murad. N.D. 'Zakat in a Post-Modern Economy', *National Zakat Foundation*, https://nzf.org.uk/news/zakat-in-a-post-modern-economy-by-shaykh-abdal-hakim-murad/ (Accessed 05/06/2020).

Sheikh, Mona. 2012. 'How Does Religion Matter?: Pathways to Religion in International Relations', *Review of International Studies*, 38 (02): 365–92.

Sidel, Mark. 2006. 'The Third Sector, Human Security and Anti-Terrorism: The United States and Beyond', *Voluntas, International Journal of Voluntary and NonProfit Organisations*, 17 (3): 199–210.

Sidel, Mark. 2011. 'Choices and Approaches: Anti-Terrorism Law and Civil Society in the United States and the United Kingdom After September 11', *The University of Toronto Law Journal*, 61 (1): 119–46.

Smith, Julianne and Filipiak, Natalia. 2007. 'Islamic Charities in Europe', pp. 81–97, in Alterman, Jon B. and von Hippel, Karin (eds), *Understanding Islamic Charities*, (Washington, DC; Center For Strategic and International Studies).

Smith, Matthew. 2016. 'Terrorist Attack in Britain Expected by 84% of People', *YouGov*, https://yougov.co.uk/topics/politics/articles-reports/2016/08/04/terrorist-attack-britain-expected-84-people (Accessed 14/08/2020).

Spalek, Basia and Lambert, Robert. 2008. 'Muslim Communities; Counter-Terrorism and Counter-Radicalisation: A Critically Reflective Approach to Engagement', *International Journal of Law, Crime and Justice*, 36 (4): 257–70.

Spencer, Jonathon. 2010. 'The Perils of Engagement: A Space for Anthropology in the Age of Security', *Current Anthropology*, 289–99.

Stanlley, Rebecca and Buckley, Ross. 2016. 'Protecting the West, Excluding the Rest: The Impact of the AML/CTF Regime on Financial Inclusion in the Pacific and Potential Responses', *Melbourne Journal of International Law*, 17 (1): 83–106.

Stirk, Chloe. 2015. 'An Act of Faith: Humanitarian Financing and Zakat', Briefing Paper, Global Humanitarian Assistance, http://devinit.org/wp-content/uploads/2015/03/ONLINE-Zakat_report_V9a.pdf (Accessed 20/08/2020).

Strindberg, Anders and Warn, Mats 2011. *Islamism: Religion, Radicalization and Resistance* (Cambridge; Polity).

Stritzel, Holger. 2007. 'Towards a Theory of Securitization: Copenhagen and Beyond', *European Consortium for Political Research*, 13 (3): 357–83.

Sunan, al-Kubra. 19049. 'Daily Hadith Online', https://www.abuaminaelias.com/dailyhadithonline/2012/08/12/not-believer-neighbor-hungry/ (Accessed 27/03/2021).

Tehmina, N. Basit. 2009. 'White British; Dual Heritage; British Muslim: Young Briton's Conceptualisation of Identity and Citizenship', *British Educational Research Journal*, 35 (5): 723–43.

Tell Mama. 2017. 'Annual Report 2016: A Constructed Threat: Identity, Prejudice, and the Impact of Anti-Muslim Hatred' (London; Faith Matters), https://tellmamauk.org/constructed-threat-identity-intolerance-impact-anti-muslim-hatred-tell-mama-annual-report-2016/ (Accessed 28/12/2017).

The 9/11 Commission Report. 2004. https://www.9-11commission.gov/report/911Report.pdf (Accessed 13/05/2020).

The Daily Telegraph. 2014. '"Corrections and Clarifications": Muslim Charities Forum', 3 October, https://www.muslimcharitiesforum.org.uk/the-daily-telegraph-article-correction-in-print-edition/ (Accessed 20/08/2020).

Thomas, Paul. 2014. 'Divorced but Still Co-habiting? Britain's Prevent/Community Cohesion Policy Tension', *British Politics*, 9 (4): 472–93.

Tierney, Michael. 2017. 'Well Funded and Dangerous: Assessing the Islamic State's Financing Operations', *Journal of Money Laundering Control*, 20 (2): 159–71.

Turner, Camilla. 2014. 'Government Donation to Muslim Charities Forum Denounced as "Madness"', *The Telegraph*, 23 September 2014, https://www.telegraph.co.uk/news/uk news/11114599/Government-donation-to-Muslim-Charities-Forum-denounced-as-madness.html (Accessed 02/06/2020).

Uddin, Ahmed. 2020. 'The Neighbours Next Door: The Story of Muslim Organisations Responding to Covid-19', Muslim Charities Forum, https://www.muslimcharitiesforum.org.uk/wp-content/uploads/2020/07/MCF-Report-The-Neighbours-Next-Door.pdf (Accessed 31/07/2020).

Ulmschneider, Georgia Wralstad and Lutz, James M. 2019. 'Terrorism Analysis and Holder V. Humanitarian Law Project: The Missing Element', *Terrorism and Political Violence*, 31 (4): 800–16.

US Government. 2004. *The 9/11 Commission Report*, U.S. Government, https://www.9-11commission.gov/report/911Report.pdf (Accessed 01/05/2018), 169.

Van Bruinessen, Martin. 2007. 'Development and Islamic Charities', *ISIM Review*, 1 (20): 5.

Vertovec, Steve. 2009. *Transnationalism* (London and New York; Routledge).

Walker, Clive. 2018. 'Terrorism Financing and the Governance of Charities', pp. 1085–115, in King, Colin, Walker, Clive and Gurule, Jimmy (eds), *The Palgrave Handbook of Criminal and Terrorism Financing Law* (Cham; Palgrave Macmillan).

Warde, Ibrahim. 2007. *The Price of Fear: The Truth Behind the Financial War on Terror* (California; University of California Press).

Ware, John. 2009. 'Response to Interpal Inquiry by Charity Commission', BBC, http://news.bbc.co.uk/panorama/hi/front_page/newsid_7915000/7915916.stm (Accessed 22/02/2020).

Warsi, Sayeeda. 2017. *The Enemy Within: A Tale of Muslim Britain* (London; Allen Lane).

Weally, Kirsty. 2019. 'Daily Mail Owner Pays £120,000 in Damages to Interpal Trustees', *Civil Society*, https://www.civilsociety.co.uk/news/daily-mail-owner-pasy-120-000-in-damages-and-apologises-to-interpal-trustees.html

Webb, Emma. 2018. 'Wolves in Sheep's Clothing: How Islamist Extremists Exploit the UK Charitable Sector', *The Henry Jackson Society*, https://henryjacksonsociety.org/publications/wolves-in-sheeps-clothing-how-islamist-extremists-exploit-the-uk-charitable-sector/ (Accessed 12/02/2021).

Weber, Max. 2001. *The Protestant Ethic and the Spirit of Capitalism* (New York; Routledge).

Werbner, Pnina. 2000. 'Divided Loyalties, Empowered Citizenship? Muslims in Britain', *Citizenship Studies*, 4 (3): 307–24.

Werbner, Pnina. 2011. 'The Predicament of Diaspora and Millennial Islam: Reflections on September 11, 2001', p. 231, in Volpi, Frederic (ed.), *Political Islam: A Critical Reader* (Abington; Routledge).

Wharton, Rachel and de Las Casas, Lucy. 2016. 'What a Difference a Faith Makes: Insights into Faith-based Charities', *NCP Report*, file:///C:/Users/sam_m/AppData/Local/Temp/What-a-difference-a-faith-makes_NPC-1.pdf

Whitehead, Harriet. 2019. 'Interpal Trustees Receive £50,000 in Damages From Jewish Chronicle', *Civil Society News*, https://www.civilsociety.co.uk/news/interpal-trustees-receive-50-000-in-damages-from-jewish-chronicle.html (Accessed 22/02/2020).

Wilson, Erin K. 2014. 'Faith-Based Organisations and Post Secularism in Contemporary International Relations', pp. 219–41, in Mavelli, Luca and Petito, Fabio (eds), *Towards a Postsecular International Politics* (New York; Palgrave Macmillan).

Wilson, Erin K. and Steger, Mandfred B. 2013. 'Religious Globalisms in the Post-Secular Age', *Globalisations*, 10 (3): 481–95.

Yasmin, Sofia and Ghafran, Choudhry. 2019. 'The Problematics of Accountability: Internal Responses to External Pressures in Exposed Organisations', *Critical Perspectives on Accounting*, 64, https://doi.org/10.1016/j.cpa.2019.01.002

Yusoof, Rizwan. 2020. 'Resilience of Muslim Giving During Covid 19', National Zakat Foundation, https://nzf.org.uk/news/resilience-of-muslim-giving-during-covid19/ (Accessed 28/07/2020).

Ziebertz, Hans-Georg and Riegal, Ulrich. 2010. 'Europe: A Post-Secular Society?', *International Journal of Practical Theology*, 13 (2): 293–308.

Index

Note: Due to the frequency of the term 'charity', this is not listed in the index.

accountability   5, 17, 66, 68, 72–3, 77, 81, 95, 129, 148, 153–4, 156, 158, 160–5, 167
   anticipatory accountability   165
Afghanistan   19, 23, 24, 35, 56, 108, 135, 137
Ahmadiyya   25, 72–3
aid   1, 11, 13, 15, 20, 23, 32, 36, 50–3, 60, 76, 89, 93, 99, 108, 114, 126, 135–6, 140, 154–5, 160–1, 163, 176–7
Al-Qaeda   35, 43, 93–4, 151
anti-money laundering (AML)   1, 30, 31, 34, 39, 41, 153, 170–1
authority (in Islam)   4, 67, 70, 81, 115–16, 140–5

bank accounts   1, 3, 48, 50, 56, 153, 155–7, 170
Al-Barakaat   3, 35–7, 40, 57, 80
belonging   15–16, 29, 100–4, 113, 117, 119–20, 133, 135–7, 144–5, 149, 174–5
Benevolence International Foundation   35, 38
Benthall, Jonathan   10, 13, 18–20, 23–4, 35, 51, 53, 59, 62–3, 80, 82, 101, 106, 116, 122, 126, 129, 135–7, 141–4, 153, 169, 176
Bin Laden, Osama   7
Britain   2, 12, 16, 19–22, 27, 30, 40, 43, 60, 62, 73, 78, 97, 99–100, 102–3, 106, 110, 113, 115, 117, 123–7, 129, 139, 144, 150, 174
British Muslims   3–4, 16–17, 19, 22, 42, 59–61, 68–9, 74, 76, 78, 97, 99–103, 105, 110, 115–16, 122–4, 133, 137, 144, 149–50, 159, 174–5
Britishness   43, 61, 100, 103, 133, 136–7, 150
Brown, Gordon   41, 82

bureaucratization   4, 143, 160–3, 167, 172
Butler, Judith   3, 15, 17, 80–1, 125, 151, 172, 175

CAFOD (Catholic Agency for Overseas Development)   21, 23, 106, 165
Catholic   124
Charity Commission for England and Wales   24–6, 32, 45–7, 59, 70, 79, 82–91, 95–7, 126, 147, 158, 161, 163, 167–70, 175
charity regulator(s)   3, 38, 40, 45, 79, 82, 97, 157, 159
Christian Aid   106, 165
Christianity   18, 51, 67, 70, 88
   Christian   23, 51, 87, 106, 165–6, 177
citizenship   10, 29, 59, 100, 102, 107, 114, 137, 145
civil society   60, 96, 121, 134
clandestine giving   61, 71
CONTEST   5, 7, 16, 41, 43, 142
   CONTEST II   7, 142, 166
counterproductive   3, 36, 55, 57, 84, 152, 154, 172–2, 176–7
counter-terror (CT)   1, 3, 7–8, 11–15, 17, 21, 29–32, 38–50, 56–7, 81, 83, 89–90, 94–6, 107, 137, 142, 147–8, 151, 169–71, 177–8
counter-terror financing (CTF)   2–5, 7, 15, 17, 27, 29–55, 64, 79–85, 88, 91, 93–7, 147–8, 151–5, 157–60, 162–3, 165–7, 170–3, 176–8
criminality   13, 20, 30, 41–3, 49, 51, 55, 160, 170–1, 177

Daesh (also ISIS; ISIL)   114, 141, 151
De Goede, Marieke   3, 8, 14, 19, 30, 34, 41, 43, 48, 56, 85, 88, 90, 93, 135, 154, 161–2, 165, 172

demographics   25, 30, 56, 60, 75, 121, 149
Department of Communities and Local Government (DCLG)   94–6
de-radicalization   7, 41, 43–4
de-risking, (banks)   4, 47, 49, 56, 147–8, 153–5, 170, 176
designated list   52–3, 89
  designated entity   20, 33–5, 40, 44, 47–8, 52, 53, 89
deviant   8, 12, 14, 17, 81, 154, 160, 171–2
diaspora   4, 36, 44, 100–6, 108–9, 117, 123–5, 132

Early Day Motion   89–90, 92
economic (critique)   127
  economic failures/insecurity   4, 22, 91, 106, 109, 117, 126–7, 144, 149, 152
  economic paradigms/systems   9–10, 19, 51, 62, 64, 97, 99, 125–6, 141, 149, 152
  economic practices   8, 160, 171–2
  economic violence   32, 37, 41, 50, 170, 176
El-Banna, Hany   20–1, 163
EU (European Union)   34, 40, 47, 52, 94
Europe   9, 12–13, 21, 34, 37, 45, 52–3, 76, 80, 89, 94, 101, 121, 123–4, 157, 171, 177
everyday practices/politics   7–9, 11, 13, 17, 24, 30, 34, 73–4, 99, 123, 125, 170, 172–3, 176
extremism   7, 20, 35, 41–2, 44, 59, 83, 86, 94–6, 142, 147, 152, 155–60, 163, 169, *see also* radicalism

faith-based organisation (faith-based charities)   4, 9–11, 19–20, 23–7, 51, 76, 79, 82–4, 88, 107, 134, 135, 139, 145, 148, 158–9, 161–2, 167, 175, 177
Financial Action Task Force (FATF)   8, 29–32, 35, 39, 47, 49, 56–7, 79–82, 147, 153–4, 162
financial exclusions   56, 170
financial War on Terror (FWoT)   1–3, 14, 17, 27, 29–30, 36, 41, 52, 80, 176
five pillars   16, 18, 61–3, 150

fraud   24, 71, 86
fundamental British values   8, 43, 77, 137
  shared-values   6, 43, 134, 142, 165

generations   4, 9, 22, 65, 100–1, 104, 107, 110, 113, 117, 119–32, 138, 144–5, 149, 166, 173–5
globalization   4, 101, 103–5, 107, 119, 132, 139, 145, 173
governmentality   80–1, 85, 88, 91, 95–6

Habitus   125, 129
Hadith   74–5, 109, 129, 162
Hamas   20, 38, 52–3, 55, 89–90, 94, 107–8, 135–6
Henry Jackson Society   20, 88
Hizbullah   94
Holder V. Humanitarian Law Project   33
Holy Land Foundation   38–9, 55, 57
House of Commons   89–90, 92, 96
humanitarian   4–5, 8, 18–19, 21, 23, 26, 27, 33, 35, 52–3, 55, 59–60, 92–3, 99, 106, 114–15, 117, 120, 125, 151, 158, 160, 164, 166–7, 169, 172–3, 176–7
Huntington, Samuel   9
  'Clash of Civilizations'   9, 59

identity   100–3, 105, 107, 110, 114, 120–1, 124, 129, 137, 149–51, 164, 174–5
immigration   7, 33, 100
  immigrant(s)   101, 104, 110, 113, 120, 122, 124
informal (financial) value systems   19, 29, 35, 37, 40, 51, 56–7, 62, 106
insecurity   4, 13, 117, 126, 152, 178
Interpal   3, 25, 39, 50, 69, 79, 80, 88–94, 96, 108, 135
IRA (Irish Republican Party)   2, 51
Iraq   23, 53, 63, 114, 132, 135, 137, 141, 154
Islam   17–18
Islam, Yusuf   20
Islamic charity   59–63, 69–71, 120
Islamic practice   23, 62, 65
  Muslim practice   61, 69
Islamic relief   19, 21–3, 25, 74, 105, 107–8, 126, 128, 135–6, 140, 147

Islamic state   140–3
    ISIS/ISIL (*see* Daesh)
Islamophobia   10, 17, 60, 87, 103, 122, 124–5, 133, 148–9, 154, 172, 174
isolation(ist)   9, 22, 69, 75–6, 102, 121, 177
Israel   20, 47, 50, 89, 92, 135–7, 139

Jihad   23, 34–5, 61, 65–6
Judaism   18, 124
    (Jewish)   87, 105, 124

Khums   69–70
'Know your Customer'   30, 47–50
Kundnani, Arun   7, 12, 38, 42, 44, 122, 132, 137, 177
Kuwait   35

liberal/liberalism   9–10, 18, 21, 43, 45, 56, 61, 142, 173
local (charitable giving)   4, 10, 70–1, 81, 96, 109, 111, 117, 126–7, 129, 131–2
London bombings   12, 41, 53
    July 7/7   16–17, 29, 41, 53, 119, 121

Mahmood, Saba   15, 18, 60, 73–4, 151, 159, 175
marginalization   55, 102, 125, 127, 133, 177
Material Support Act   30, 32–4
media   1, 4, 8–9, 12, 25, 27, 32, 36, 44–5, 49, 59–60, 81–2, 85, 87–8, 90–7, 99, 101, 103, 117, 132, 137–40, 143–5, 148, 151, 154, 158, 163–4, 172–3
minority   4, 9, 29, 42, 73, 102, 105, 107, 110, 113, 117, 150
Al-Mizan   22, 126
Mosque   6–7, 20, 24–5, 42, 50, 63, 65–6, 69–74, 76, 106, 109, 111, 144
multiculturalism   74, 102, 120
mundane   7–8, 11, 13, 30, 83, 173, 178
Muslim Aid   19–21
Muslim Association of Britain   76, 110
Muslim Brotherhood   20, 141
Muslim Charities Forum (MCF)   6, 25, 94–5, 163
Muslim charity   16, 27, 71, 88, 101, 105, 126, 149, 166

Muslim communities   2, 4, 11, 15, 17–18, 23, 76, 103, 105–6, 119, 121, 126, 128, 133, 137, 165, 169
Muslim Council of Britain (MCB)   69, 102–3
Muslimness   100–3, 107, 122, 129, 132–3, 137, 144, 149, 151

National Security   1, 45, 82, 93, 172
National Zakat Foundation   22, 68, 126, 128
the needy   64, 66, 72, 75, 110, 128, 138
neoliberal(ism)   9–10, 19, 99, 126, 132, 149, 158–64, 171–2
9/11   1–3, 12, 16–17, 22, 29–31, 35, 38–9, 41, 44, 46, 49, 51, 54–5, 59, 65, 78, 80, 81, 93, 101–2, 121–2, 129, 130, 135, 148–51, 153, 160, 163, 169, 172, 174, 178
non-government organizations (NGOs)   1, 9–11, 15, 19, 21, 24, 34, 38, 48, 59, 95, 129, 135, 152, 158–66, 169, 172–3, 176–7
'norm adopter'   3, 37, 40, 79
'normal'   2, 8, 12, 14, 21, 32, 42, 44, 57, 81, 160, 164, 171–2
Northern Ireland   2, 40, 171

Office of the Scottish Charity Regulator (OSCR)   19, 32, 79–82, 85–6, 92, 97
orphans   20, 22, 52–3, 67, 136, 139
Oxfam   21, 23, 77–8, 121

Pakistan   23, 102–3, 105, 113, 115, 120, 131
Palestine   1, 22, 38–9, 50–3, 89, 92, 107, 127, 135–7, 140, 154
    Gaza   52–3, 92, 94, 107, 139–40
Palestinian *Zakat* Committee   38, 51, 136
PATRIOT Act   34, 49
Penny Appeal   7, 22, 26
performativity   15, 73, 101, 123, 125, 175
    performative acts   60, 103, 132
personhood   74, 174
petty-sovereigns   3, 4, 17, 43, 49, 79–82, 88, 90, 94–7, 148, 153–4, 157, 163, 170, 172
Pickles, Eric (MP)   94–5, 97

Index

political loyalty   39, 114–16, 119, 133
　disloyalty   1, 97, 99–100, 103, 114, 133, 174
politicized (aid)   50–1, 92
Portes, Alejandro   100–1, 107, 120, 131–2, 174
poverty   4, 22, 26, 63, 75, 99, 110–13, 117, 120–1, 126–8, 131, 133, 139, 152, 154
pre-emptive   1, 30, 49
President Bush   1, 30, 36, 44
prevent   7, 17, 31, 42–4, 46, 86, 91, 96, 169
Prophet Muhammad   1, 52, 69, 74–5, 109, 129, 138, 141, 143
　prophetic tradition   104, 126
proportionate/proportionality   32, 48, 54, 56, 82, 84–5, 155, 170
protestant   70

Al-Qaradawi, Yusuf   63, 65, 78
Quran   61, 104, 109, 113, 116

racism   102–3, 125
radicalism   44, 160
　radicalization   7, 42–5, 102
rationalization   161–3
Red Cross   21, 38
religion   8–11, 13, 15, 18, 23–4, 26, 45, 60, 66, 73–4, 83, 88, 100, 103, 105, 113, 120–1, 130, 134, 137, 143, 153, 172–3
religious practice   10, 12, 61, 64, 121
remittances   36, 100, 113, 120

Sadaqah   25, 59, 61–2, 68–9, 73–4, 76–8, 105, 107, 109, 117, 121, 133, 173
Sassen, Saskia   104–5, 107, 137, 145
Saudi Arabia   24, 35, 116
secular (secularization; secularism)   4, 8–10, 16, 18, 20–4, 26, 43, 45, 51, 60–1, 76, 79, 82–3, 94, 100, 106–7, 119, 121, 123, 139, 142, 145, 149, 159, 163, 167, 171–3
securitization   3, 7–9, 11–14, 32, 34, 51, 149, 172
security   7, 10–13, 34–7, 45, 48, 51, 55, 101, 135–6, 154, 173, 177–8
Shariah   61, 65, 143, 162, 173

Shawcross, William   83–4
Shia   18, 25, 65, 69–70, 141–2
　Shi'ism   70
social cohesion   1, 59, 75–6, 78, 102, 121, 134, 137, 177
soft power   11, 177
Somalia   35–7, 56, 133, 154
speculative   13, 30, 34, 43, 165
Sudan   108, 127, 154, 157
surveillance   1, 7, 12–14, 30–1, 33, 40, 54–7, 80, 93, 108, 122, 156–7, 170–1
suspicious activity reports (SARs)   54–5, 88, 154, 156
SWIFT   34

Taliban   13, 108
terrorism   1–3, 7–8, 12–14, 17, 23–4, 27, 29–31, 34–5, 37–46, 49, 51–2, 54–5, 60, 82–4, 86, 90, 93–4, 96, 100, 132, 135–6, 154, 158, 167, 170–1, 176–7
the 9/11 Commission Report   2, 78
transnational   4, 11, 15, 39, 94, 100–1, 103, 106–7, 109, 112–13, 117, 119–20, 122–4, 127, 129, 131–3, 135, 138, 144–5, 172–4
　transnationalism   100, 105, 122, 129
trustee   27, 46, 82, 87, 90, 92, 96, 149, 151, 163, 166, 169

Ummah   4, 10, 18, 99–100, 103–5, 117, 119, 132–3, 136–7, 144, 174
unaccountable   3–4, 17, 79, 162
　non-accountable   82, 157, 172
United Arab Emirates   135
United Kingdom (UK)   1–4, 7, 10–25, 29–32, 37–43, 45, 53–7, 59–64, 68–71, 73–5, 77, 79, 82–3, 87–91, 93, 95, 97, 99–113, 115, 117, 119–35, 138, 142–5, 147, 149, 151–2, 159–60, 162, 166, 169–71, 175, 177
United Nations   21, 38, 57
　UN Security Council   39–40
　UNRWA   135
United States   17, 24, 27, 29–30, 34, 37, 38, 40, 46, 49–50, 52, 57, 61, 80–2, 88–9, 94, 96, 102, 108, 169, 176

Vertovec, Steve   101, 105, 110, 113, 122–5, 129

violence   1–3, 5, 9, 12–15, 20, 23–4, 29–30, 32, 37–9, 41–3, 45, 48–54, 57, 71, 81, 84, 86, 89, 94, 122, 141, 148, 154–5, 167, 169–72, 176–8
'vulnerable'   3, 29, 31, 35, 37, 41, 43–4, 49, 51, 59, 72, 125, 162, 169, 172, 176

War On Terror (WoT)   1, 8, 29–30, 51, 80, 84, 148, 152, 160, 176
Warde, Ibrahim   2, 17, 31–2, 34–7, 39, 47, 49–50, 52–4, 80, 89, 154, 169–70, 172, 176
Weber, Max   159, 161–3
  disenchantment   161–3

welfare provisions   4, 19, 32, 52–3, 62, 100, 112–14, 117, 126, 133–4, 149, 158–9, 174, 177
  welfare state   10, 110, 117, 126–7, 134–5, 174
Werbner, Pnina   103, 125, 144–5
world-check   48

youth(s)   7, 18, 23, 41, 76, 121–3, 129–34, 144, 149–50

zakat   3–4, 18–20, 22, 25–6, 35, 37–8, 51, 59, 61–73, 75–8, 99, 103–21, 126–9, 131–3, 136, 138, 140–5, 160–1, 169, 173–4
  rightful recipients   59, 61, 65–6

www.ingramcontent.com/pod-product-compliance
Lightning Source LLC
Chambersburg PA
CBHW060953230426
43665CB00015B/2178